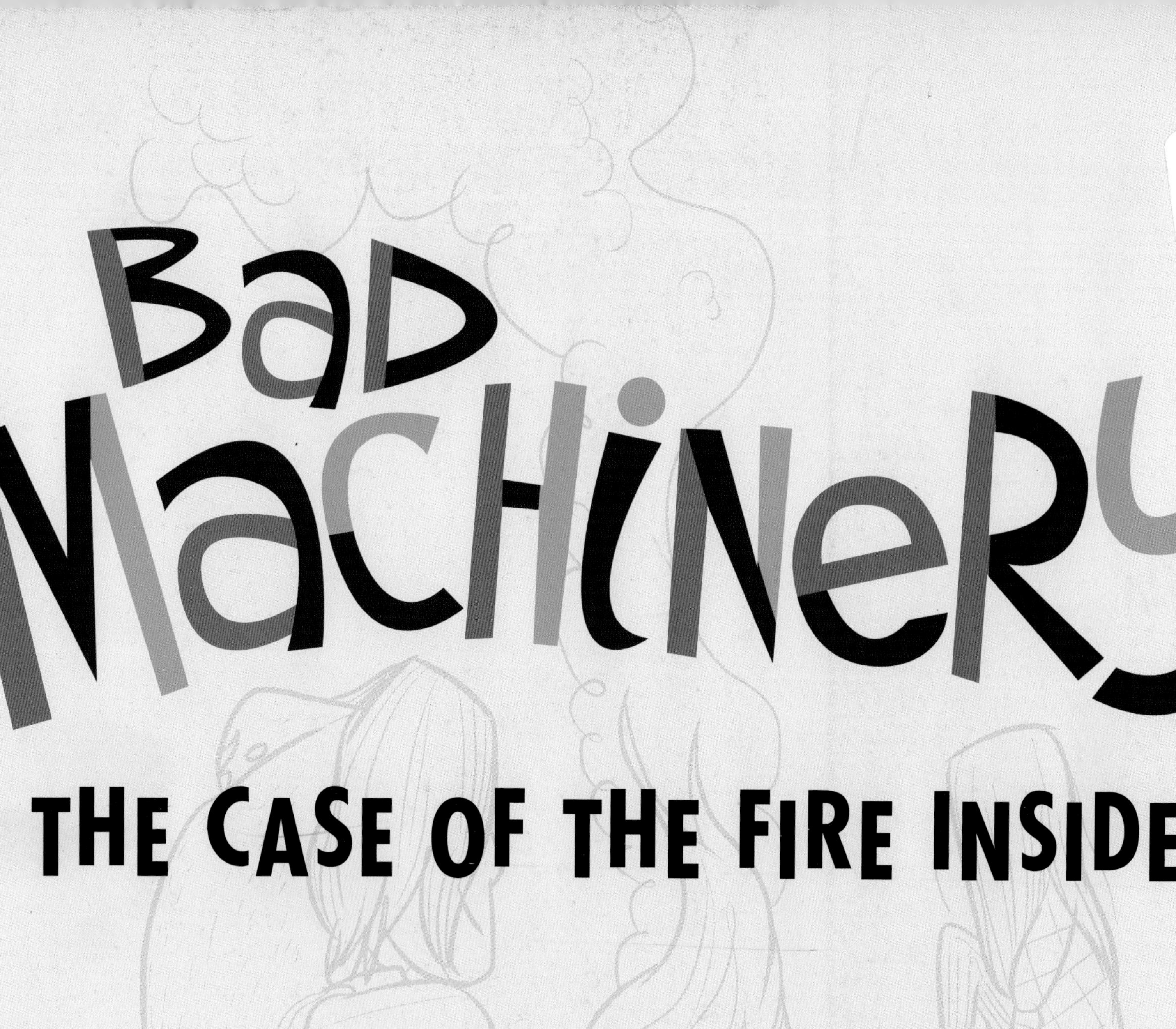

Bad Machinery™

THE CASE OF THE FIRE INSIDE

AN ONI PRESS PUBLICATION

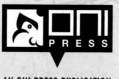

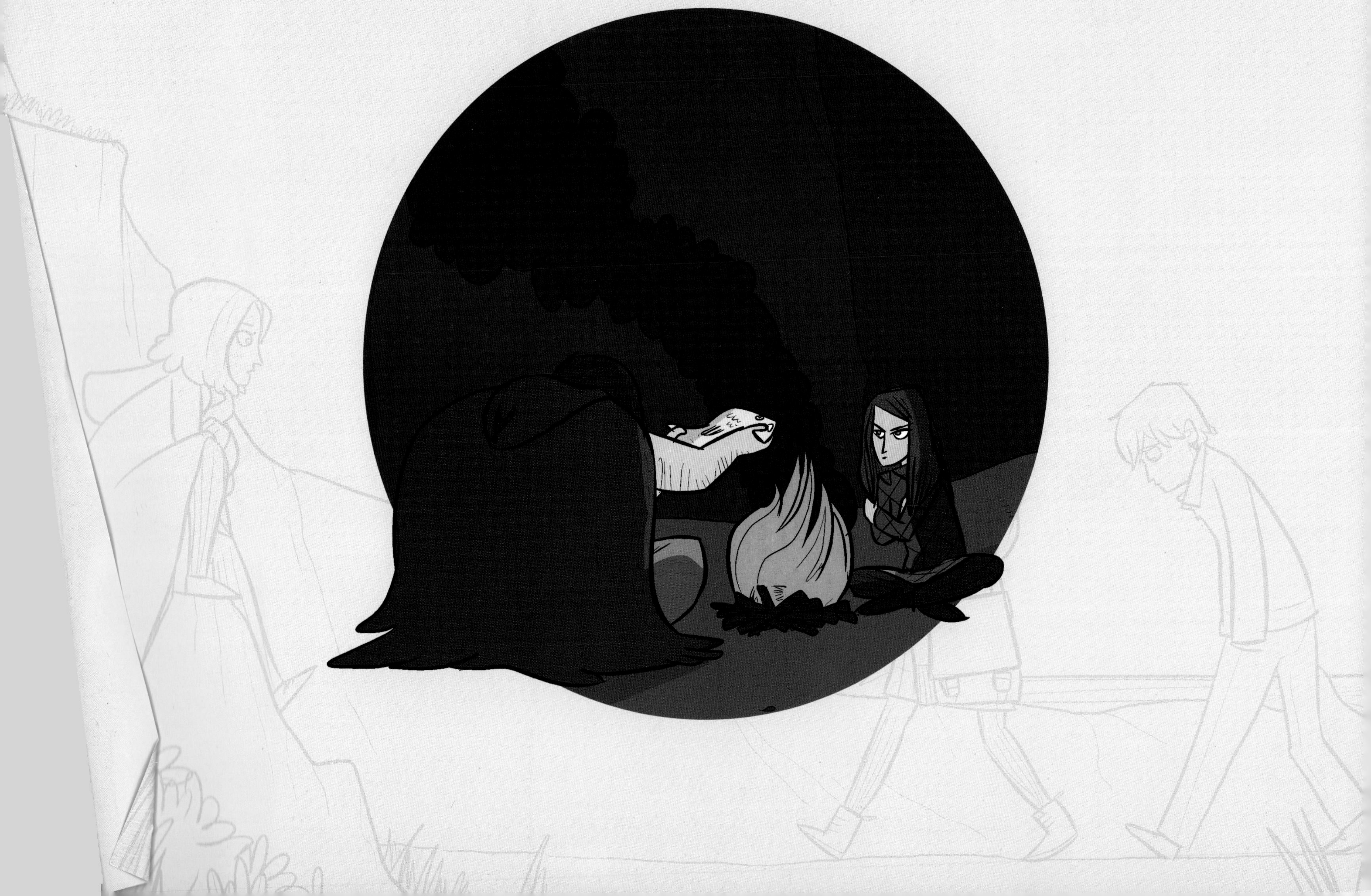

Bad Machinery™

The Case of the Fire Inside

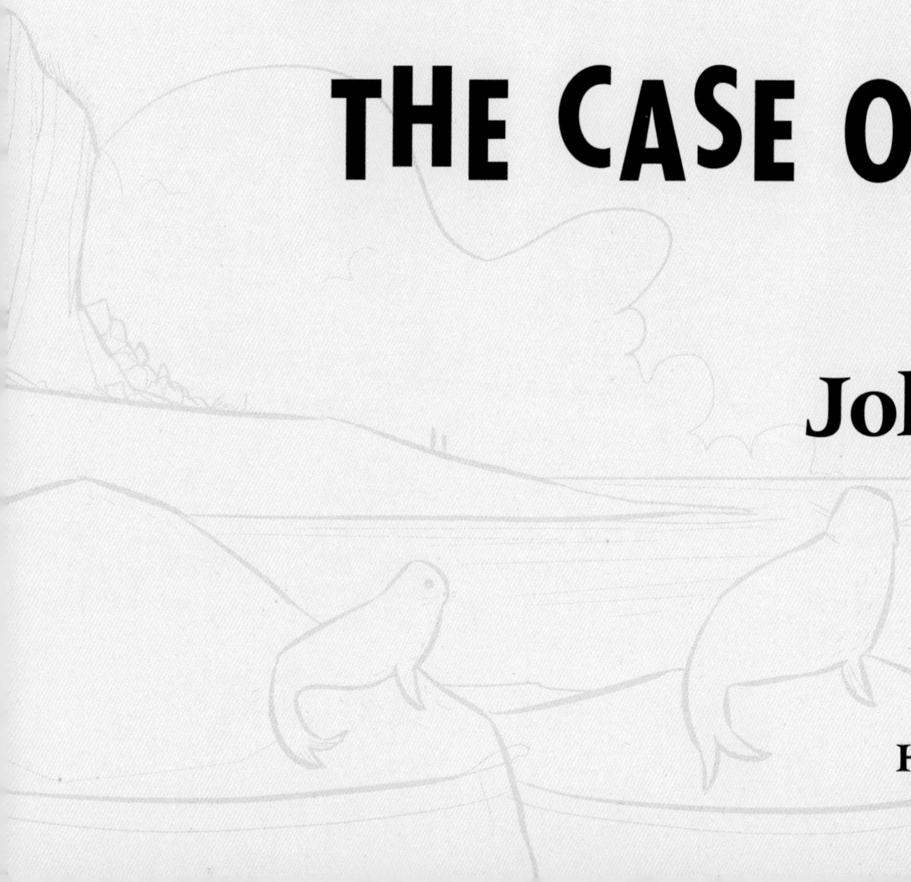

By
John Allison

Edited by
Ari Yarwood

Designed by
Hilary Thompson

Published by Oni Press, Inc.

publisher, Joe Nozemack

editor in chief, James Lucas Jones

director of sales, Cheyenne Allott

marketing coordinator, Amber O'Neill

publicity coordinator, Rachel Reed

director of design & production, Troy Look

graphic designer, Hilary Thompson

digital art technician, Jared Jones

managing editor, Ari Yarwood

senior editor, Charlie Chu

editor, Robin Herrera

editorial assistant, Bess Pallares

director of logistics, Brad Rooks

office assistant, Jung Lee

onipress.com
facebook.com/onipress
twitter.com/onipress
onipress.tumblr.com
instagram.com/onipress
badmachinery.com

First Edition: April 2016

ISBN 978-1-62010-297-8
eISBN 978-1-62010-298-5

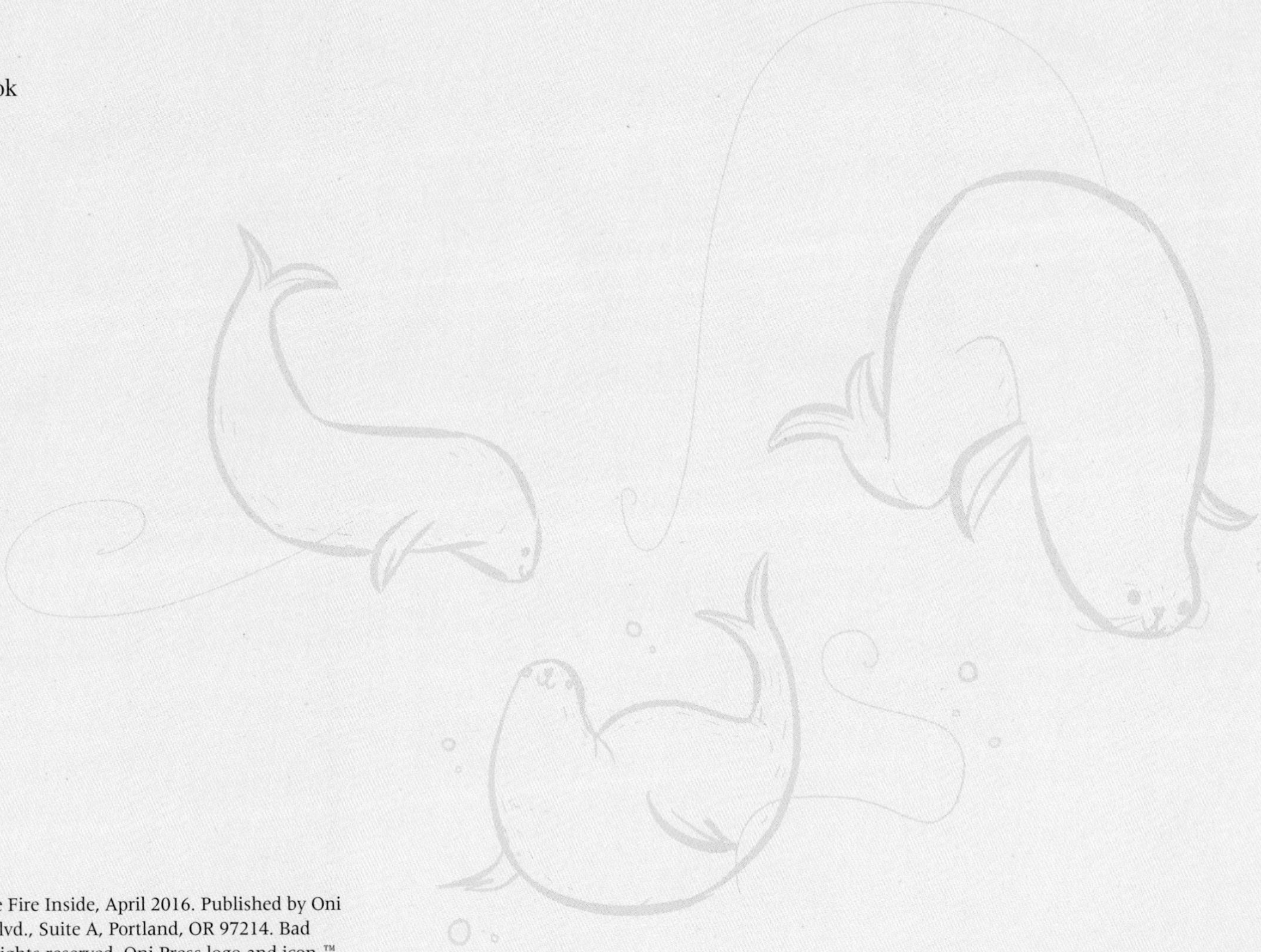

Bad Machinery Volume Five: The Case of the Fire Inside, April 2016. Published by Oni Press, Inc. 1305 SE Martin Luther King Jr. Blvd., Suite A, Portland, OR 97214. Bad Machinery is ™ & © 2016 John Allison. All rights reserved. Oni Press logo and icon ™ & © 2016 Oni Press, Inc. All rights reserved. Oni Press logo and icon artwork created by Keith A. Wood. The events, institutions, and characters presented in this book are fictional. Any resemblance to actual persons, living or dead, is purely coincidental. No portion of this publication may be reproduced, by any means, without the express written permission of the copyright holders.

Printed in China.

Library of Congress Control Number: 2012953355

1 2 3 4 5 6 7 8 9 10

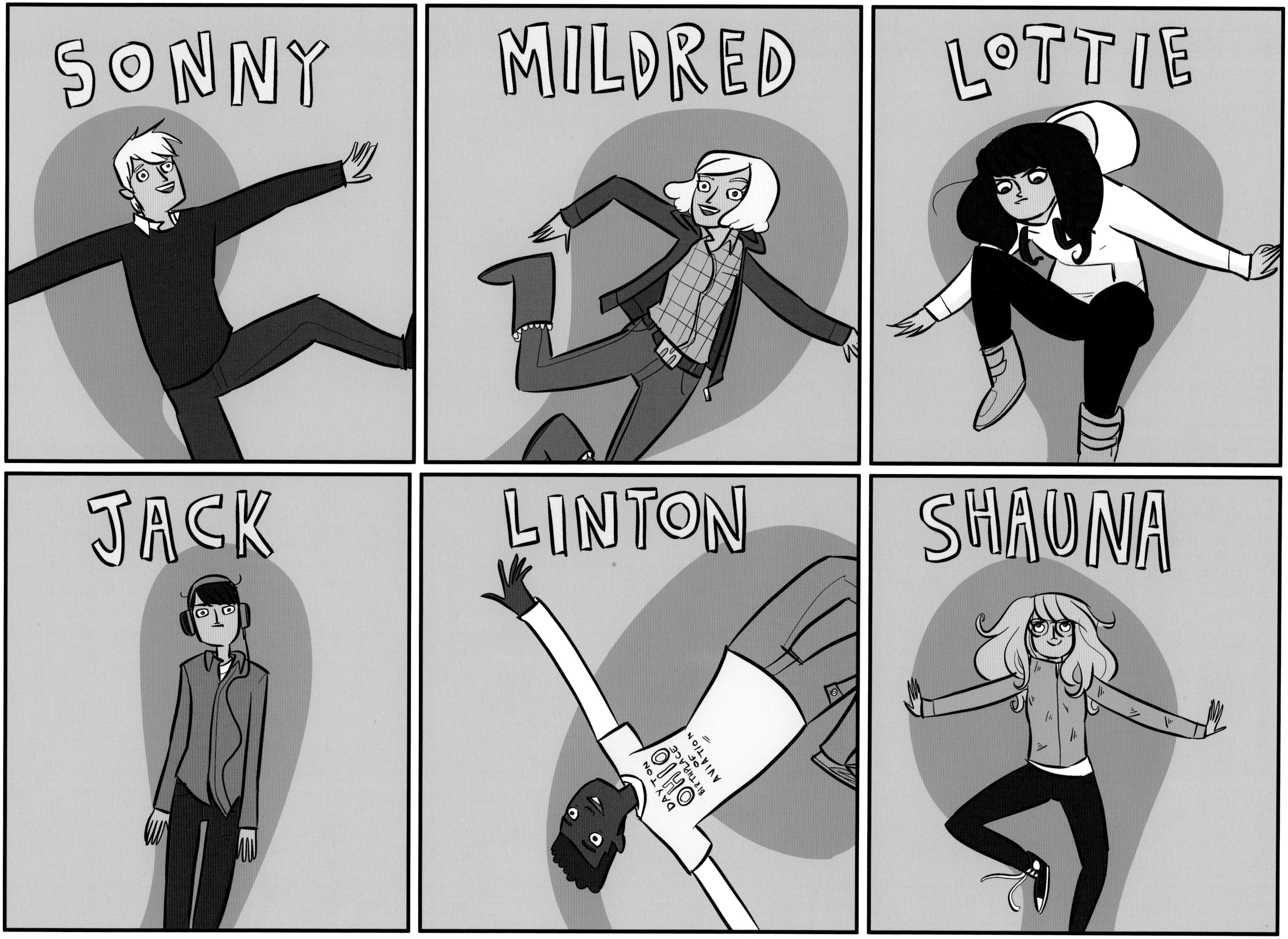
SONNY
MILDRED
LOTTIE
JACK
LINTON
DAYTON OHIO BIRTHPLACE OF AVIATION
SHAUNA

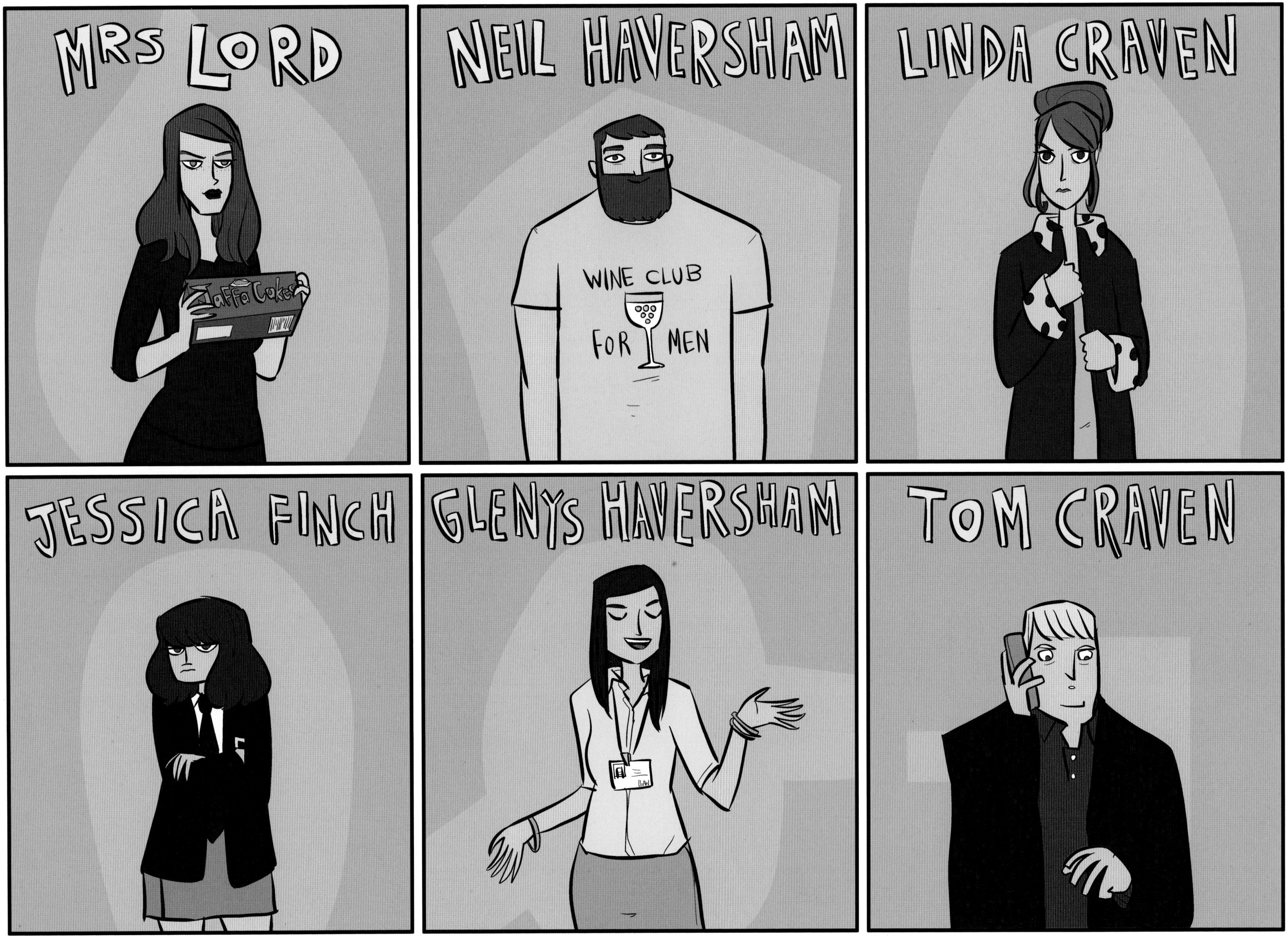
MRS LORD
Jaffa Cakes
NEIL HAVERSHAM
WINE CLUB FOR MEN
LINDA CRAVEN
JESSICA FINCH
GLENYS HAVERSHAM
TOM CRAVEN

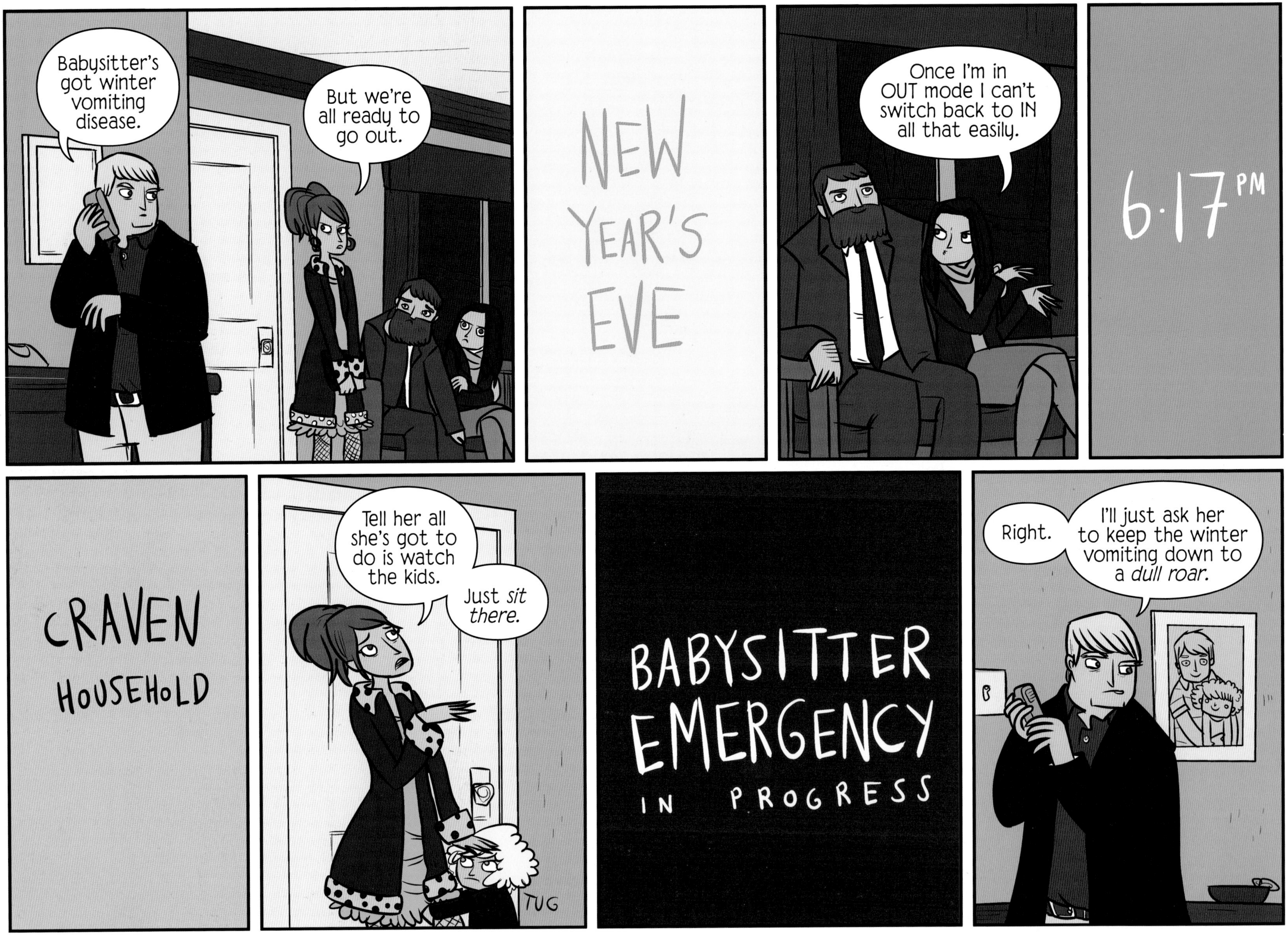
Babysitter's got winter vomiting disease.
But we're all ready to go out.
NEW YEAR'S EVE
Once I'm in OUT mode I can't switch back to IN all that easily.
6·17 PM
CRAVEN HOUSEHOLD
Tell her all she's got to do is watch the kids.
Just *sit there.*
TUG
BABYSITTER EMERGENCY IN PROGRESS
Right.
I'll just ask her to keep the winter vomiting down to a *dull roar.*

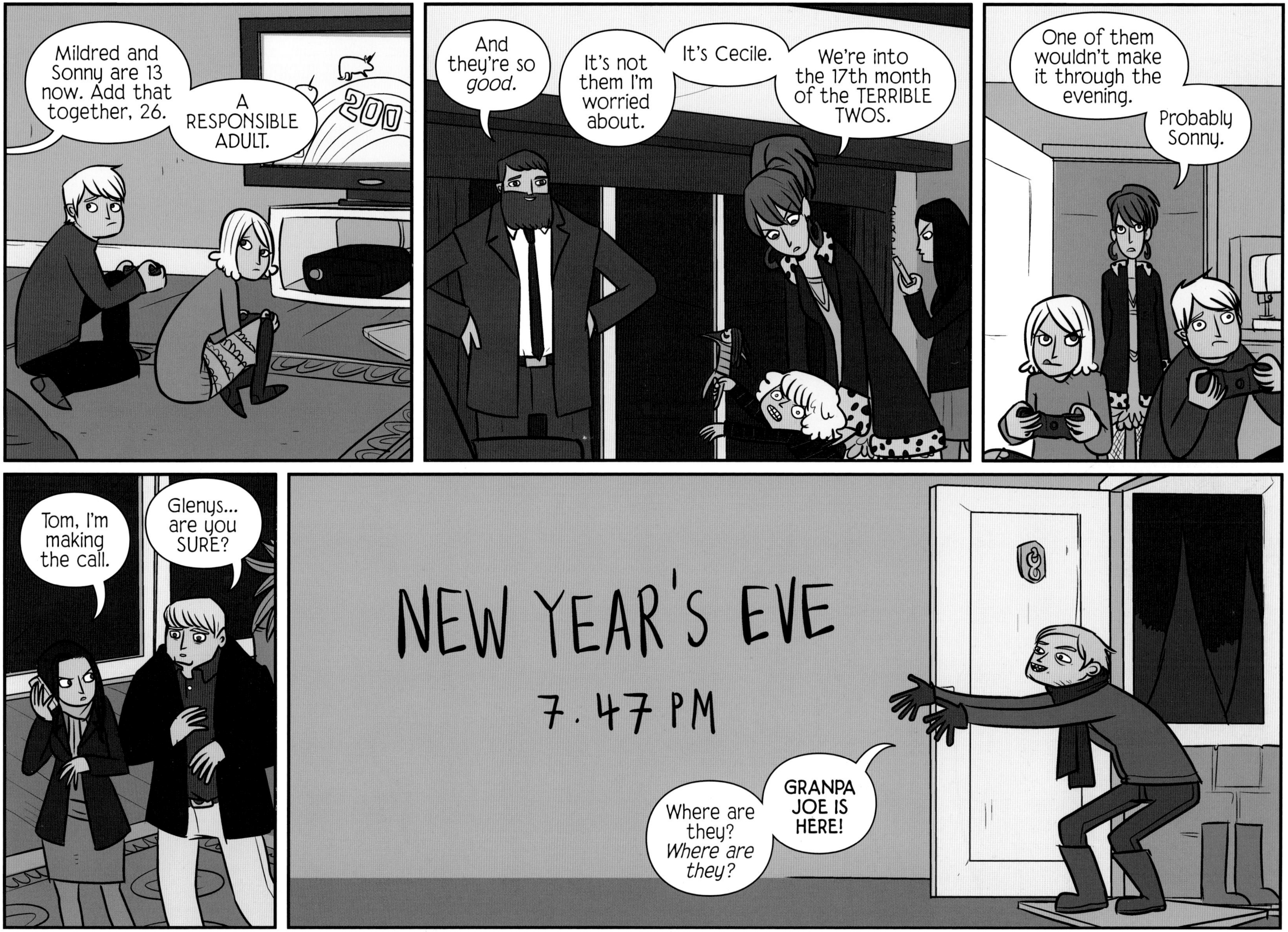
Mildred and Sonny are 13 now. Add that together, 26.
A RESPONSIBLE ADULT.
And they're so *good.*
It's not them I'm worried about.
It's Cecile.
We're into the 17th month of the TERRIBLE TWOS.
One of them wouldn't make it through the evening.
Probably Sonny.
Tom, I'm making the call.
Glenys... are you SURE?
NEW YEAR'S EVE
7.47 PM
GRANPA JOE IS HERE!
Where are they? *Where are they?*

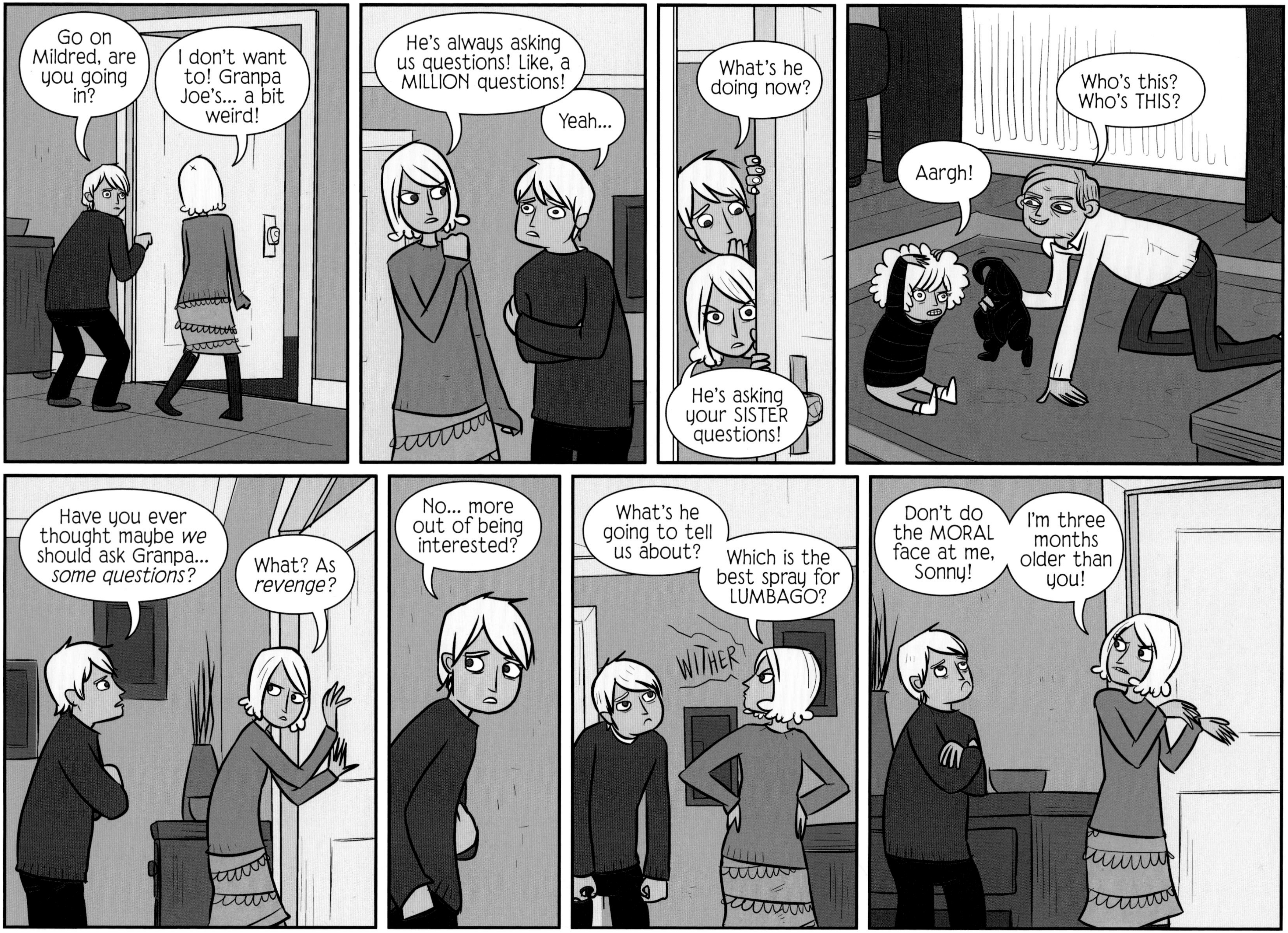
Go on Mildred, are you going in?
I don't want to! Granpa Joe's... a bit weird!
He's always asking us questions! Like, a MILLION questions!
Yeah...
What's he doing now?
He's asking your SISTER questions!
Who's this? Who's THIS?
Aargh!
Have you ever thought maybe *we* should ask Granpa... *some questions?*
What? As *revenge?*
No... more out of being interested?
What's he going to tell us about?
Which is the best spray for LUMBAGO?
WITHER
Don't do the MORAL face at me, Sonny!
I'm three months older than you!

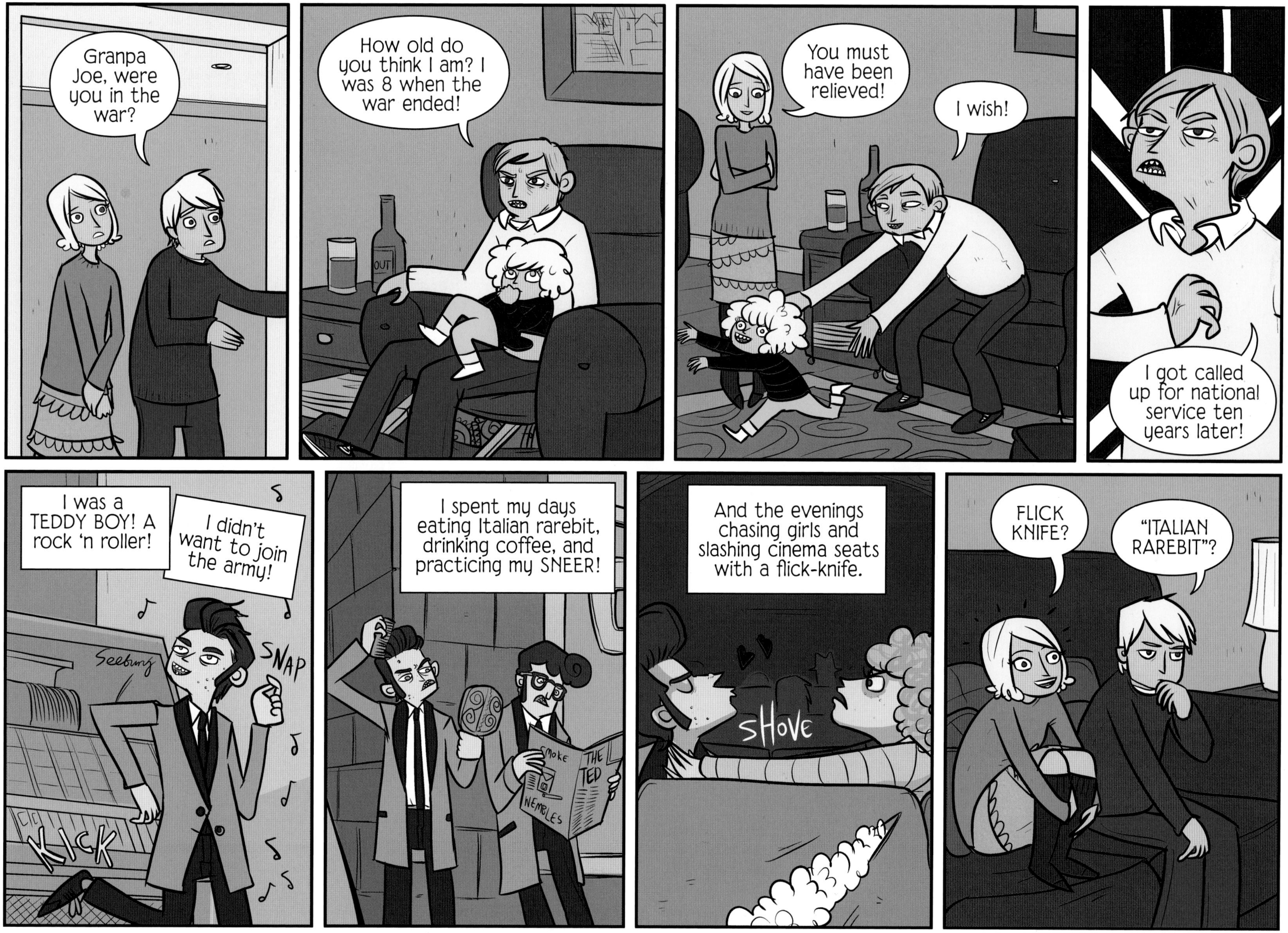
Granpa Joe, were you in the war?
How old do you think I am? I was 8 when the war ended!
OUT
You must have been relieved!
I wish!
I got called up for national service ten years later!
I was a TEDDY BOY! A rock 'n roller!
I didn't want to join the army!
Seeburg
SNAP
KICK
I spent my days eating Italian rarebit, drinking coffee, and practicing my SNEER!
SMOKE
THE TED
WEMBLES
And the evenings chasing girls and slashing cinema seats with a flick-knife.
SHOVE
FLICK KNIFE?
"ITALIAN RAREBIT"?

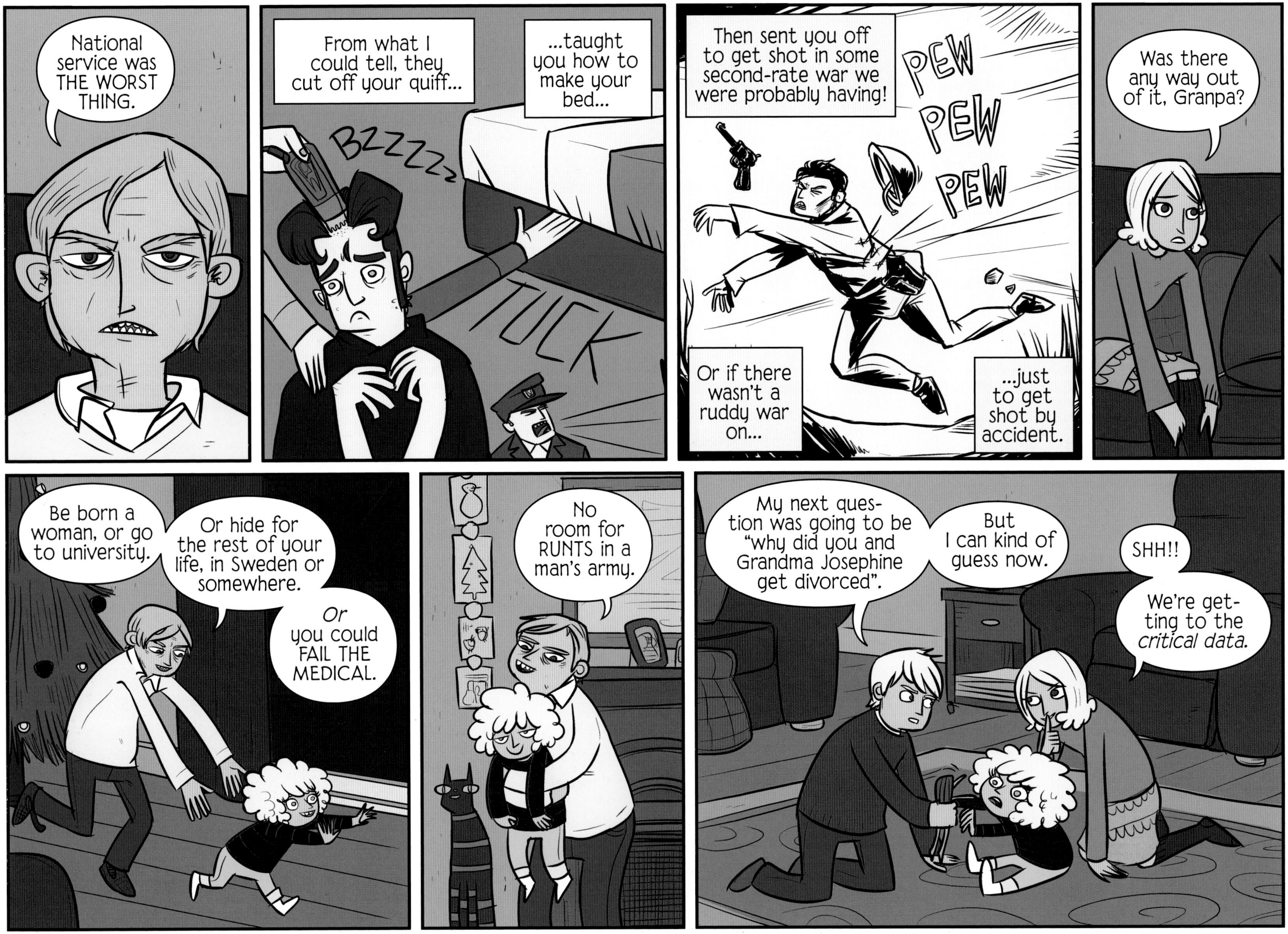
National service was THE WORST THING.
From what I could tell, they cut off your quiff...
BZZZZZz
...taught you how to make your bed...
TUCK
Then sent you off to get shot in some second-rate war we were probably having!
PEW
PEW
PEW
Or if there wasn't a ruddy war on...
...just to get shot by accident.
Was there any way out of it, Granpa?
Be born a woman, or go to university.
Or hide for the rest of your life, in Sweden or somewhere.
Or you could FAIL THE MEDICAL.
No room for RUNTS in a man's army.
My next question was going to be "why did you and Grandma Josephine get divorced".
But I can kind of guess now.
SHH!!
We're getting to the *critical data.*

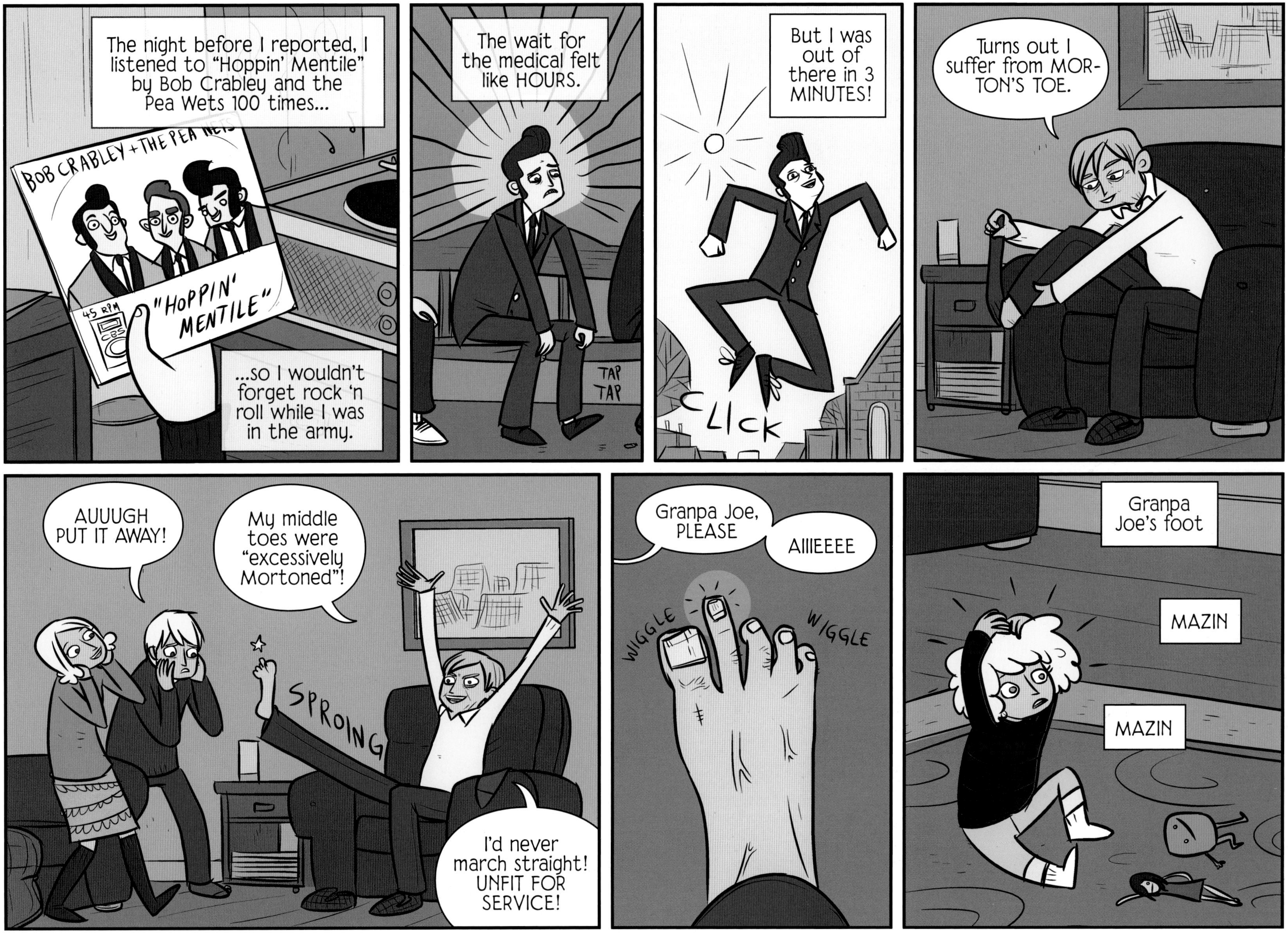
The night before I reported, I listened to "Hoppin' Mentile" by Bob Crabley and the Pea Wets 100 times...
BOB CRABLEY + THE PEA WETS
"HOPPIN' MENTILE"
45 RPM
CBS
...so I wouldn't forget rock 'n roll while I was in the army.
The wait for the medical felt like HOURS.
TAP TAP
But I was out of there in 3 MINUTES!
CLICK
Turns out I suffer from MORTON'S TOE.
AUUUGH PUT IT AWAY!
My middle toes were "excessively Mortoned"!
SPROING
I'd never march straight! UNFIT FOR SERVICE!
Granpa Joe, PLEASE
AIIIEEEE
WIGGLE
WIGGLE
Granpa Joe's foot
MAZIN
MAZIN

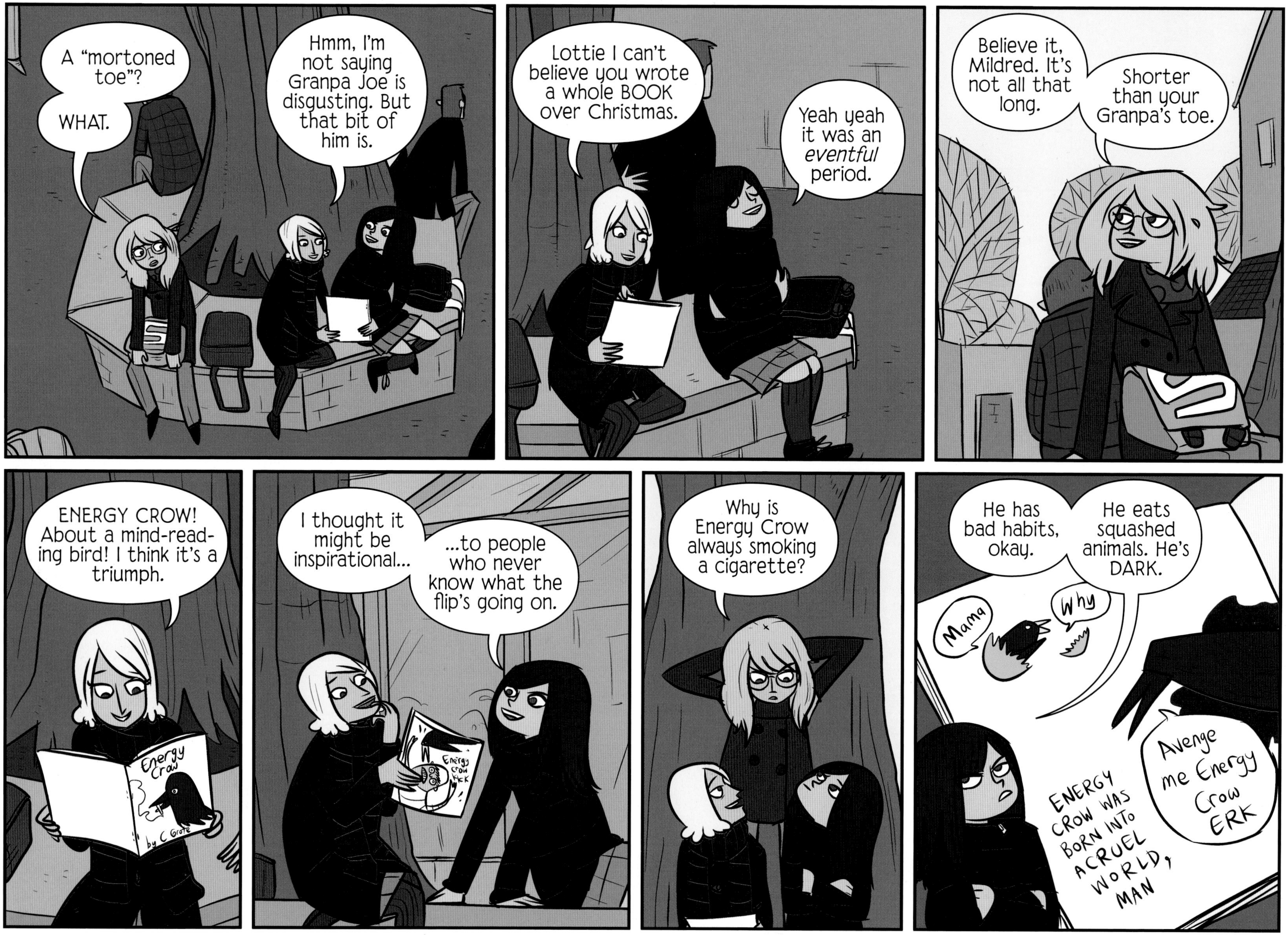
A "mortoned toe"?
WHAT.
Hmm, I'm not saying Granpa Joe is disgusting. But that bit of him is.
Lottie I can't believe you wrote a whole BOOK over Christmas.
Yeah yeah it was an *eventful* period.
Believe it, Mildred. It's not all that long.
Shorter than your Granpa's toe.
ENERGY CROW! About a mind-reading bird! I think it's a triumph.
Energy Crow
by C Grote
I thought it might be inspirational...
...to people who never know what the flip's going on.
Why is Energy Crow always smoking a cigarette?
He has bad habits, okay.
He eats squashed animals. He's DARK.
Mama
Why
ENERGY CROW WAS BORN INTO A CRUEL WORLD, MAN
Avenge me Energy Crow ERK

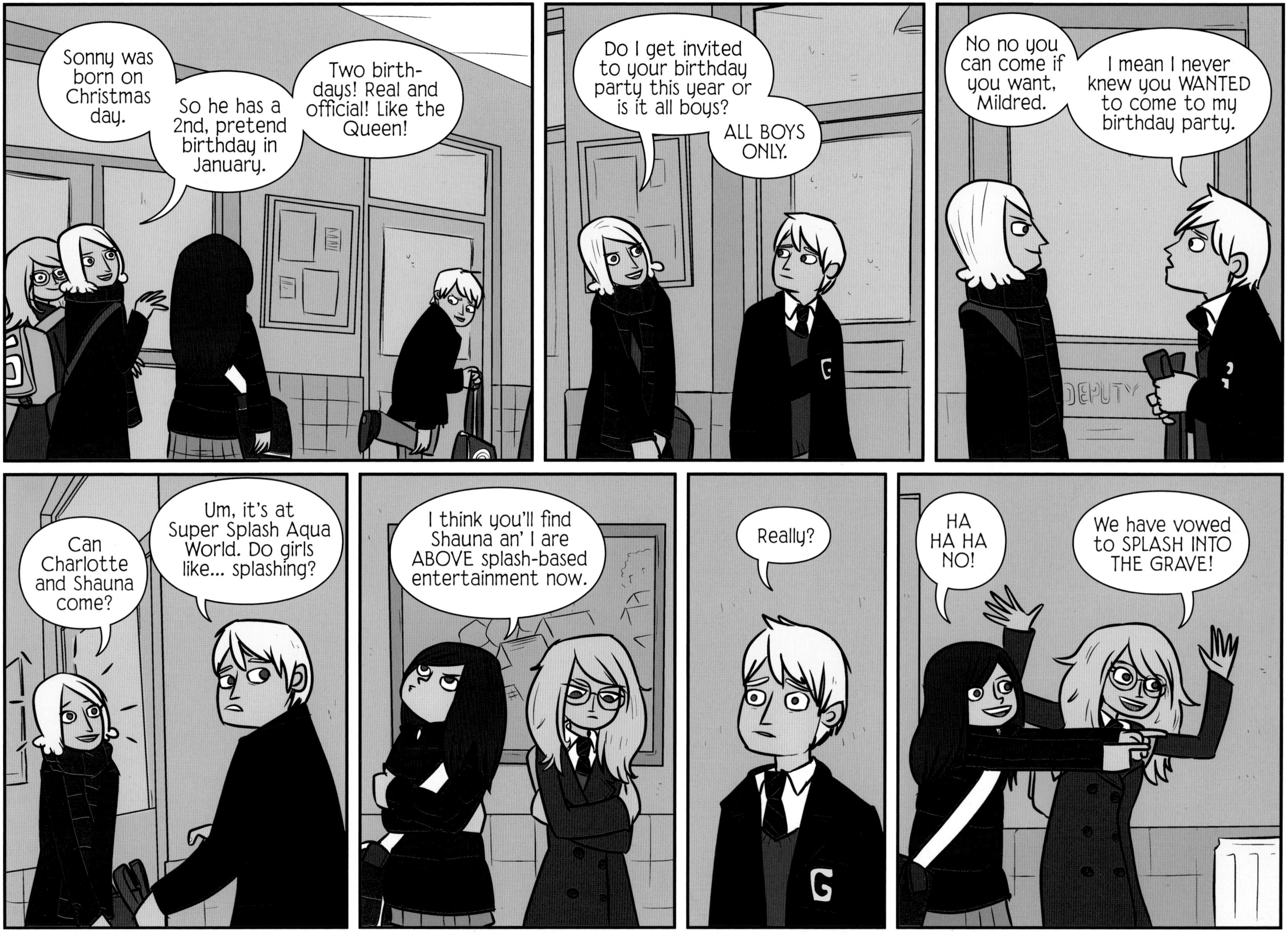
Sonny was born on Christmas day.
So he has a 2nd, pretend birthday in January.
Two birth-days! Real and official! Like the Queen!
Do I get invited to your birthday party this year or is it all boys?
ALL BOYS ONLY.
No no you can come if you want, Mildred.
I mean I never knew you WANTED to come to my birthday party.
DEPUTY
Can Charlotte and Shauna come?
Um, it's at Super Splash Aqua World. Do girls like... splashing?
I think you'll find Shauna an' I are ABOVE splash-based entertainment now.
Really?
HA HA HA NO!
We have vowed to SPLASH INTO THE GRAVE!
G

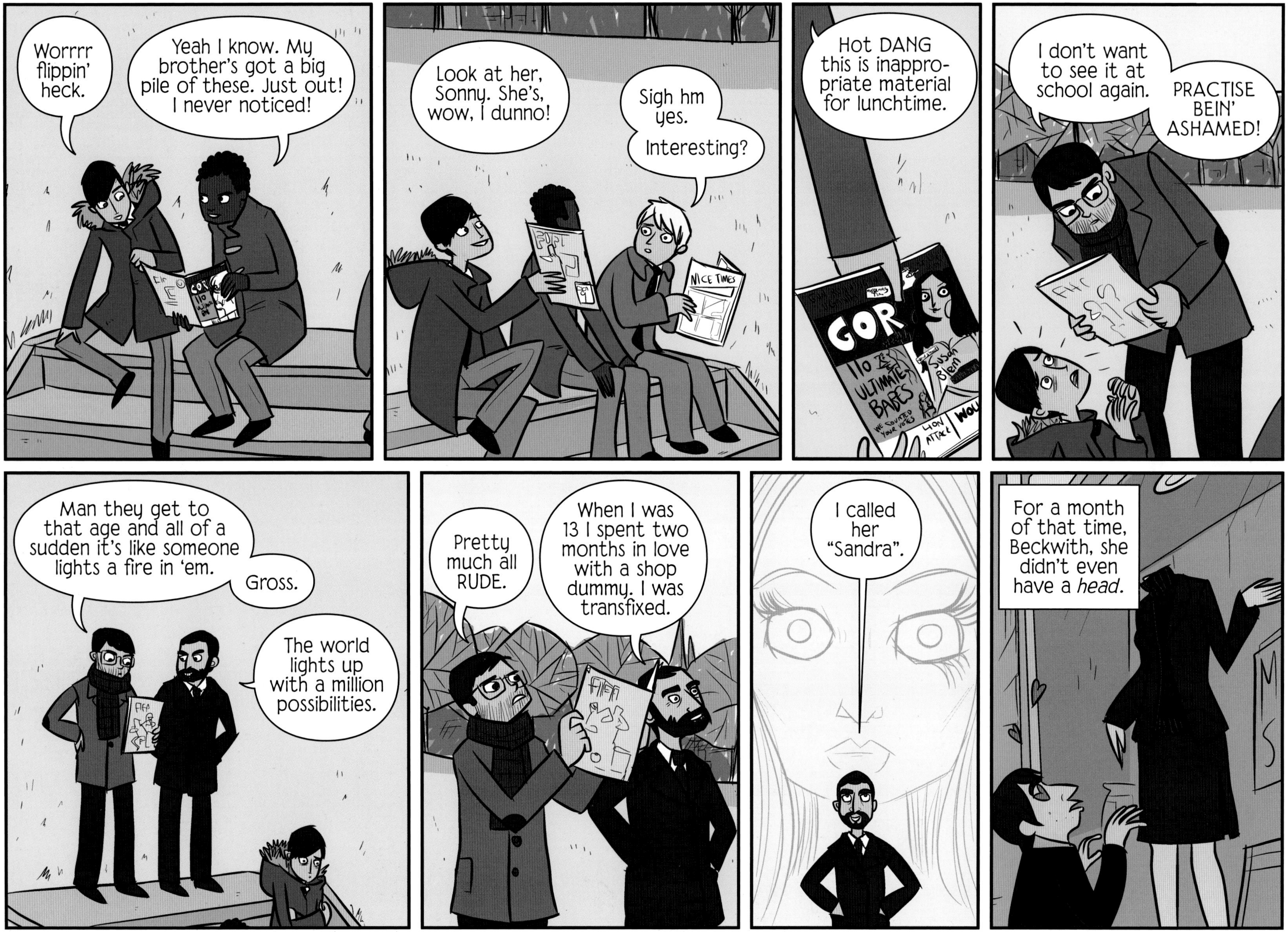
Worrrr flippin' heck.
Yeah I know. My brother's got a big pile of these. Just out! I never noticed!
Look at her, Sonny. She's, wow, I dunno!
Sigh hm yes.
Interesting?
NICE TIMES
Hot DANG this is inappropriate material for lunchtime.
GOR
110 ULTIMATE BABES
WE COUNTED YOUR VOTES
Susan Blem
LION ATTACK
I don't want to see it at school again.
PRACTISE BEIN' ASHAMED!
Man they get to that age and all of a sudden it's like someone lights a fire in 'em.
Gross.
The world lights up with a million possibilities.
Pretty much all RUDE.
When I was 13 I spent two months in love with a shop dummy. I was transfixed.
I called her "Sandra".
For a month of that time, Beckwith, she didn't even have a *head*.

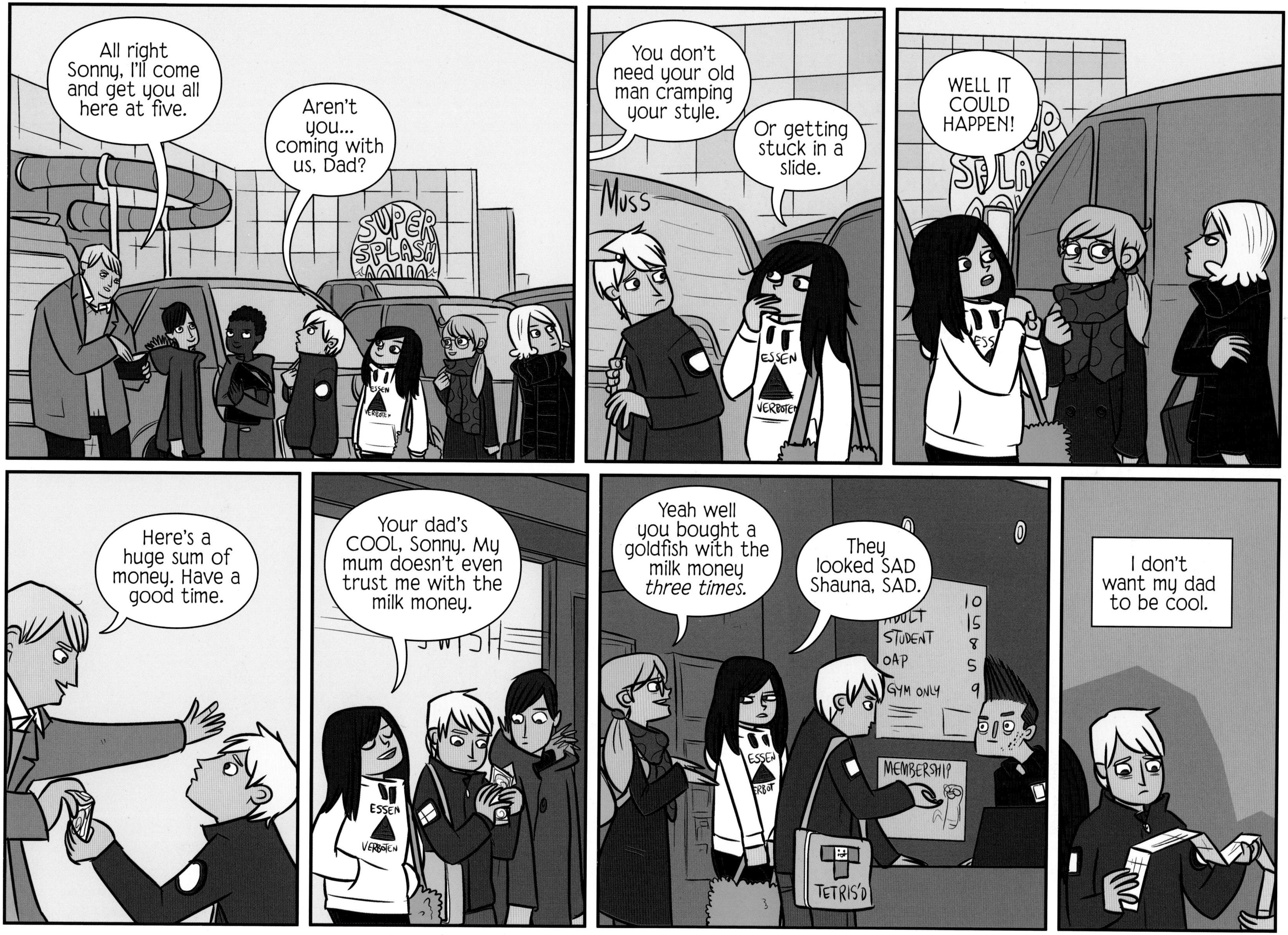
All right Sonny, I'll come and get you all here at five.
Aren't you... coming with us, Dad?
SUPER SPLASH
ESSEN VERBOTEN
You don't need your old man cramping your style.
Or getting stuck in a slide.
MUSS
WELL IT COULD HAPPEN!
Here's a huge sum of money. Have a good time.
Your dad's COOL, Sonny. My mum doesn't even trust me with the milk money.
Yeah well you bought a goldfish with the milk money *three times.*
They looked SAD Shauna, SAD.
STUDENT 8
OAP 5
GYM ONLY 9
MEMBERSHIP
TETRIS'D
I don't want my dad to be cool.

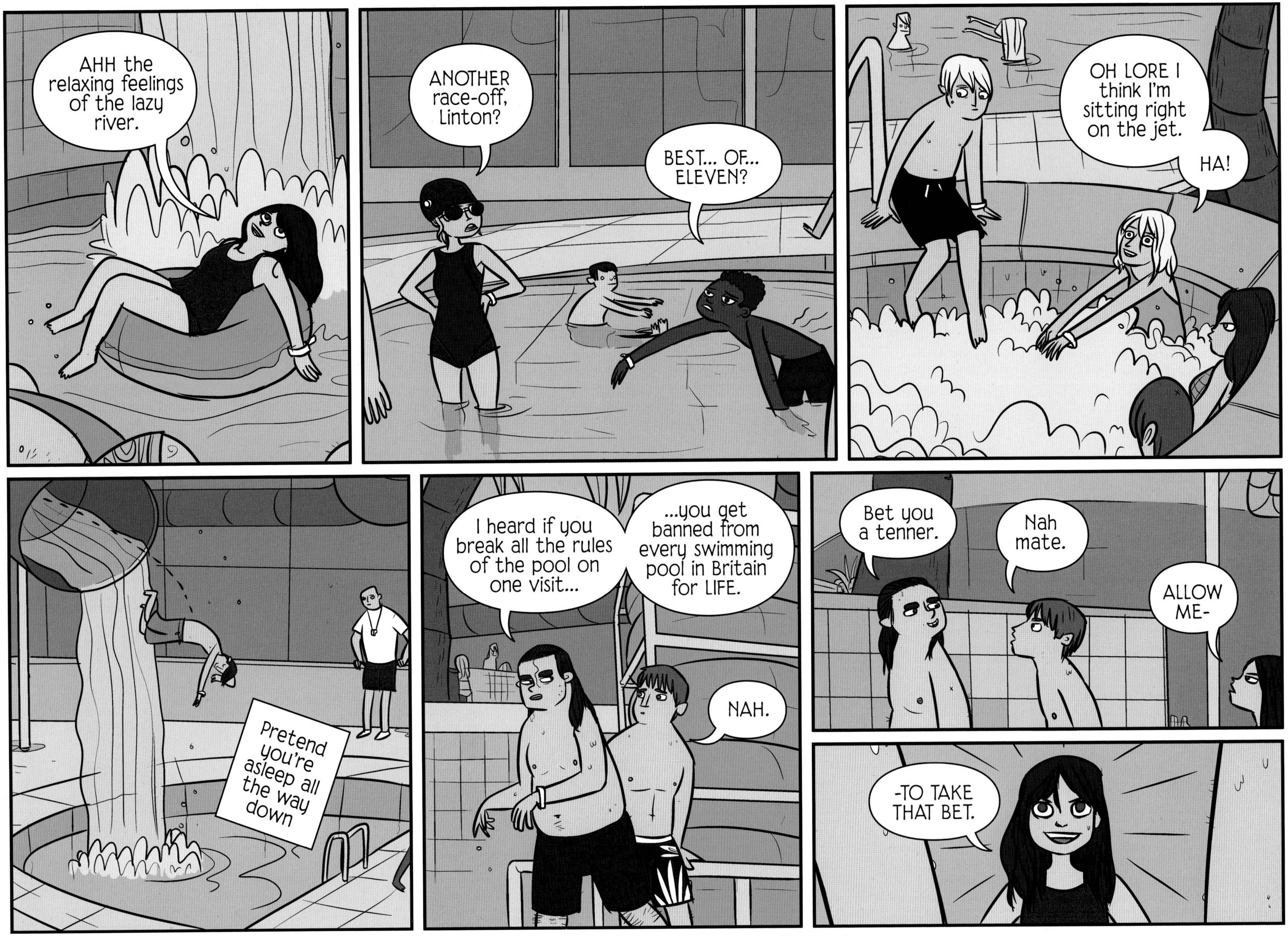

AHH the relaxing feelings of the lazy river.
ANOTHER race-off, Linton?
BEST... OF... ELEVEN?
OH LORE I think I'm sitting right on the jet.
HA!
Pretend you're asleep all the way down
I heard if you break all the rules of the pool on one visit...
...you get banned from every swimming pool in Britain for LIFE.
NAH.
Bet you a tenner.
Nah mate.
ALLOW ME-
-TO TAKE THAT BET.

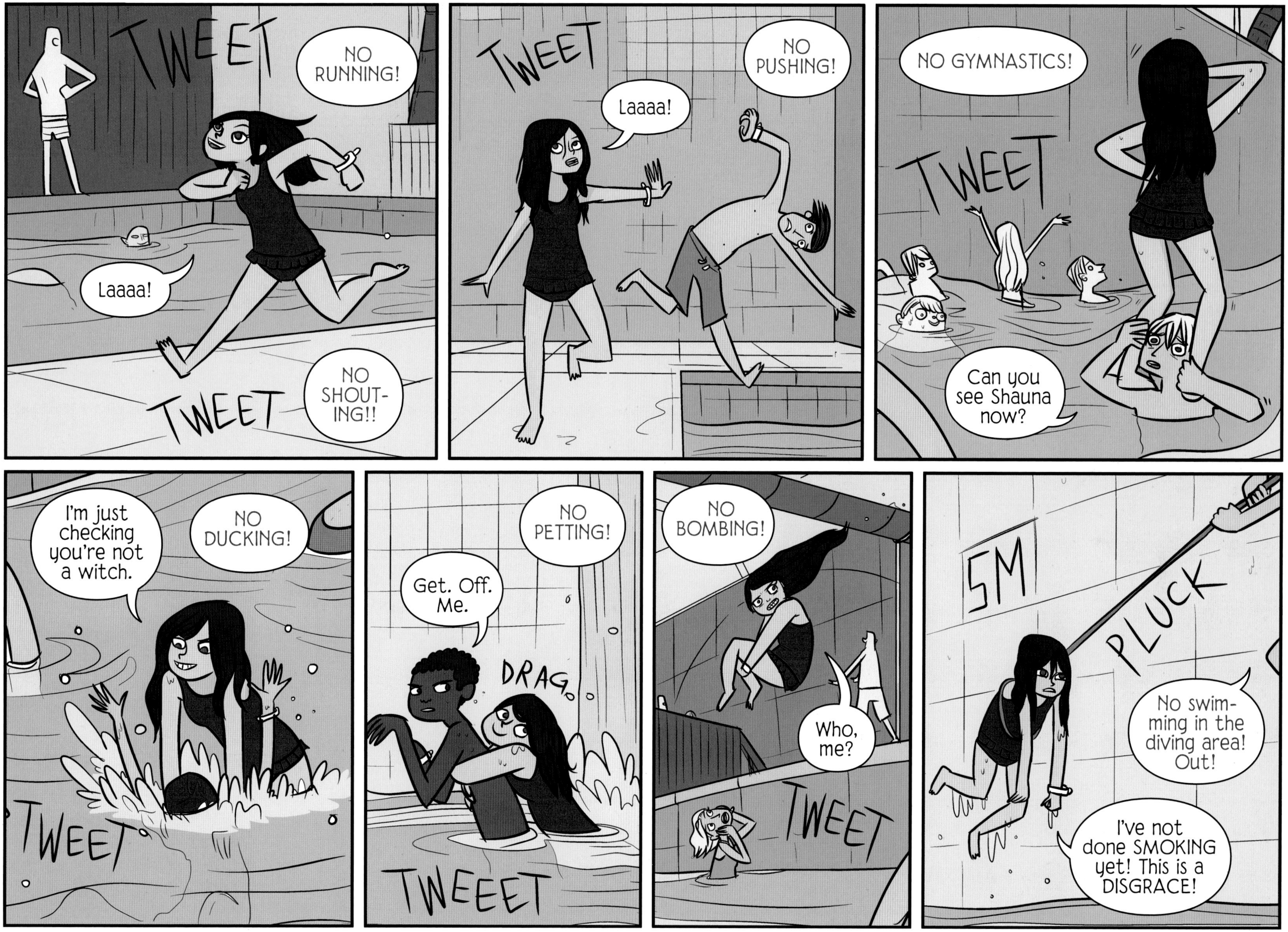
TWEET
NO RUNNING!
Laaaa!
TWEET
NO SHOUTING!!
TWEET
NO PUSHING!
Laaaa!
NO GYMNASTICS!
TWEET
Can you see Shauna now?
I'm just checking you're not a witch.
NO DUCKING!
TWEET
NO PETTING!
Get. Off. Me.
DRAG
TWEEET
NO BOMBING!
Who, me?
TWEET
5M
PLUCK
No swimming in the diving area! Out!
I've not done SMOKING yet! This is a DISGRACE!

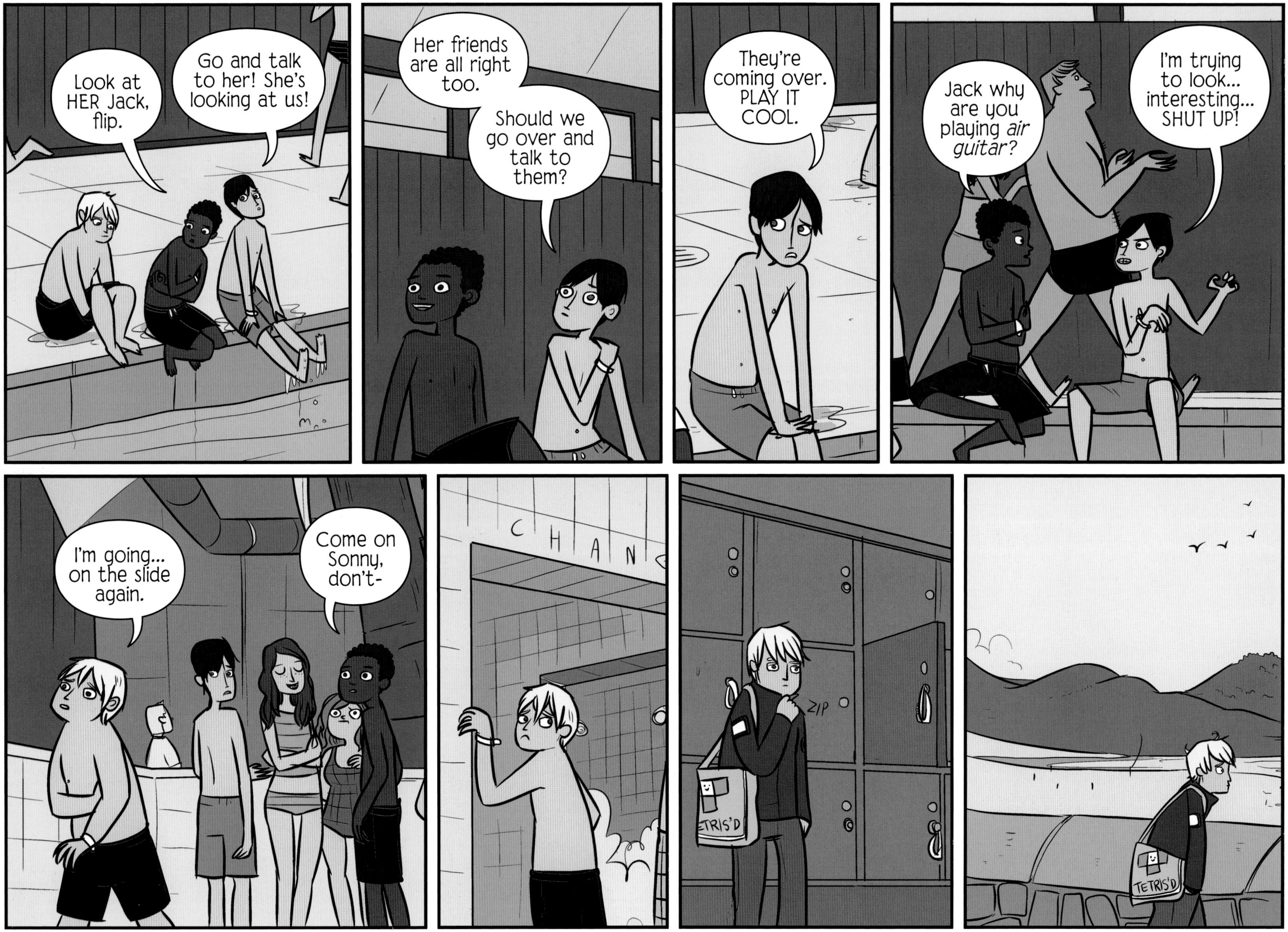
Look at HER Jack, flip.
Go and talk to her! She's looking at us!
Her friends are all right too.
Should we go over and talk to them?
They're coming over. PLAY IT COOL.
Jack why are you playing *air guitar?*
I'm trying to look... interesting... SHUT UP!
I'm going... on the slide again.
Come on Sonny, don't-
CHAN
ZIP
TETRIS'D
TETRIS'D

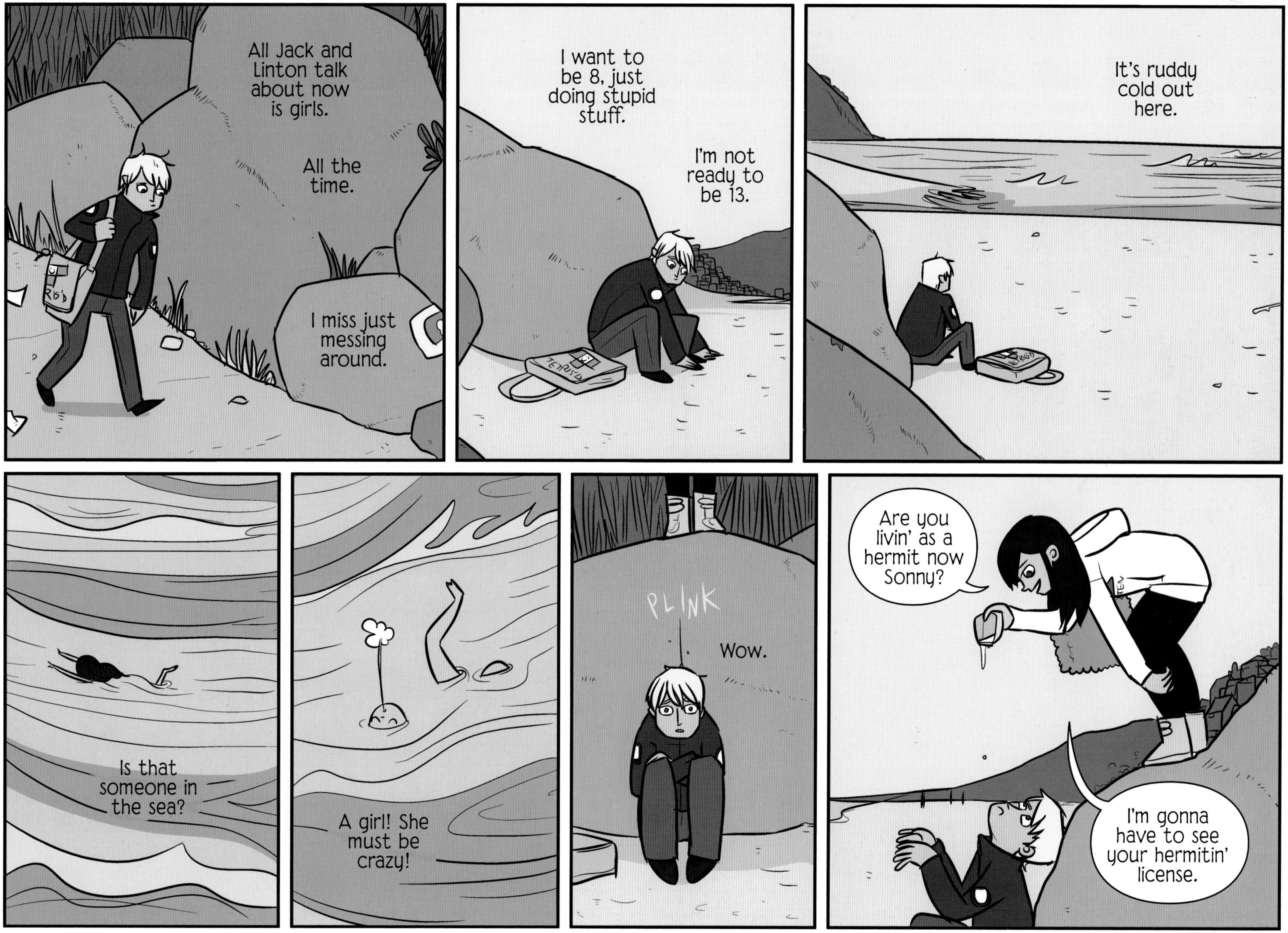
All Jack and Linton talk about now is girls.
All the time.
I miss just messing around.
I want to be 8, just doing stupid stuff.
I'm not ready to be 13.
It's ruddy cold out here.
Is that someone in the sea?
A girl! She must be crazy!
PLINK
Wow.
Are you livin' as a hermit now Sonny?
I'm gonna have to see your hermitin' license.

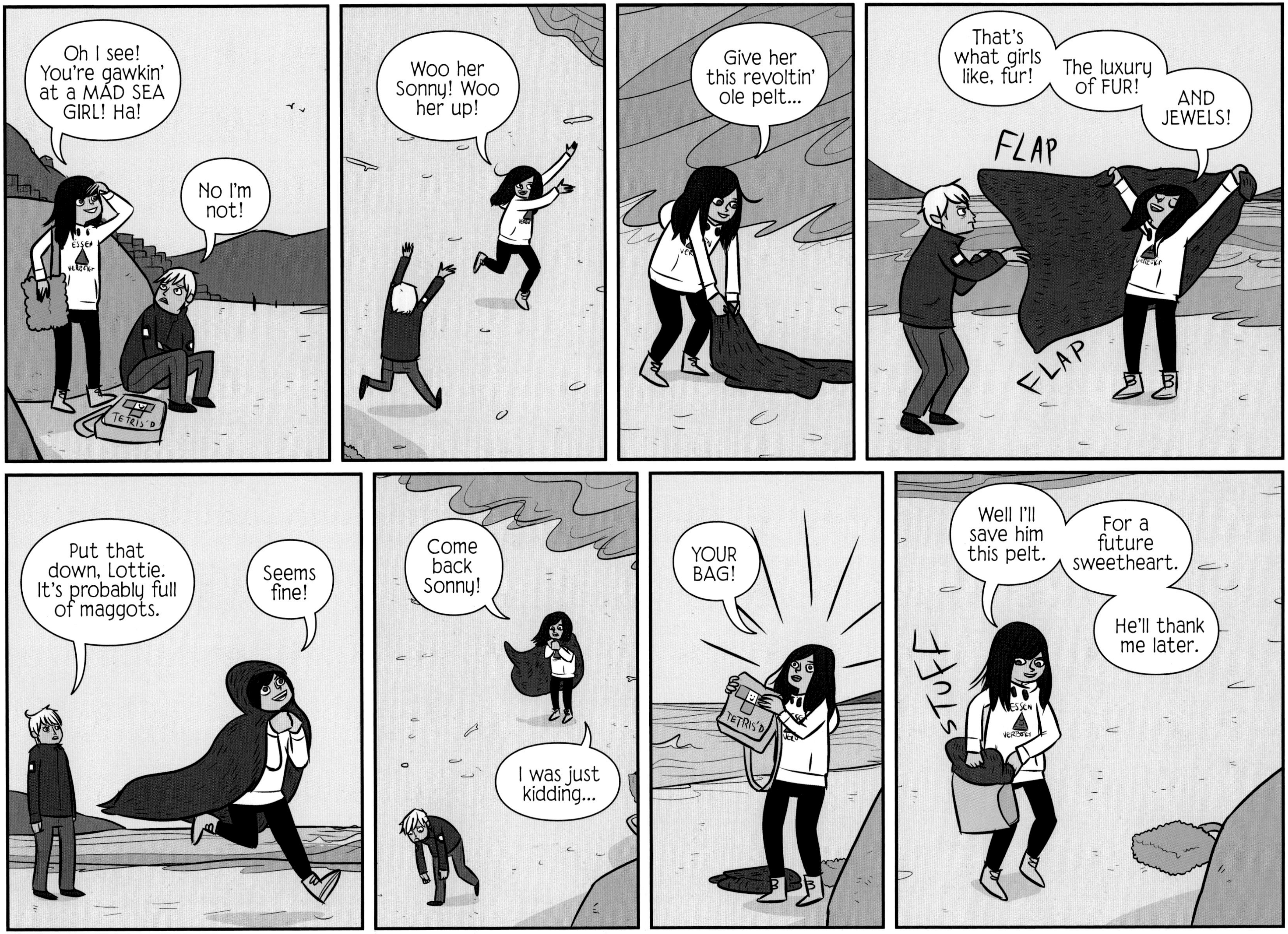
Oh I see! You're gawkin' at a MAD SEA GIRL! Ha!
No I'm not!
TETRIS'D
Woo her Sonny! Woo her up!
Give her this revoltin' ole pelt...
That's what girls like, fur!
The luxury of FUR!
AND JEWELS!
FLAP
FLAP
Put that down, Lottie. It's probably full of maggots.
Seems fine!
Come back Sonny!
I was just kidding...
YOUR BAG!
TETRIS'D
STUFF
Well I'll save him this pelt.
For a future sweetheart.
He'll thank me later.

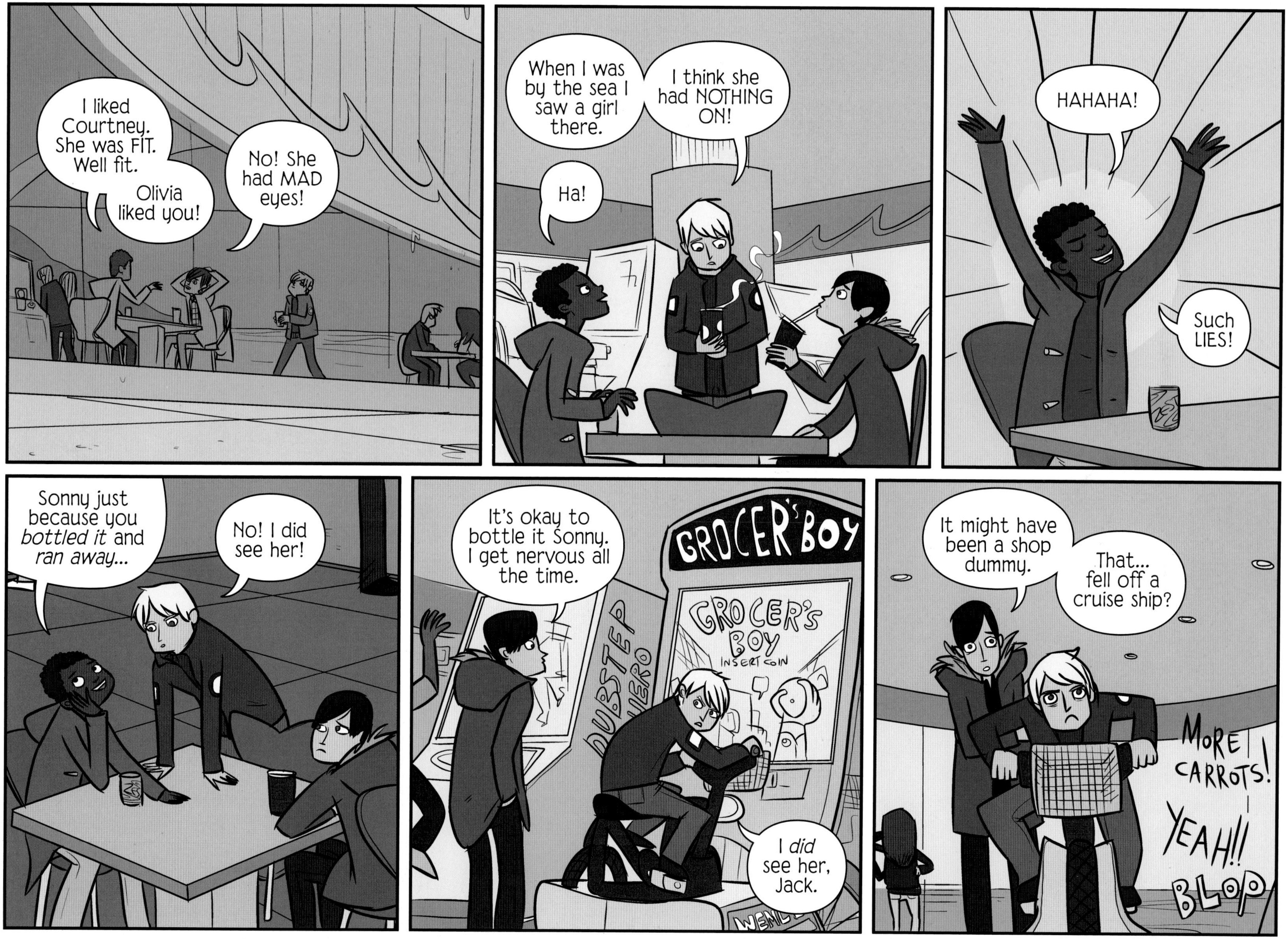
I liked Courtney. She was FIT. Well fit.
Olivia liked you!
No! She had MAD eyes!
When I was by the sea I saw a girl there.
I think she had NOTHING ON!
Ha!
HAHAHA!
Such LIES!
Sonny just because you *bottled it* and *ran away...*
No! I did see her!
It's okay to bottle it Sonny. I get nervous all the time.
GROCER'S BOY
GROCER'S BOY
INSERT COIN
DUBSTEP HERO
I *did* see her, Jack.
It might have been a shop dummy.
That... fell off a cruise ship?
MORE CARROTS!
YEAH!!
BLOP

Bad Machinery, Volume Five

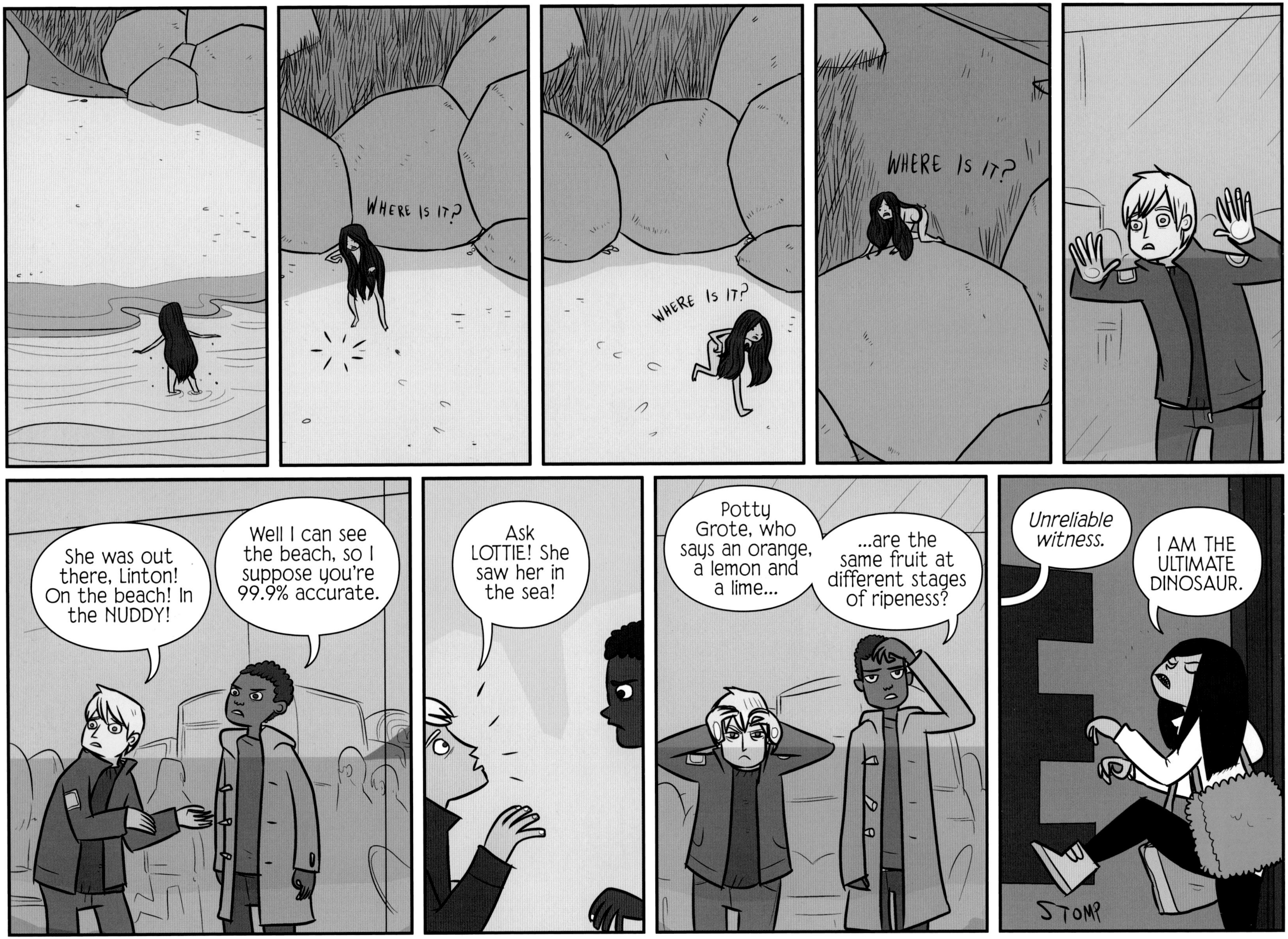
WHERE IS IT?
WHERE IS IT?
WHERE IS IT?
She was out there, Linton! On the beach! In the NUDDY!
Well I can see the beach, so I suppose you're 99.9% accurate.
Ask LOTTIE! She saw her in the sea!
Potty Grote, who says an orange, a lemon and a lime...
...are the same fruit at different stages of ripeness?
Unreliable witness.
I AM THE ULTIMATE DINOSAUR.
STOMP

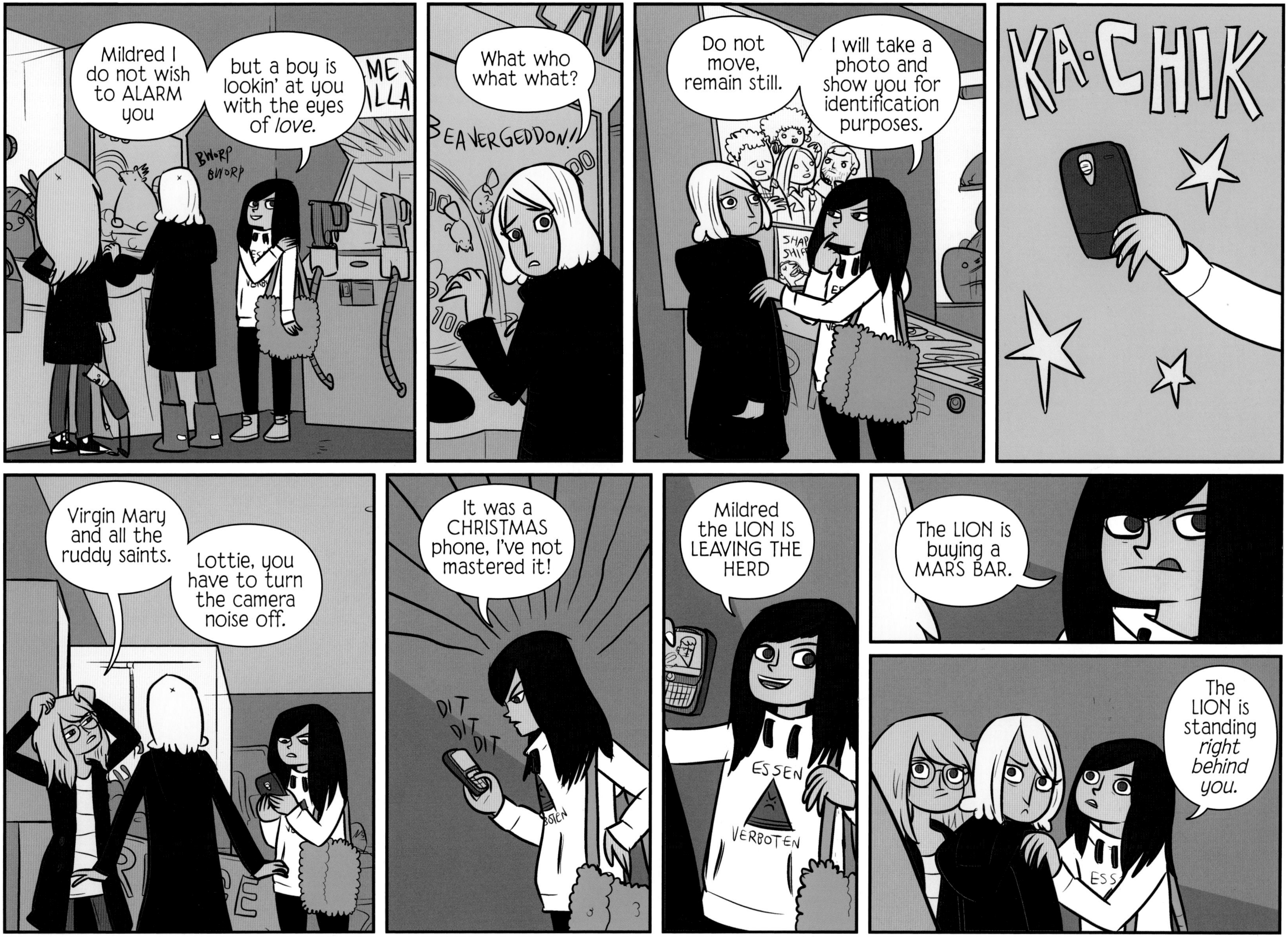
Mildred I do not wish to ALARM you
but a boy is lookin' at you with the eyes of *love.*
BWORP BWORP
What who what what?
BEAVERGEDDON!
Do not move, remain still.
I will take a photo and show you for identification purposes.
KA-CHIK
Virgin Mary and all the ruddy saints.
Lottie, you have to turn the camera noise off.
It was a CHRISTMAS phone, I've not mastered it!
DIT DIT DIT
Mildred the LION IS LEAVING THE HERD
ESSEN
VERBOTEN
The LION is buying a MARS BAR.
The LION is standing *right behind* you.

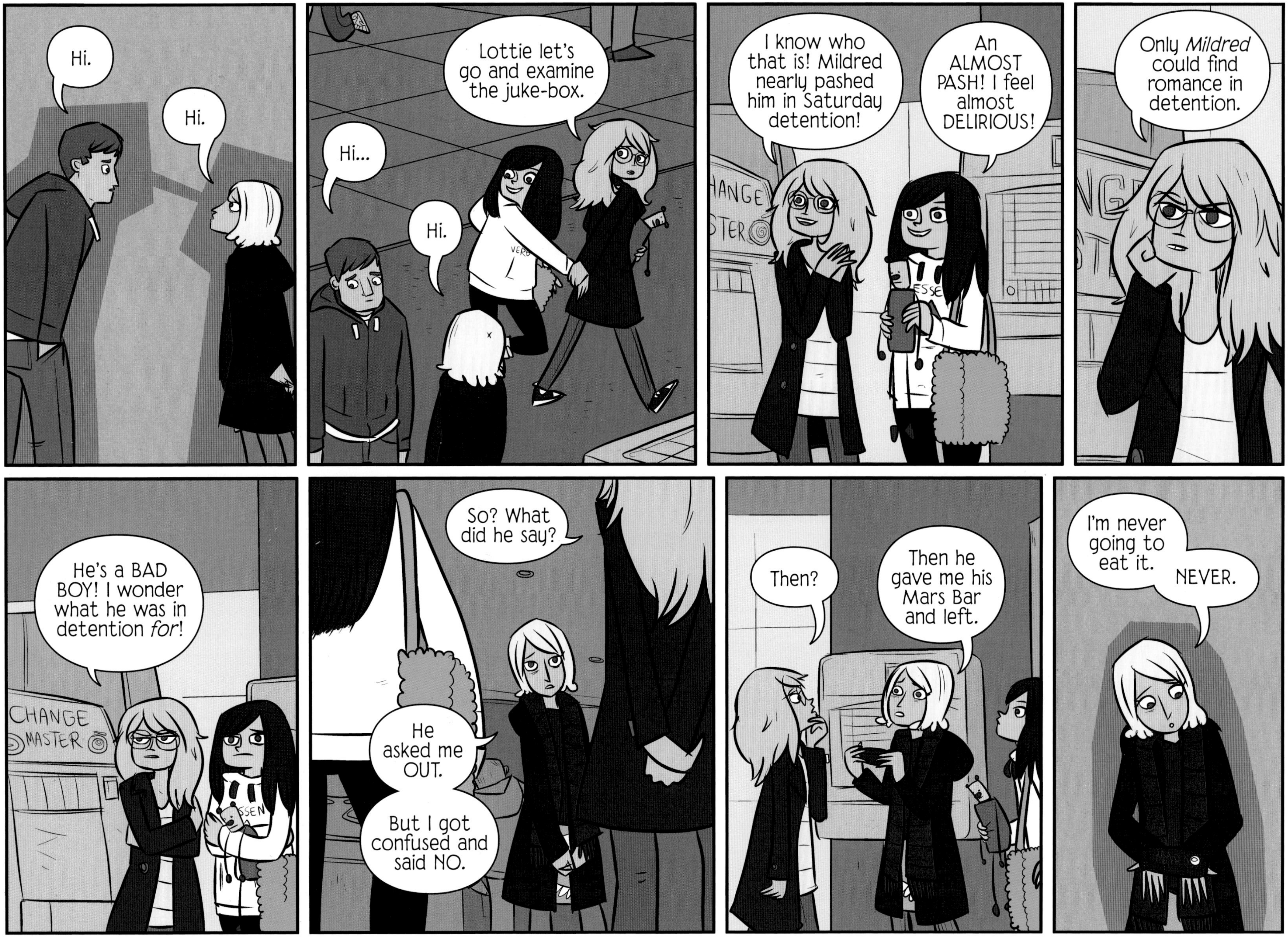
Hi.
Hi.
Lottie let's go and examine the juke-box.
Hi...
Hi.
VERO
I know who that is! Mildred nearly pashed him in Saturday detention!
An ALMOST PASH! I feel almost DELIRIOUS!
HANGE
STER
ESSE
Only *Mildred* could find romance in detention.
He's a BAD BOY! I wonder what he was in detention *for*!
CHANGE
MASTER
SSEN
So? What did he say?
He asked me OUT.
But I got confused and said NO.
Then?
Then he gave me his Mars Bar and left.
I'm never going to eat it.
NEVER.

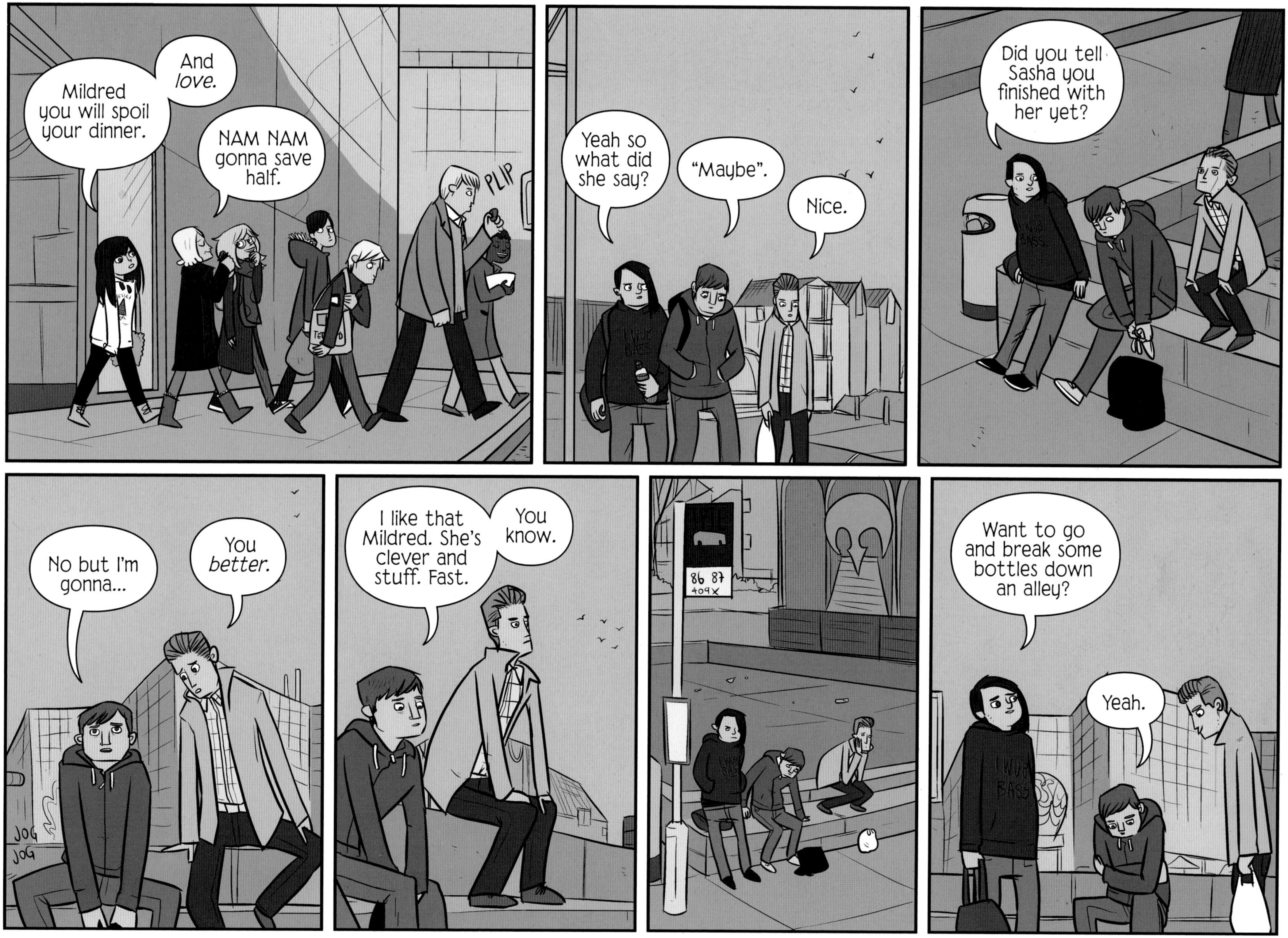
Mildred you will spoil your dinner.
And *love.*
NAM NAM gonna save half.
PLIP
Yeah so what did she say?
"Maybe".
Nice.
Did you tell Sasha you finished with her yet?
No but I'm gonna...
You *better.*
JOG JOG
I like that Mildred. She's clever and stuff. Fast.
You know.
86 87
409X
Want to go and break some bottles down an alley?
Yeah.

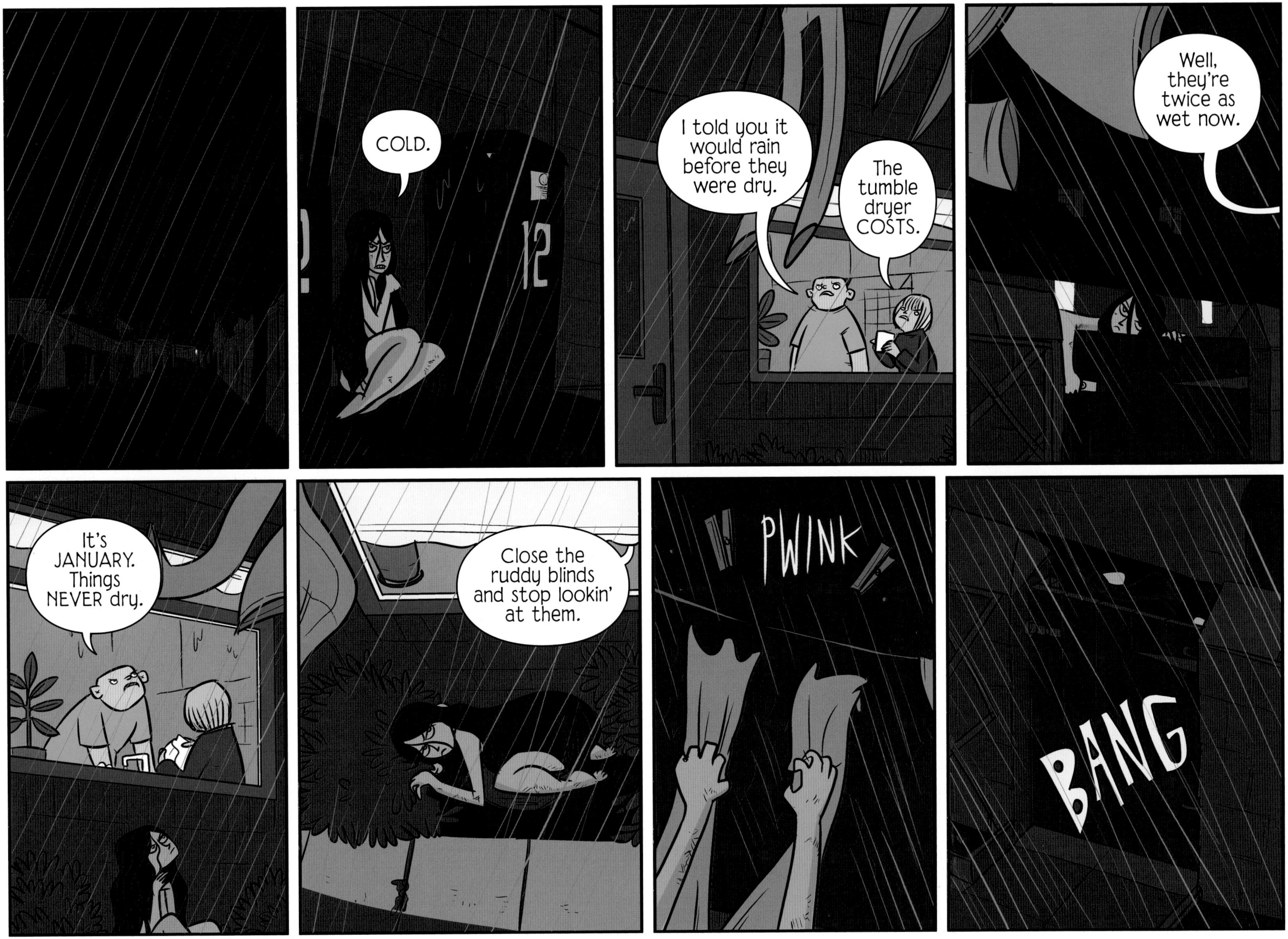
COLD.
12
I told you it would rain before they were dry.
The tumble dryer COSTS.
Well, they're twice as wet now.
It's JANUARY. Things NEVER dry.
Close the ruddy blinds and stop lookin' at them.
PWINK
BANG

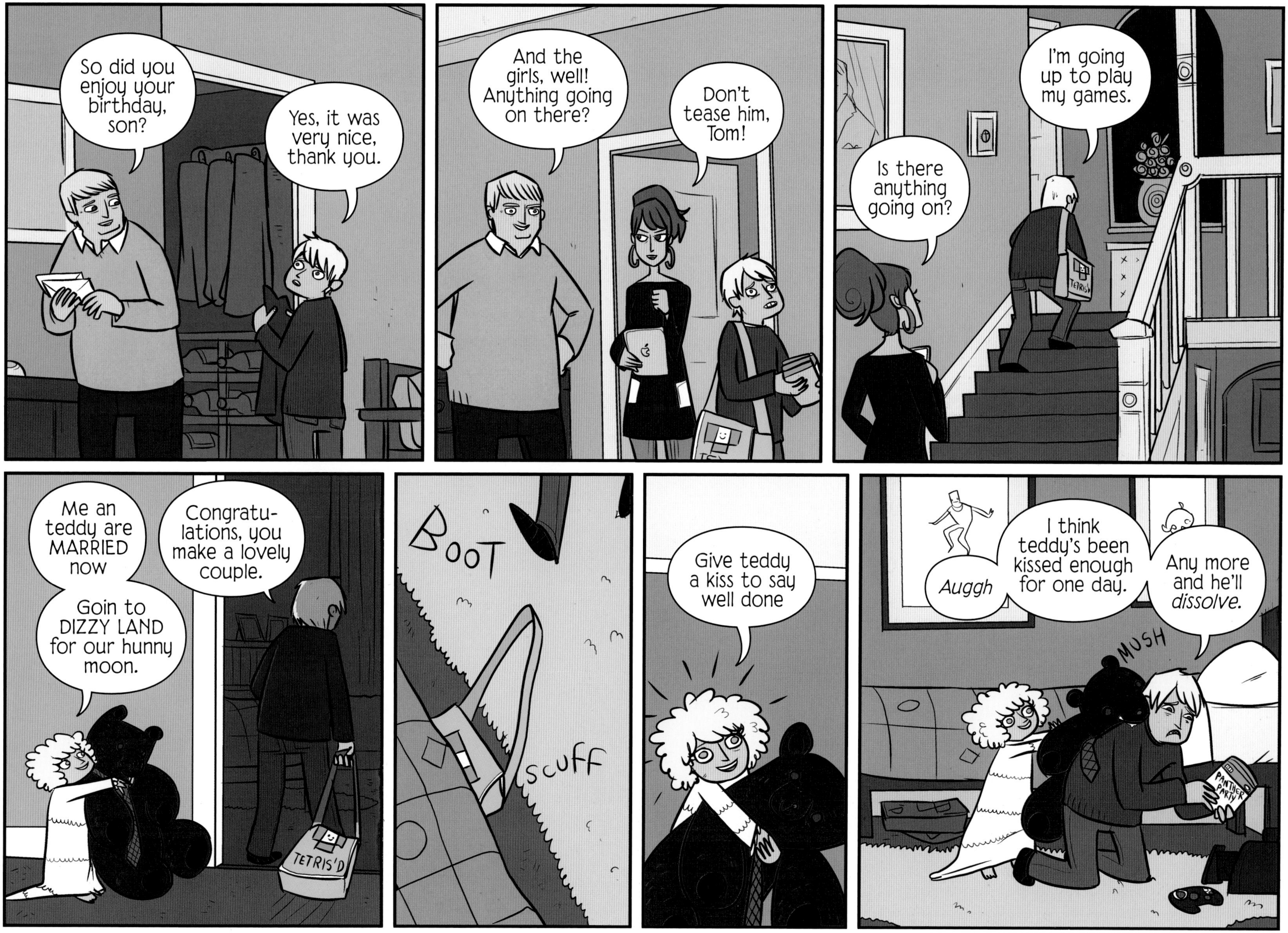
So did you enjoy your birthday, son?
Yes, it was very nice, thank you.
And the girls, well! Anything going on there?
Don't tease him, Tom!
I'm going up to play my games.
Is there anything going on?
TETRIS'D
Me an teddy are MARRIED now
Congratu-lations, you make a lovely couple.
Goin to DIZZY LAND for our hunny moon.
TETRIS'D
BOOT
SCUFF
Give teddy a kiss to say well done
Augh
I think teddy's been kissed enough for one day.
Any more and he'll *dissolve.*
MUSH
PANTHER PARTY

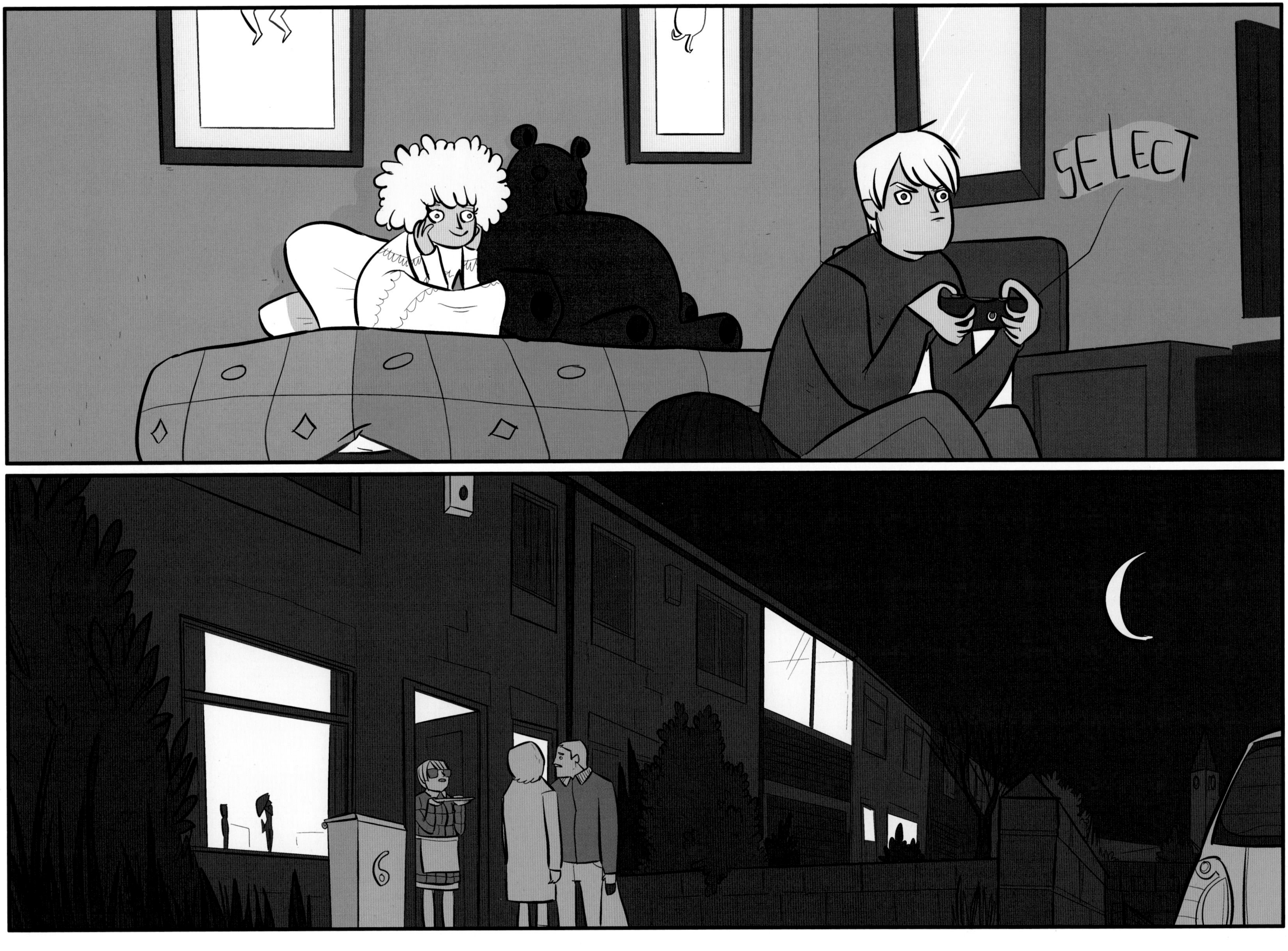
SELECT
6

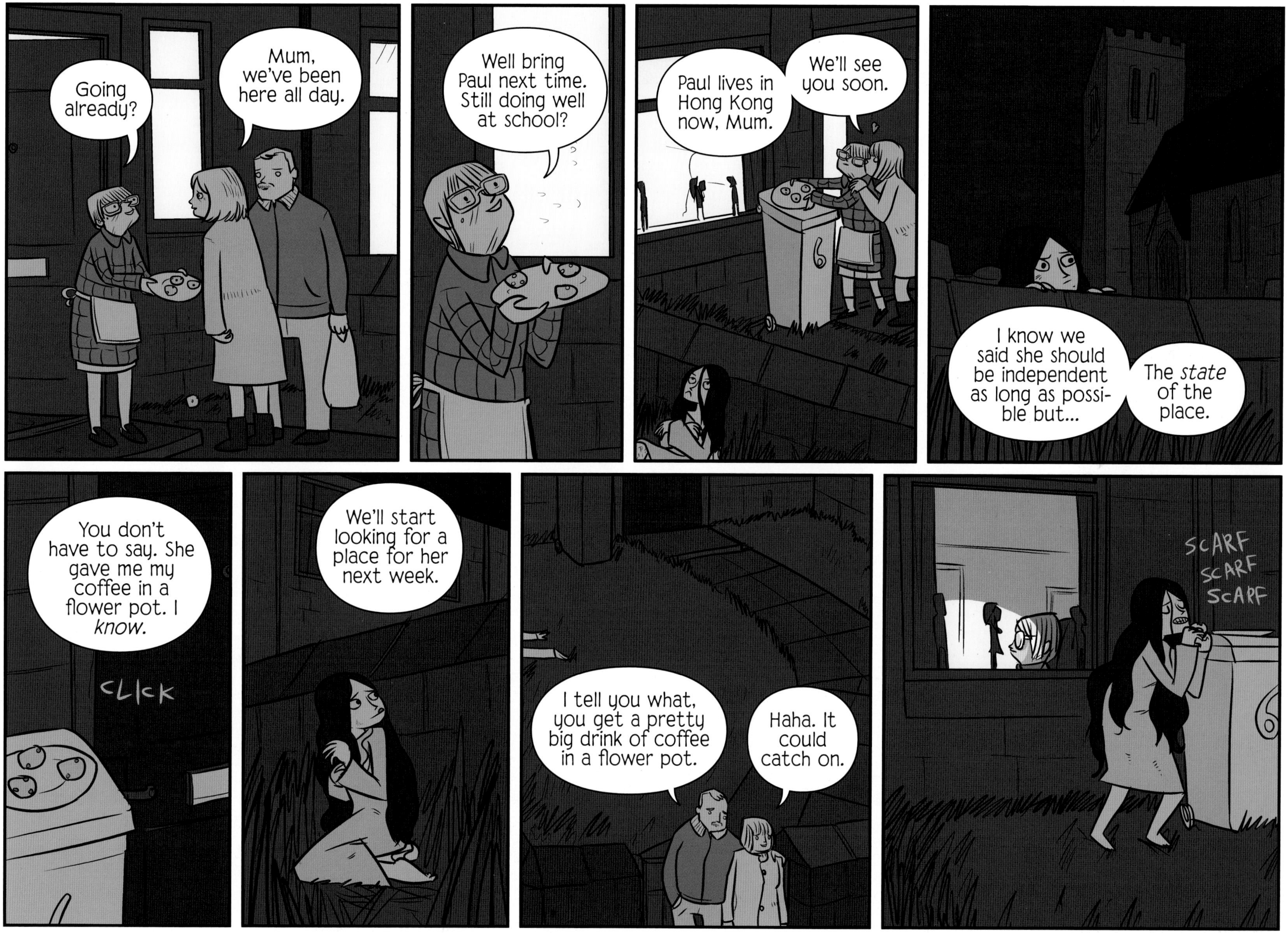
Going already?
Mum, we've been here all day.
Well bring Paul next time. Still doing well at school?
Paul lives in Hong Kong now, Mum.
We'll see you soon.
I know we said she should be independent as long as possible but...
The *state* of the place.
You don't have to say. She gave me my coffee in a flower pot. I *know.*
CLICK
We'll start looking for a place for her next week.
I tell you what, you get a pretty big drink of coffee in a flower pot.
Haha. It could catch on.
SCARF
SCARF
SCARF

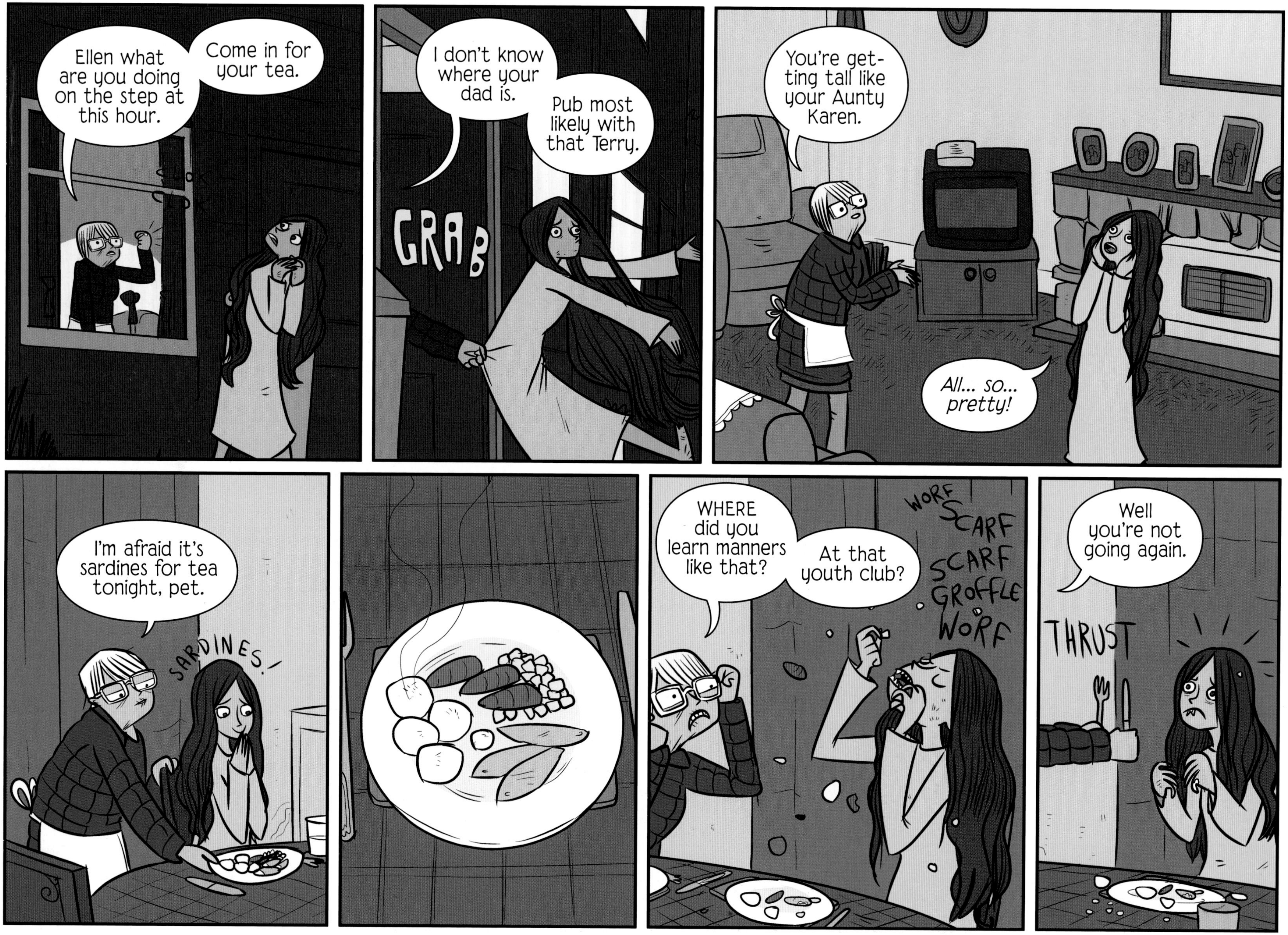
Ellen what are you doing on the step at this hour.
Come in for your tea.
I don't know where your dad is.
Pub most likely with that Terry.
GRAB
You're getting tall like your Aunty Karen.
All... so... pretty!
I'm afraid it's sardines for tea tonight, pet.
SARDINES!
WHERE did you learn manners like that?
At that youth club?
WORF
SCARF
SCARF
GROFFLE
WORF
Well you're not going again.
THRUST

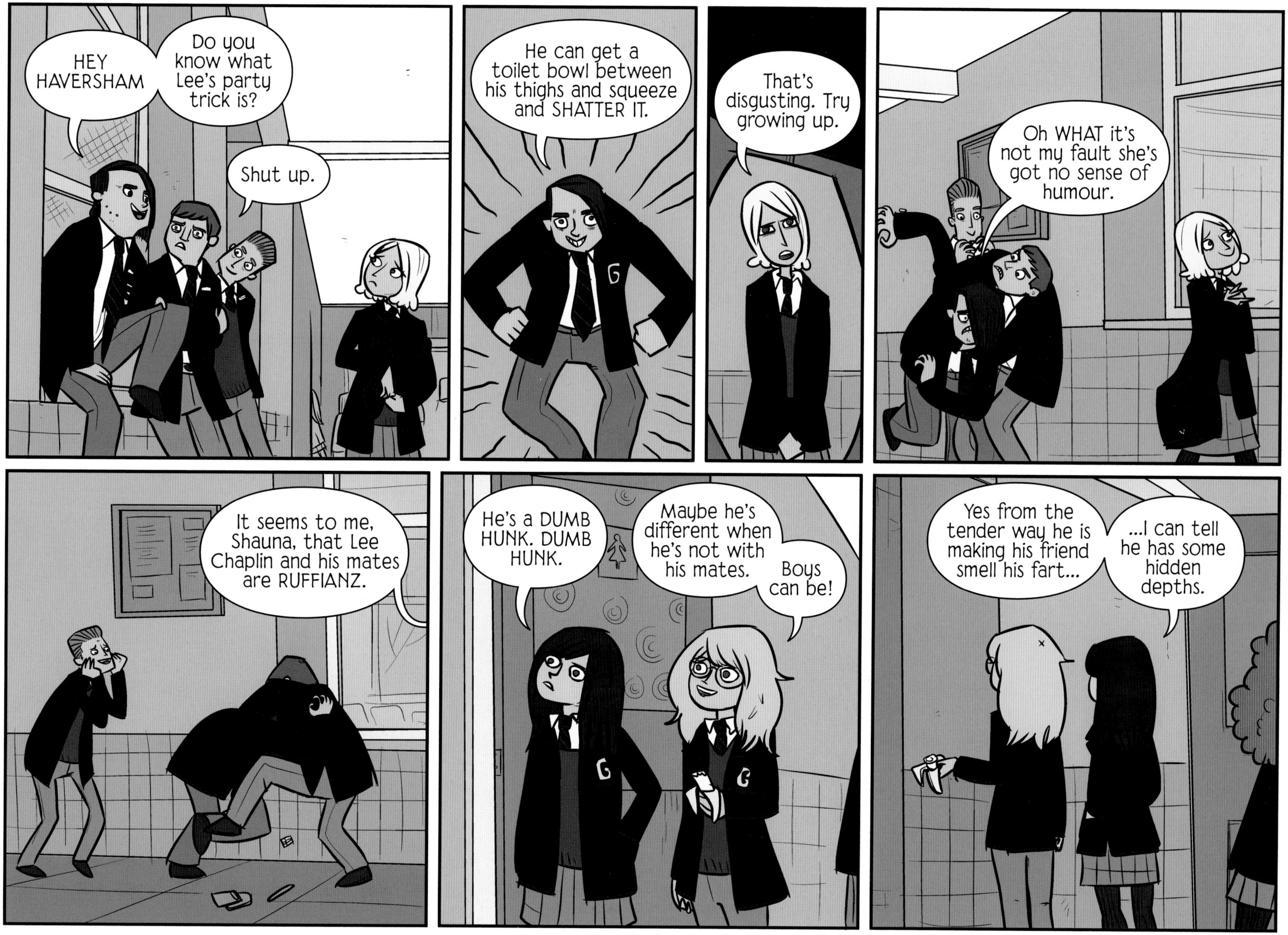
HEY HAVERSHAM
Do you know what Lee's party trick is?
Shut up.
He can get a toilet bowl between his thighs and squeeze and SHATTER IT.
That's disgusting. Try growing up.
Oh WHAT it's not my fault she's got no sense of humour.
It seems to me, Shauna, that Lee Chaplin and his mates are RUFFIANZ.
He's a DUMB HUNK. DUMB HUNK.
Maybe he's different when he's not with his mates.
Boys can be!
Yes from the tender way he is making his friend smell his fart...
...I can tell he has some hidden depths.

Bad Machinery, Volume Five

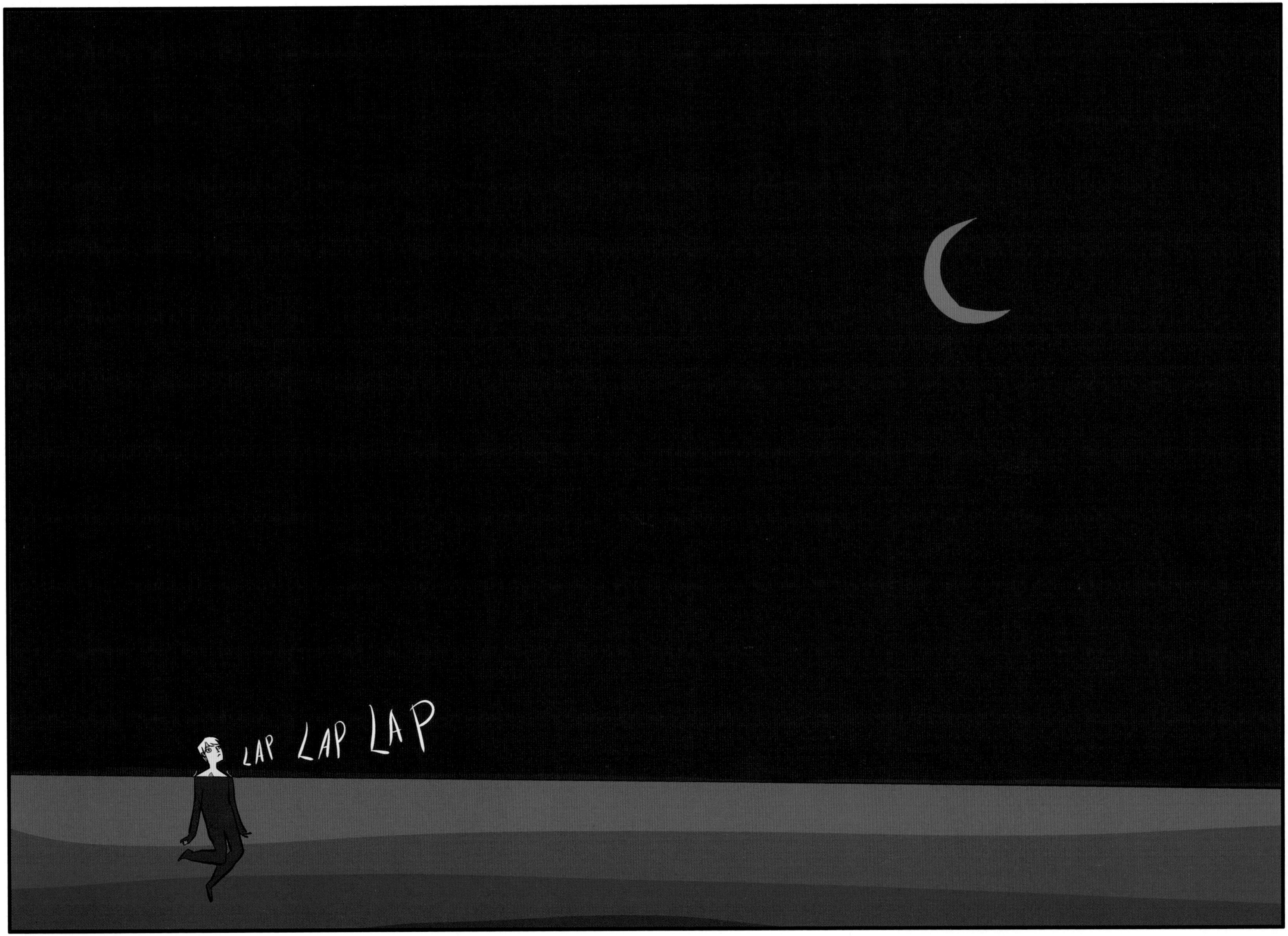
LAP LAP LAP

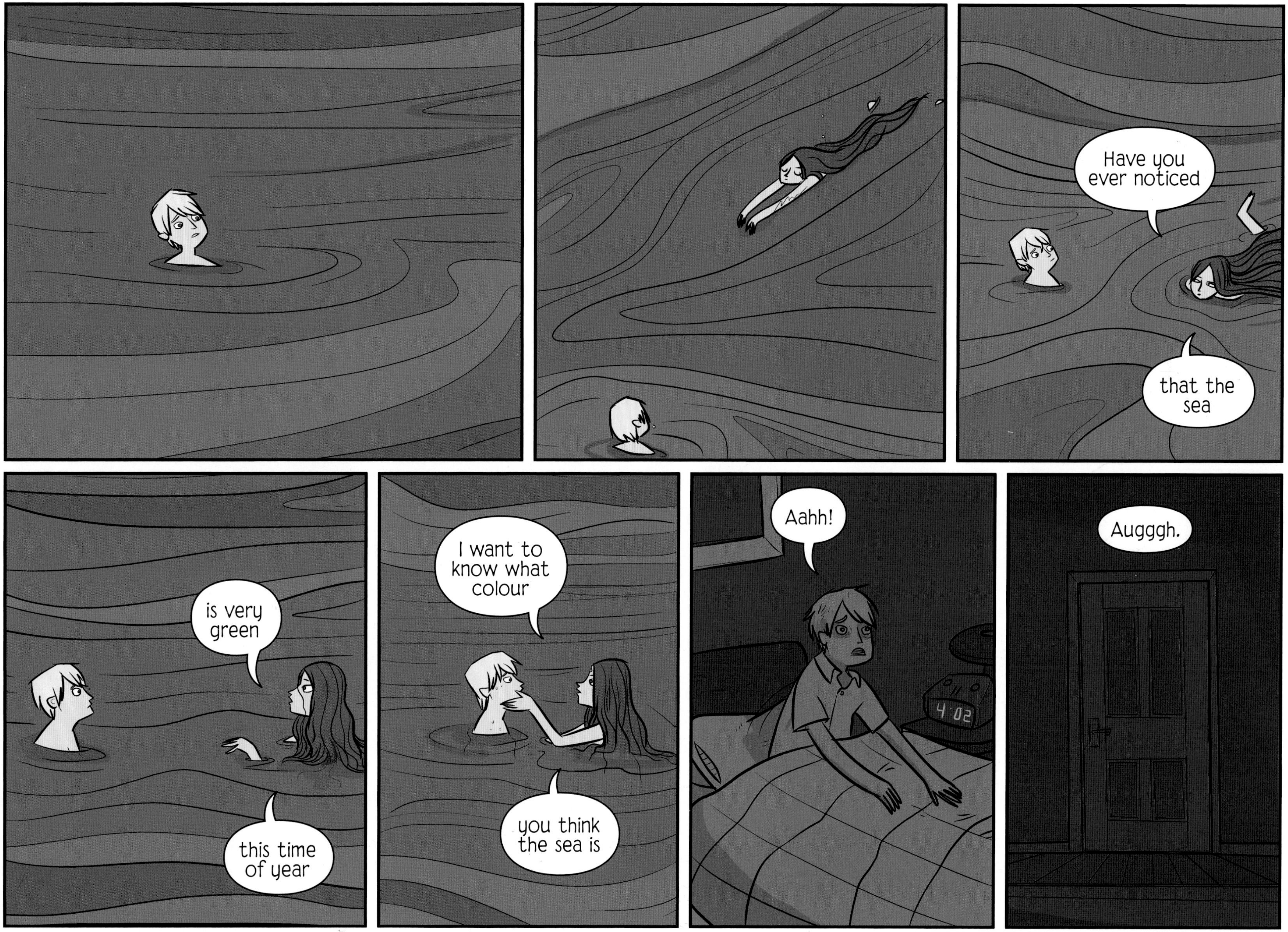
Have you ever noticed
that the sea
is very green
this time of year
I want to know what colour
you think the sea is
Aahh!
4:02
Augggh.

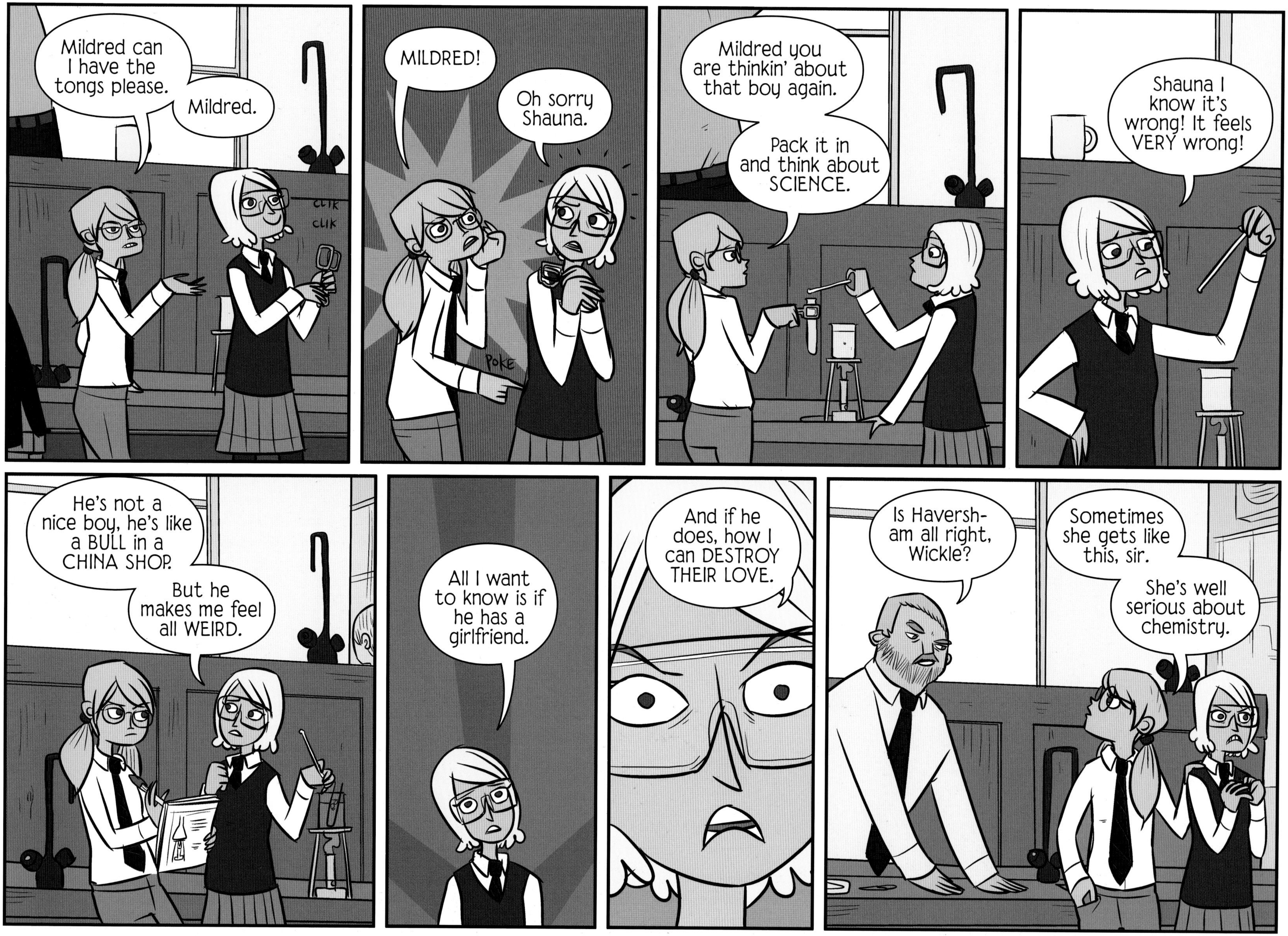
Mildred can I have the tongs please.
Mildred.
CLIK
CLIK
MILDRED!
Oh sorry Shauna.
POKE
Mildred you are thinkin' about that boy again.
Pack it in and think about SCIENCE.
Shauna I know it's wrong! It feels VERY wrong!
He's not a nice boy, he's like a BULL in a CHINA SHOP.
But he makes me feel all WEIRD.
All I want to know is if he has a girlfriend.
And if he does, how I can DESTROY THEIR LOVE.
Is Haversh-am all right, Wickle?
Sometimes she gets like this, sir.
She's well serious about chemistry.

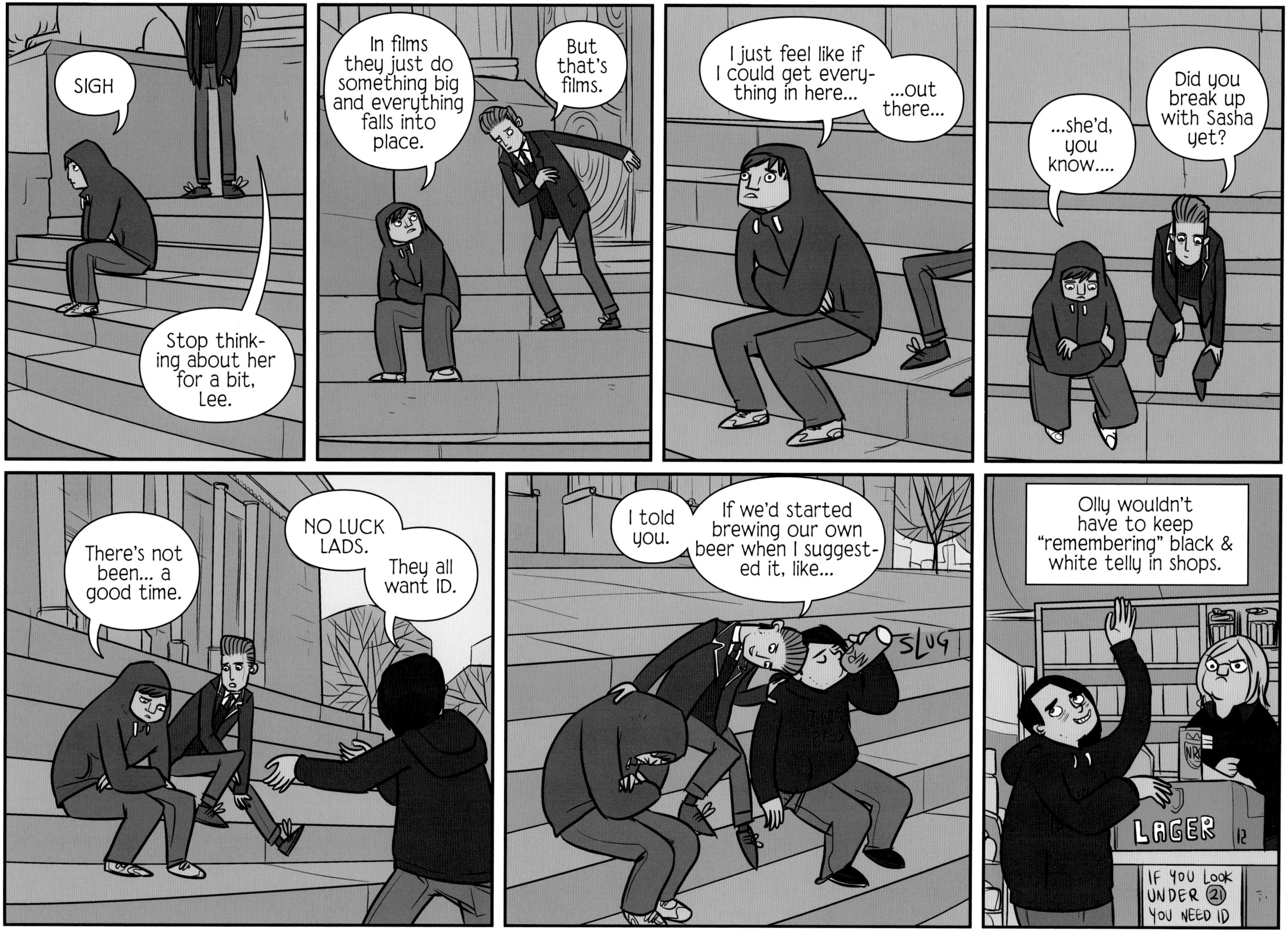
SIGH
Stop think-ing about her for a bit, Lee.
In films they just do something big and everything falls into place.
But that's films.
I just feel like if I could get every-thing in here...
...out there...
...she'd, you know....
Did you break up with Sasha yet?
There's not been... a good time.
NO LUCK LADS.
They all want ID.
I told you.
If we'd started brewing our own beer when I suggest-ed it, like...
SLUG
Olly wouldn't have to keep "remembering" black & white telly in shops.
LAGER
IF YOU LOOK UNDER 21 YOU NEED ID

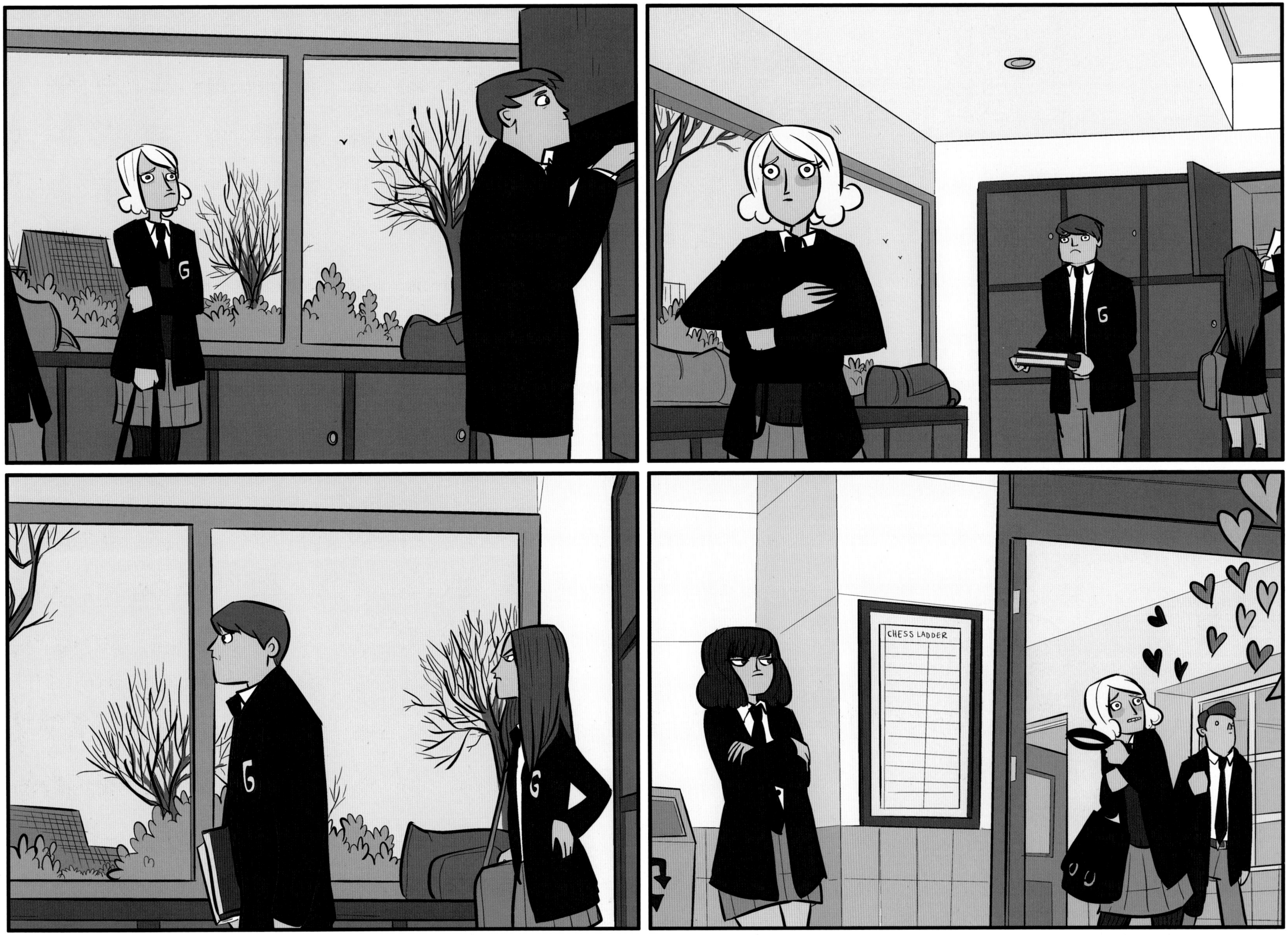
CHESS LADDER

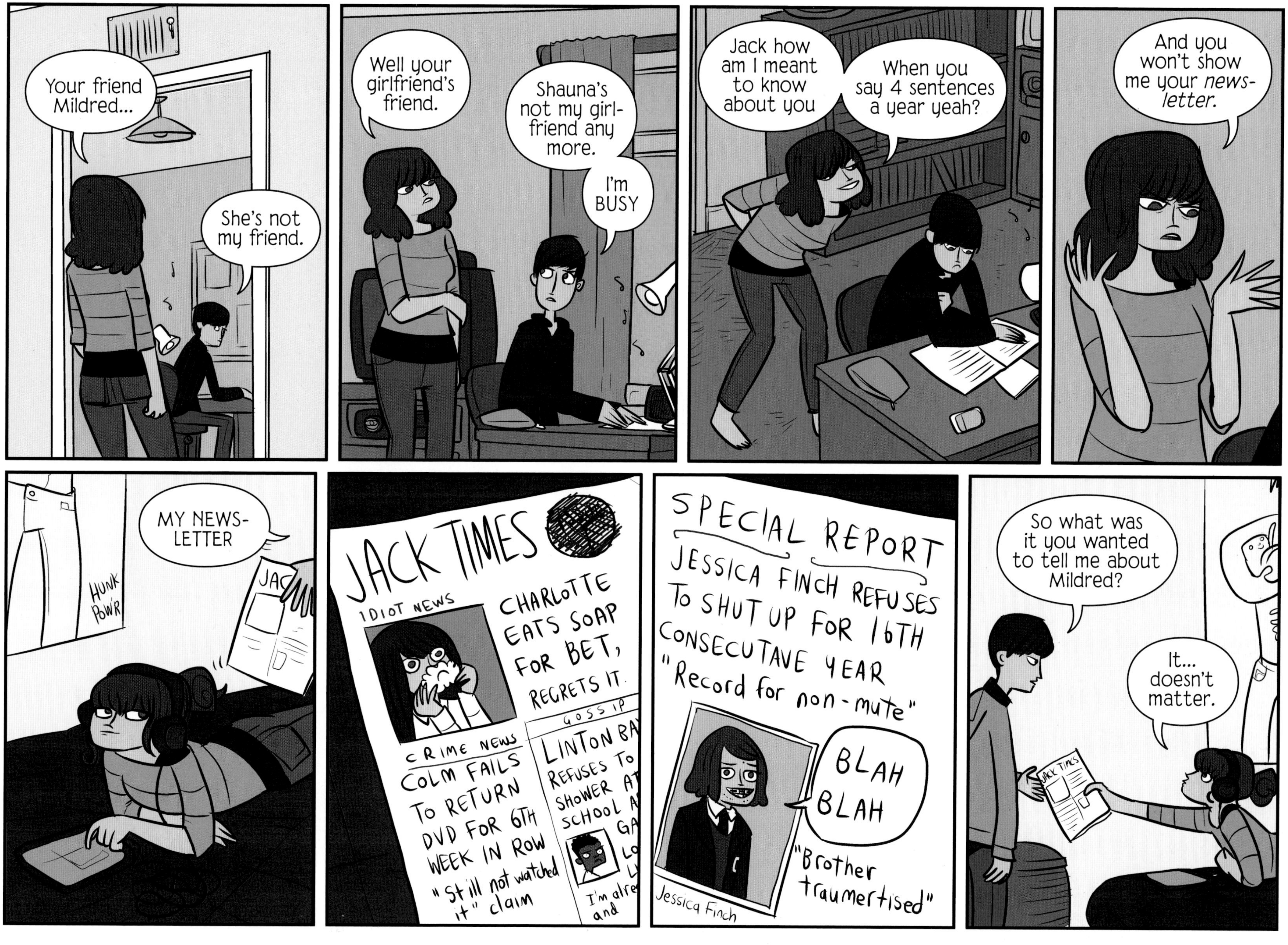
Your friend Mildred...
She's not my friend.
Well your girlfriend's friend.
Shauna's not my girl-friend any more.
I'm BUSY
Jack how am I meant to know about you
When you say 4 sentences a year yeah?
And you won't show me your *news-letter.*
MY NEWS-LETTER
HUNK POW'R
JACK TIMES
IDIOT NEWS
CHARLOTTE EATS SOAP FOR BET, REGRETS IT.
CRIME NEWS
COLM FAILS TO RETURN DVD FOR 6TH WEEK IN ROW
"Still not watched it" claim
GOSSIP
SPECIAL REPORT
JESSICA FINCH REFUSES TO SHUT UP FOR 16TH CONSECUTAVE YEAR
"Record for non-mute"
BLAH BLAH
Jessica Finch
"Brother traumertised"
So what was it you wanted to tell me about Mildred?
It... doesn't matter.
JACK TIMES

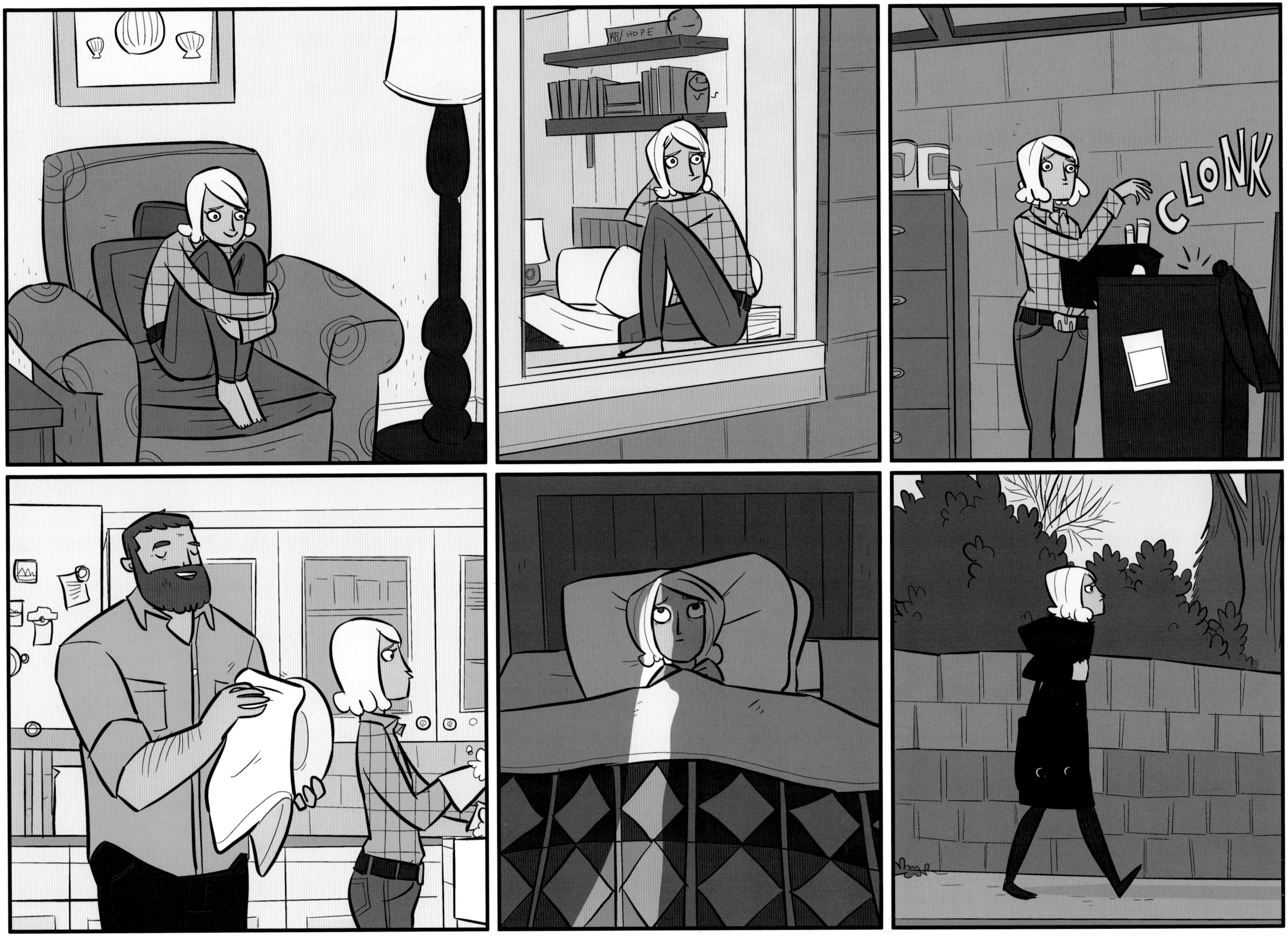
MB/ HOPE
CLONK

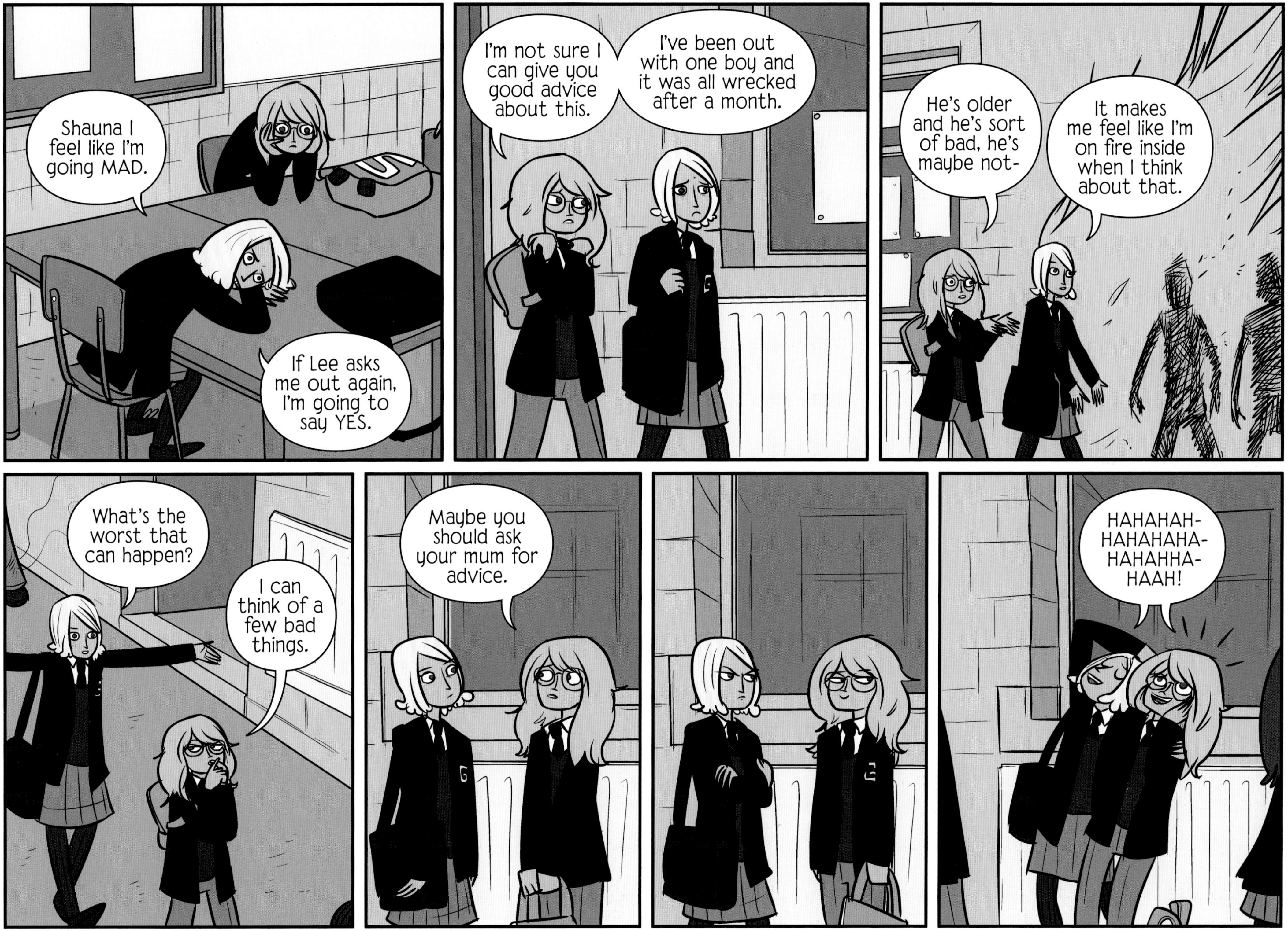
Shauna I feel like I'm going MAD.
If Lee asks me out again, I'm going to say YES.
I'm not sure I can give you good advice about this.
I've been out with one boy and it was all wrecked after a month.
He's older and he's sort of bad, he's maybe not-
It makes me feel like I'm on fire inside when I think about that.
What's the worst that can happen?
I can think of a few bad things.
Maybe you should ask your mum for advice.
HAHAHAH-
HAHAHAHA-
HAHAHHA-
HAAH!

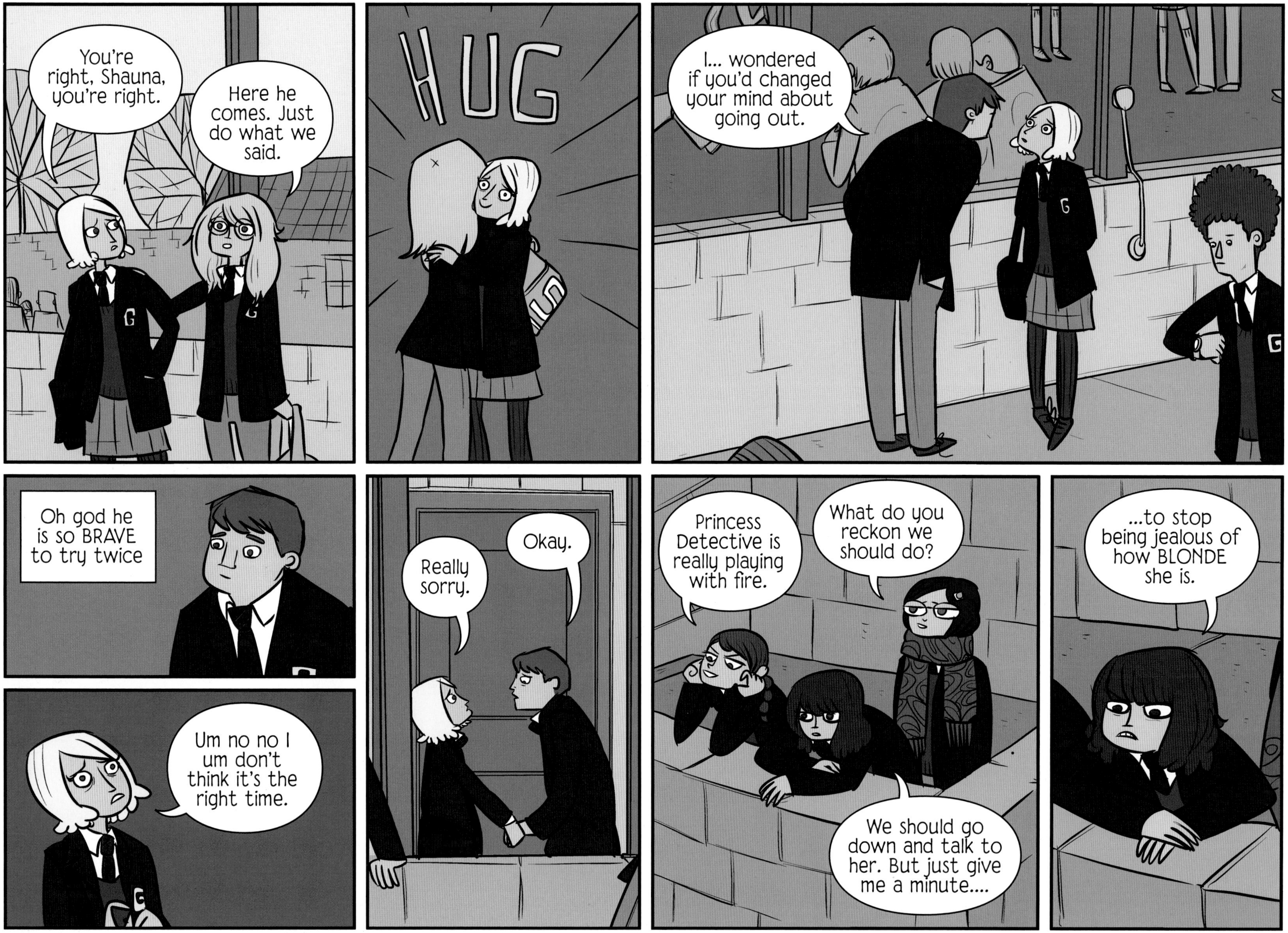
You're right, Shauna, you're right.
Here he comes. Just do what we said.
HUG
I... wondered if you'd changed your mind about going out.
Oh god he is so BRAVE to try twice
Um no no I um don't think it's the right time.
Really sorry.
Okay.
Princess Detective is really playing with fire.
What do you reckon we should do?
We should go down and talk to her. But just give me a minute....
...to stop being jealous of how BLONDE she is.

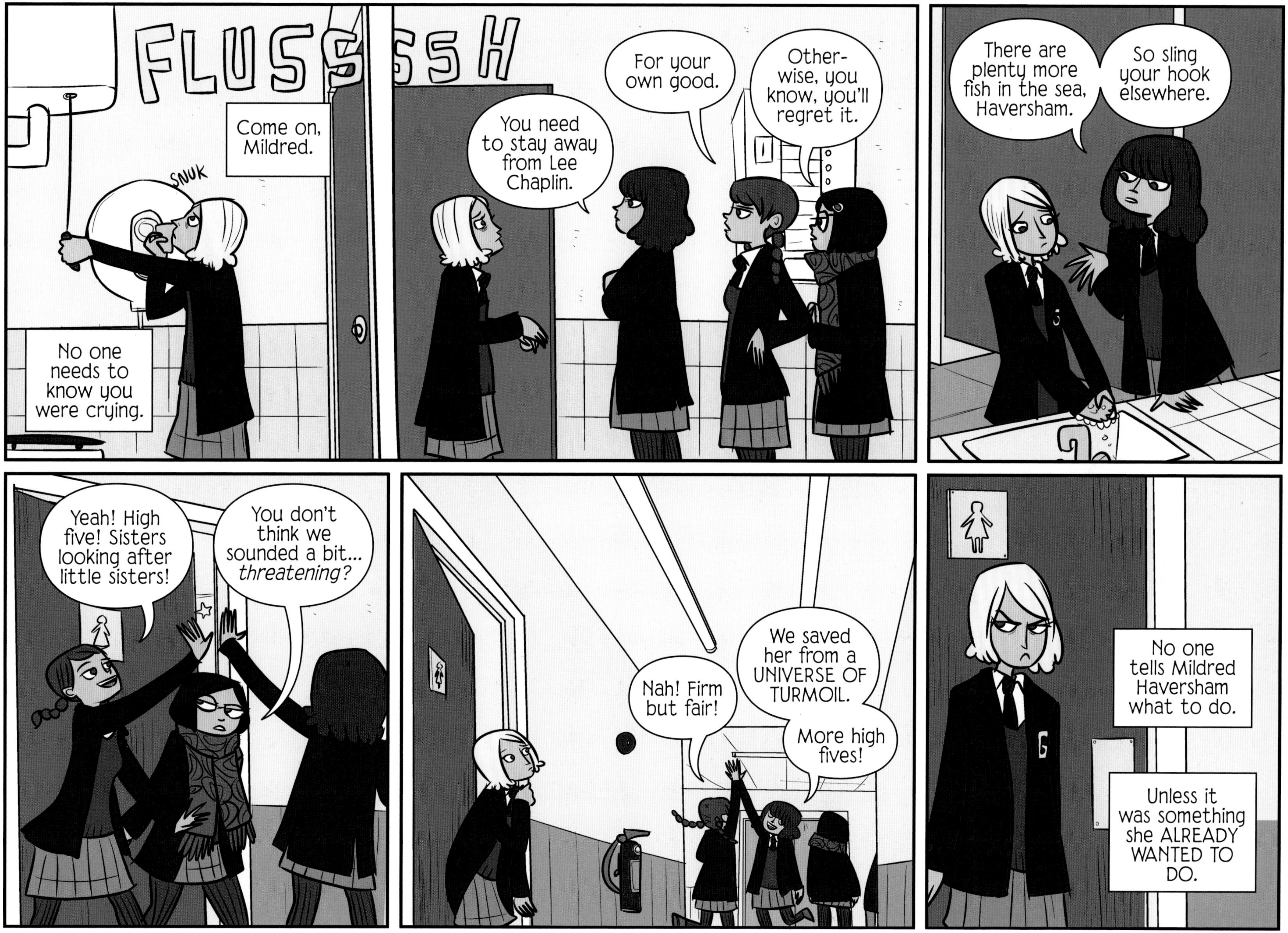
FLUSSSSH
SNUK
No one needs to know you were crying.
Come on, Mildred.
You need to stay away from Lee Chaplin.
For your own good.
Other-wise, you know, you'll regret it.
There are plenty more fish in the sea, Haversham.
So sling your hook elsewhere.
Yeah! High five! Sisters looking after little sisters!
You don't think we sounded a bit... *threatening?*
Nah! Firm but fair!
We saved her from a UNIVERSE OF TURMOIL.
More high fives!
No one tells Mildred Haversham what to do.
Unless it was something she ALREADY WANTED TO DO.

Bad Machinery, Volume Five

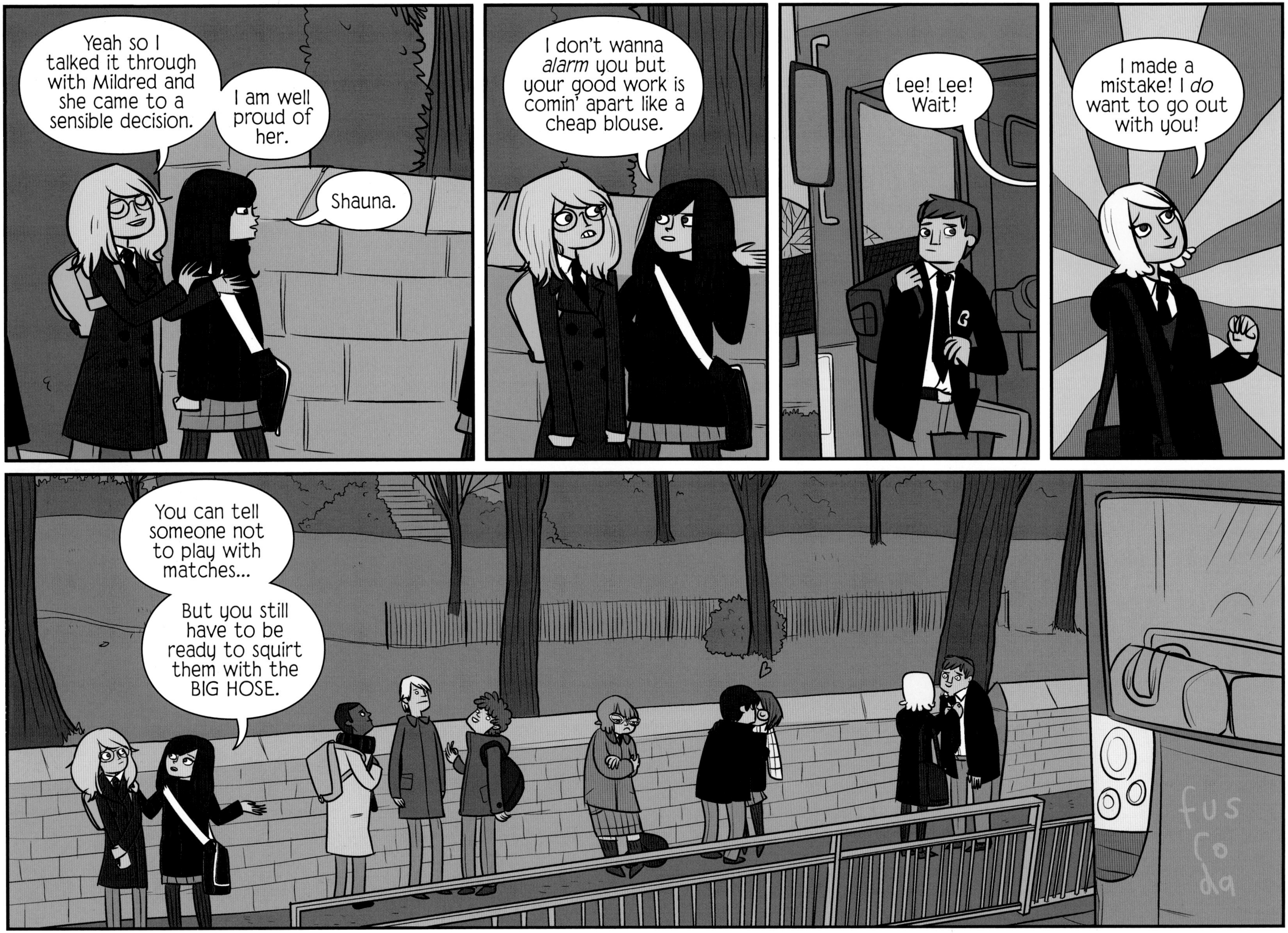
Yeah so I talked it through with Mildred and she came to a sensible decision.
I am well proud of her.
Shauna.
I don't wanna *alarm* you but your good work is comin' apart like a cheap blouse.
Lee! Lee! Wait!
I made a mistake! I *do* want to go out with you!
You can tell someone not to play with matches...
But you still have to be ready to squirt them with the BIG HOSE.

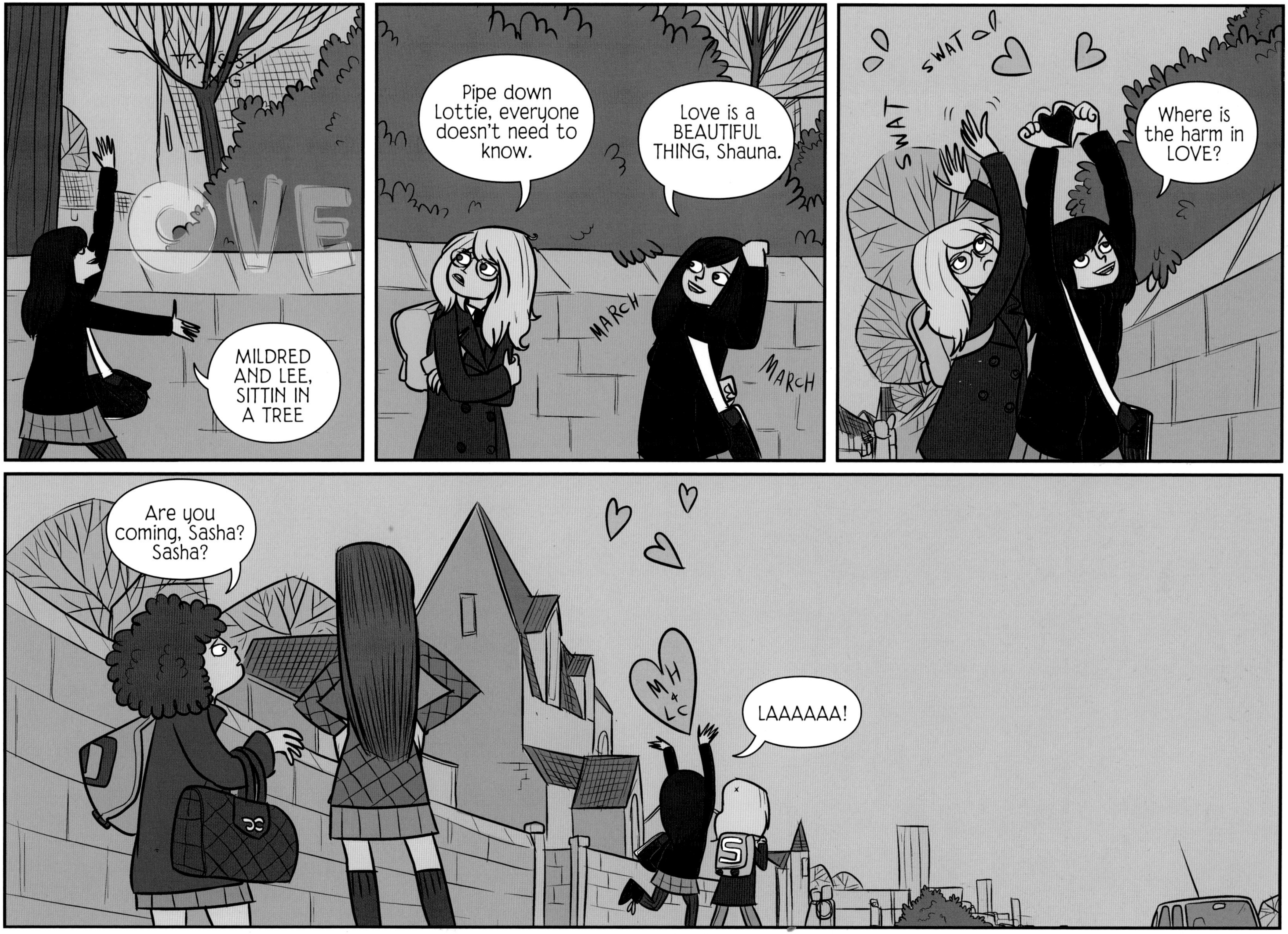
MILDRED AND LEE, SITTIN IN A TREE
Pipe down Lottie, everyone doesn't need to know.
MARCH
Love is a BEAUTIFUL THING, Shauna.
MARCH
SWAT
SWAT
Where is the harm in LOVE?
Are you coming, Sasha? Sasha?
LAAAAAA!

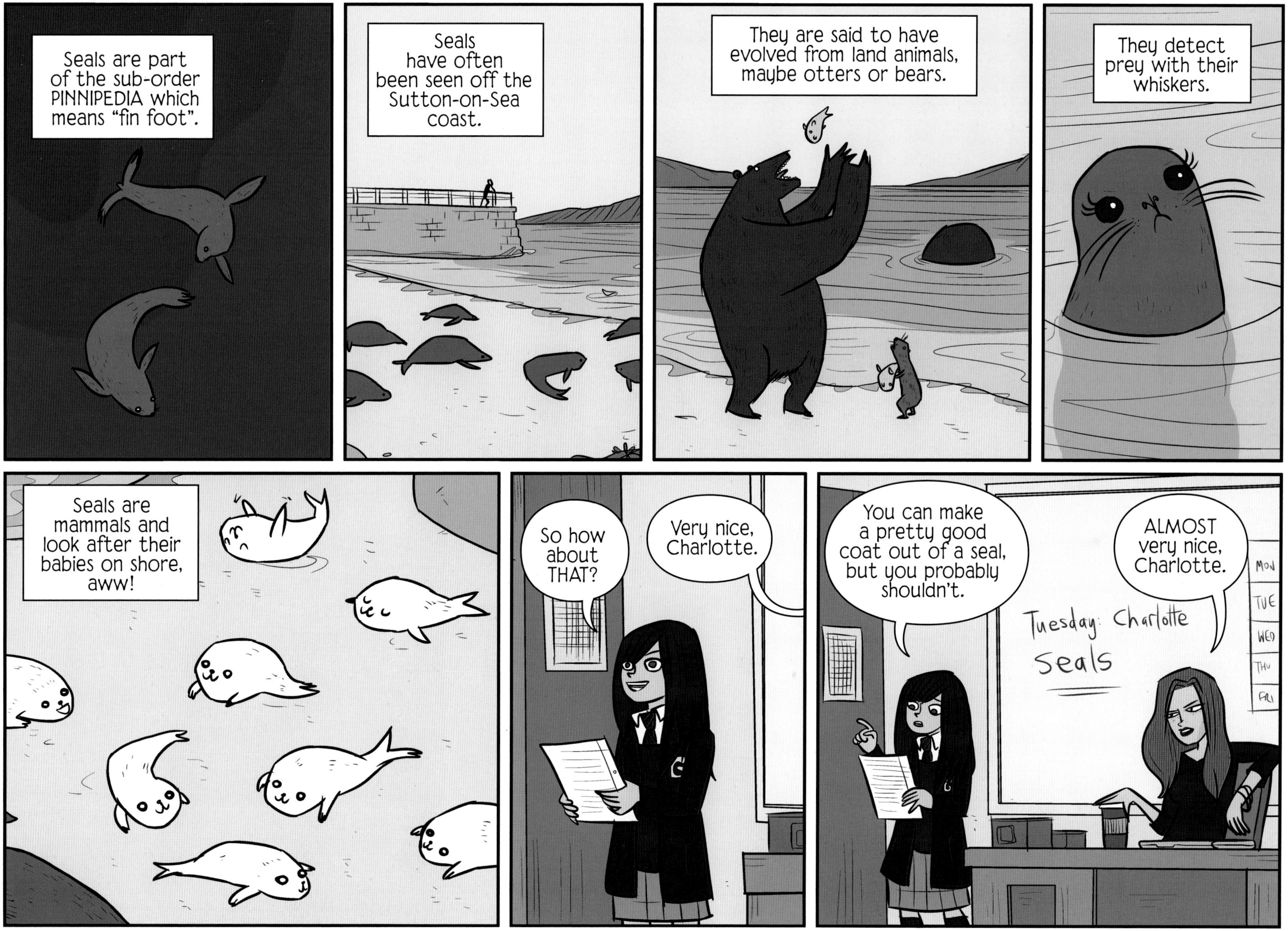
Seals are part of the sub-order PINNIPEDIA which means "fin foot".
Seals have often been seen off the Sutton-on-Sea coast.
They are said to have evolved from land animals, maybe otters or bears.
They detect prey with their whiskers.
Seals are mammals and look after their babies on shore, aww!
So how about THAT?
Very nice, Charlotte.
You can make a pretty good coat out of a seal, but you probably shouldn't.
ALMOST very nice, Charlotte.
Tuesday: Charlotte
Seals
MON
TUE
WED
THU
FRI

Bad Machinery, Volume Five

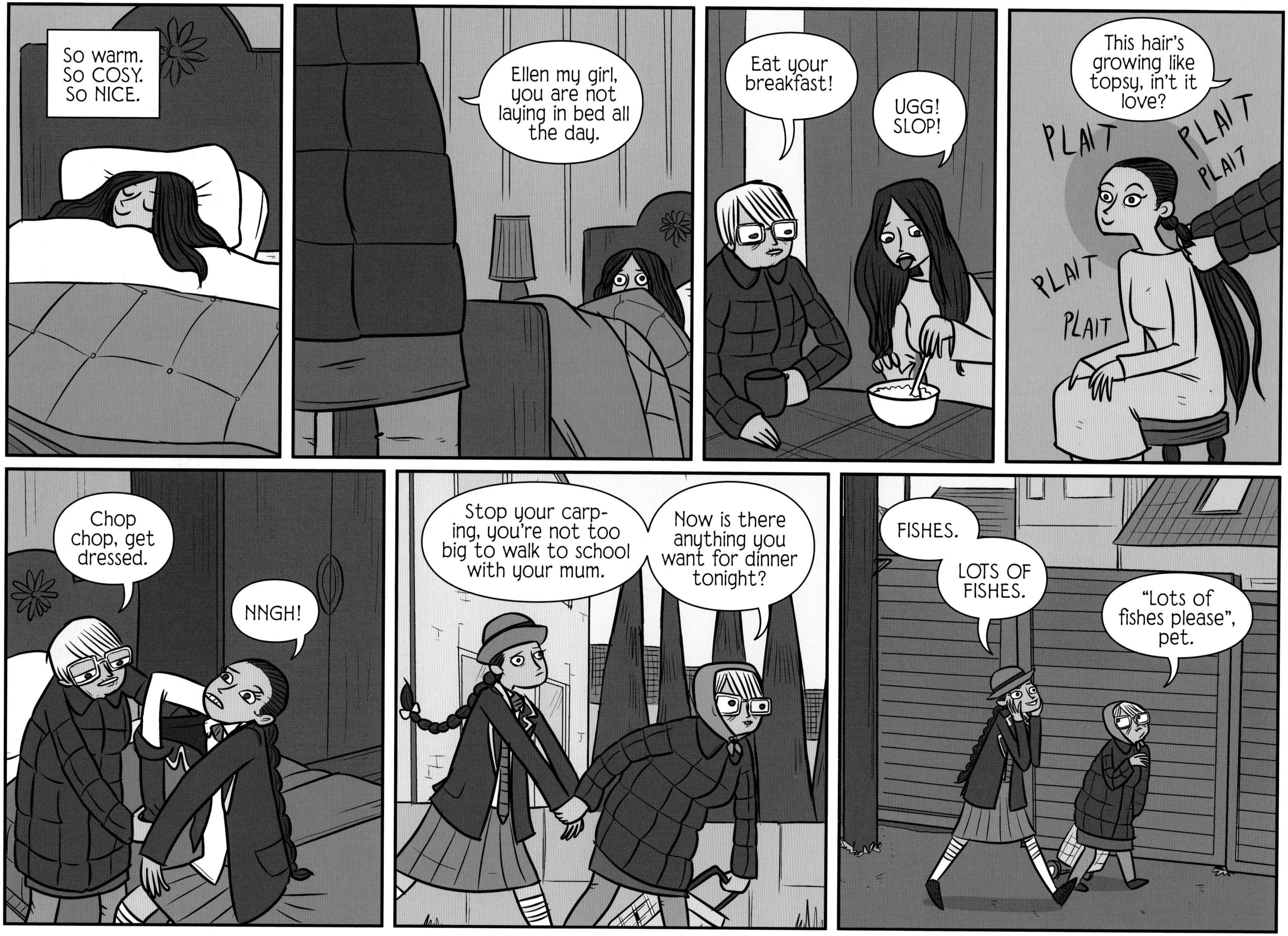
So warm. So COSY. So NICE.
Ellen my girl, you are not laying in bed all the day.
Eat your breakfast!
UGG! SLOP!
This hair's growing like topsy, in't it love?
PLAIT
PLAIT
PLAIT
PLAIT
PLAIT
Chop chop, get dressed.
NNGH!
Stop your carp-ing, you're not too big to walk to school with your mum.
Now is there anything you want for dinner tonight?
FISHES.
LOTS OF FISHES.
"Lots of fishes please", pet.

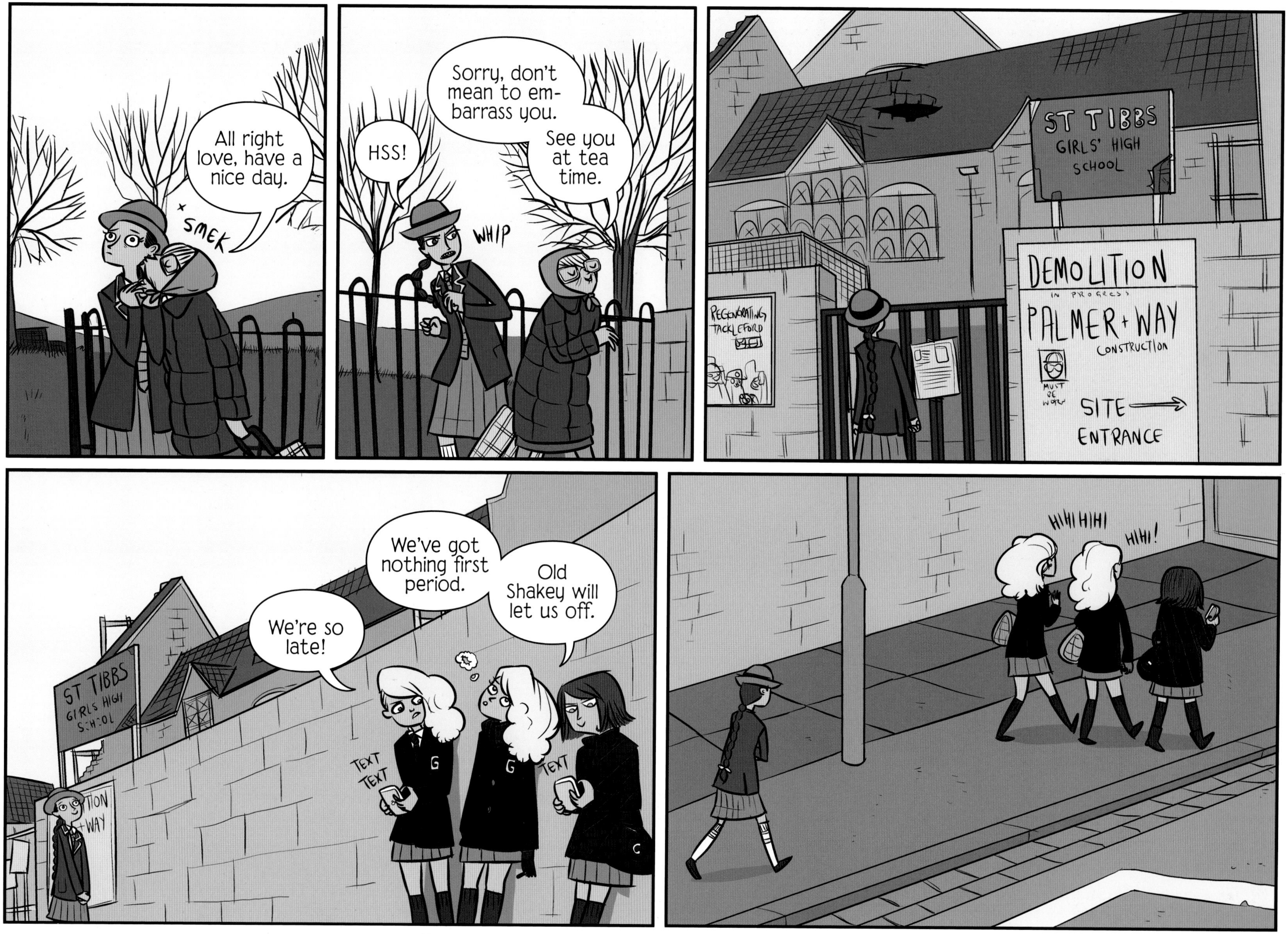
All right love, have a nice day.
SMEK
HSS!
Sorry, don't mean to em-barrass you.
See you at tea time.
WHIP
ST TIBBS GIRLS' HIGH SCHOOL
REGENERATING TACKLEFORD
DEMOLITION
IN PROGRESS
PALMER + WAY CONSTRUCTION
MUST BE WORN
SITE ENTRANCE
ST TIBBS GIRLS HIGH SCHOOL
We're so late!
We've got nothing first period.
Old Shakey will let us off.
TEXT TEXT
TEXT
HIHI HIHI
HIHI!

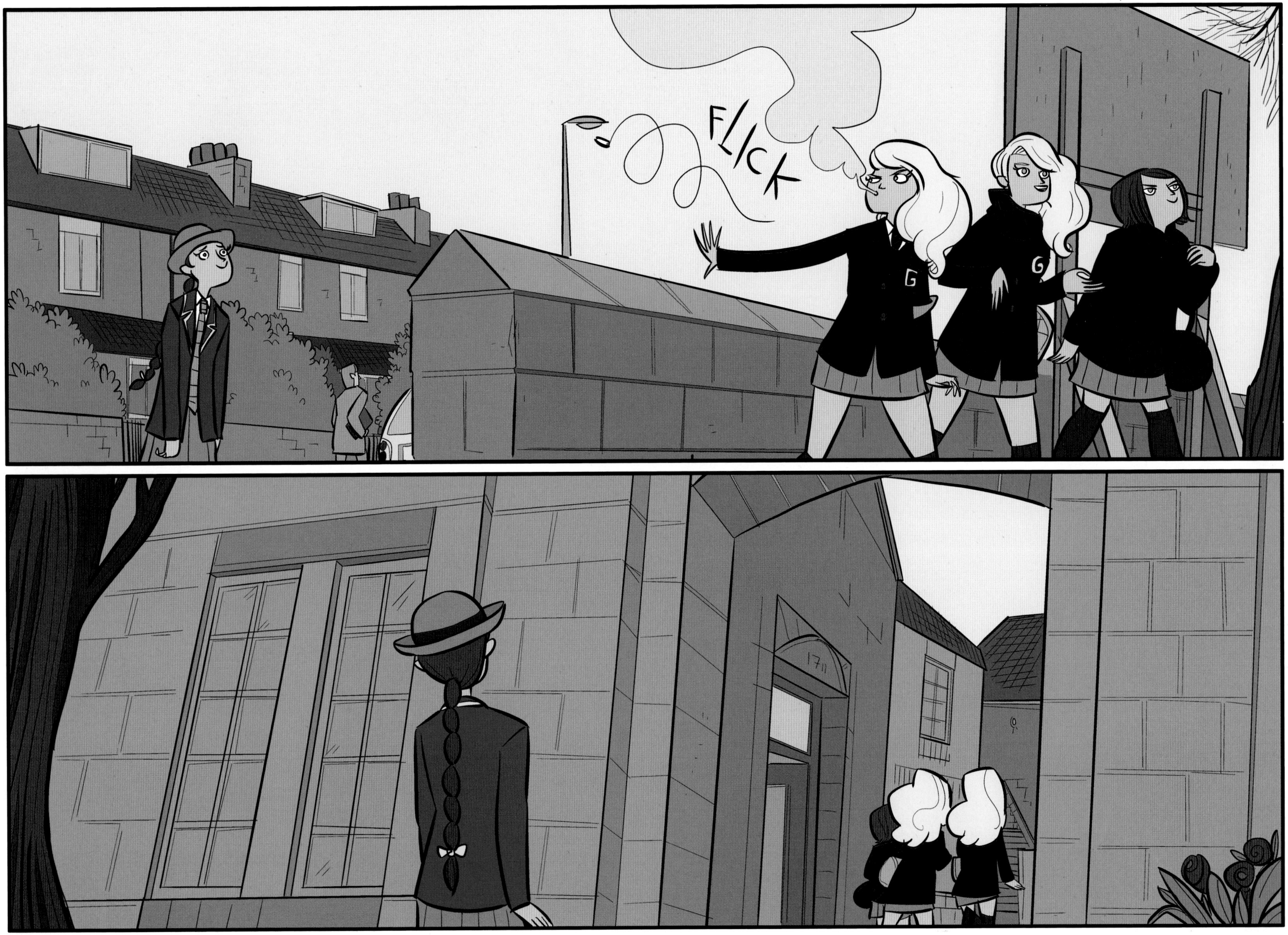
FLICK
1711

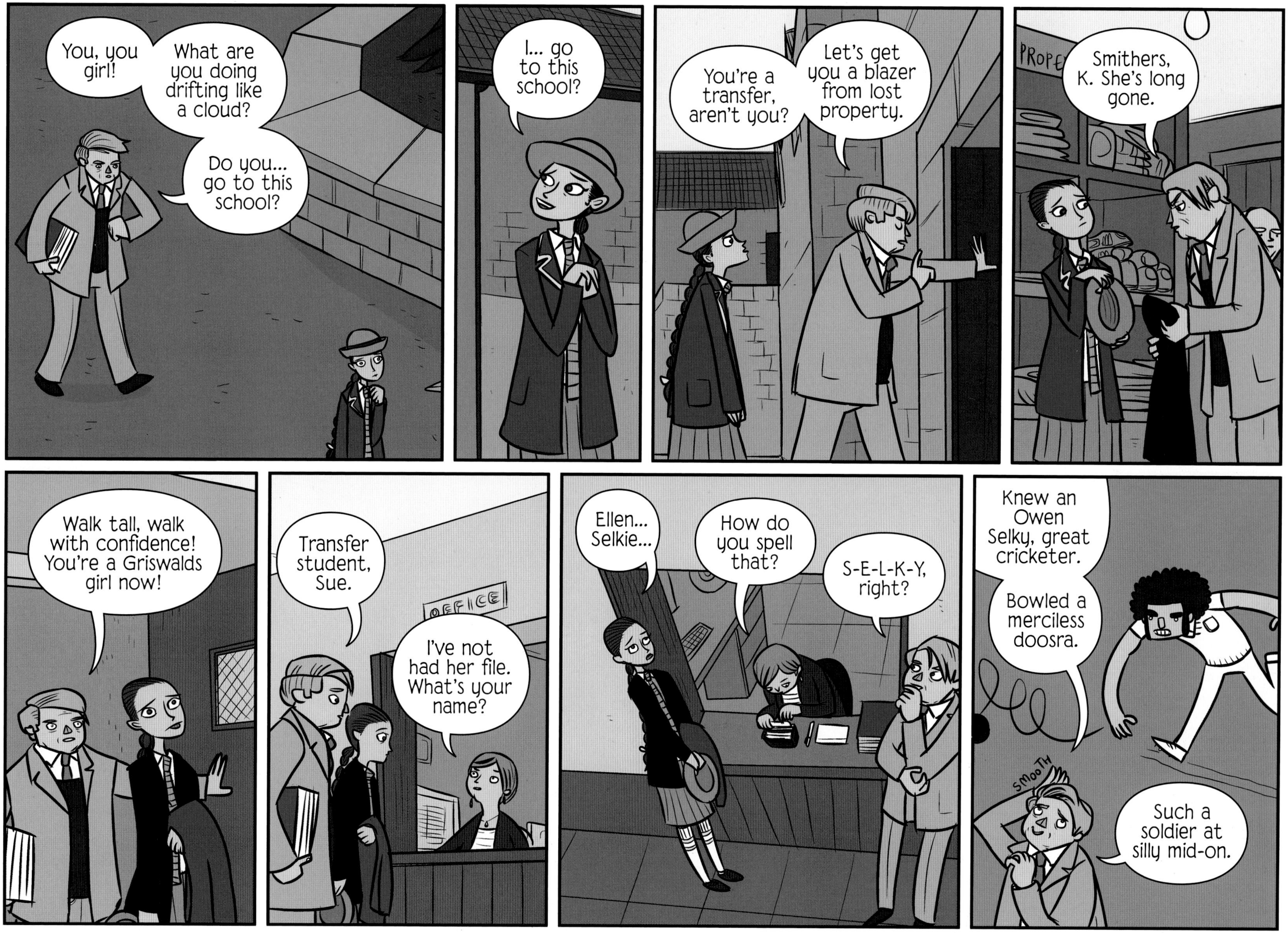
You, you girl!
What are you doing drifting like a cloud?
Do you... go to this school?
I... go to this school?
You're a transfer, aren't you?
Let's get you a blazer from lost property.
PROPE
Smithers, K. She's long gone.
Walk tall, walk with confidence! You're a Griswalds girl now!
Transfer student, Sue.
OFFICE
I've not had her file. What's your name?
Ellen... Selkie...
How do you spell that?
S-E-L-K-Y, right?
Knew an Owen Selky, great cricketer.
Bowled a merciless doosra.
SMOOTH
Such a soldier at silly mid-on.

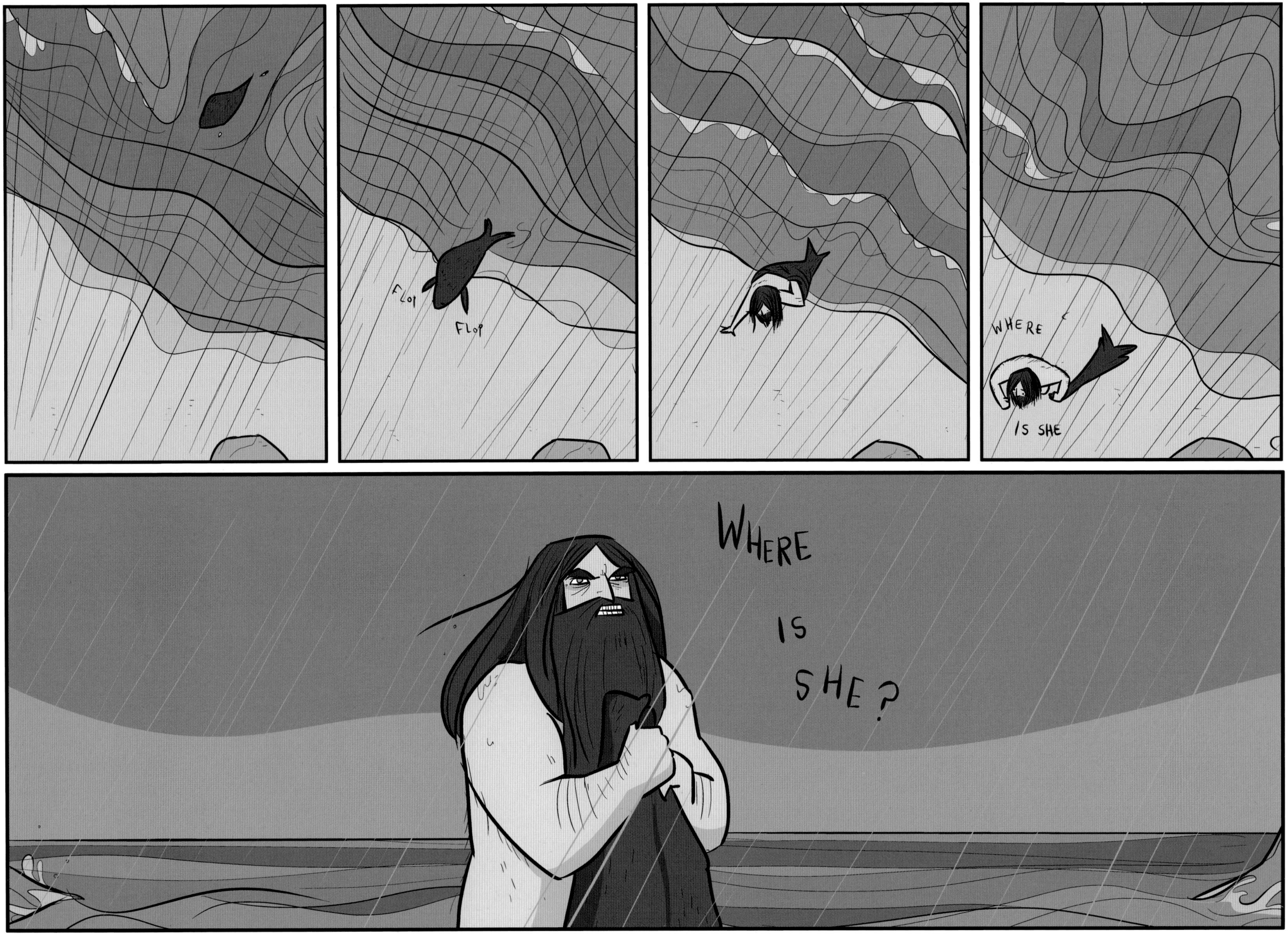
FLOP
FLOP
WHERE
IS SHE
WHERE
IS
SHE?

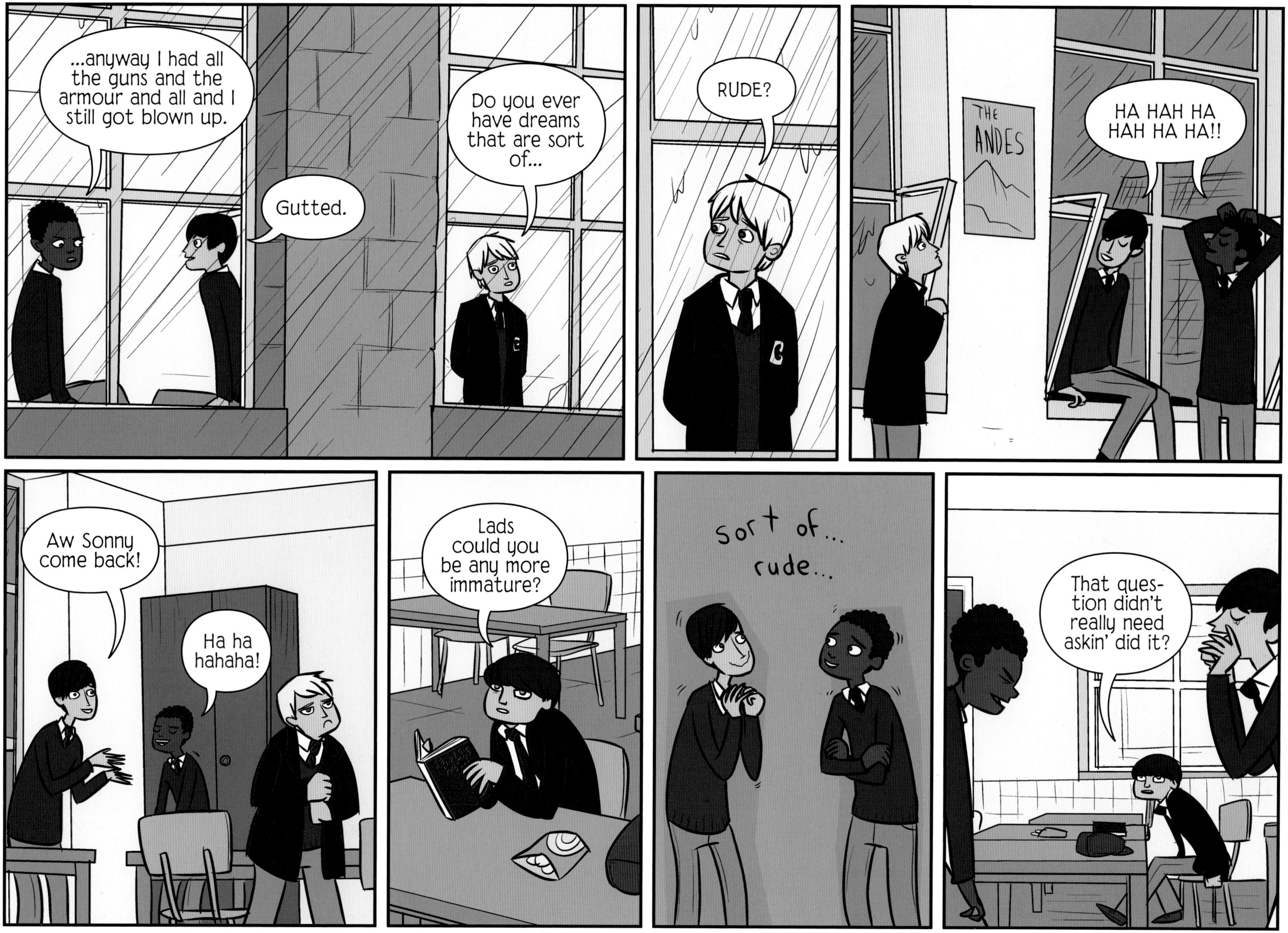
...anyway I had all the guns and the armour and all and I still got blown up.
Gutted.
Do you ever have dreams that are sort of...
RUDE?
THE ANDES
HA HAH HA HAH HA HA!!
Aw Sonny come back!
Ha ha hahaha!
Lads could you be any more immature?
sort of... rude...
That question didn't really need askin' did it?

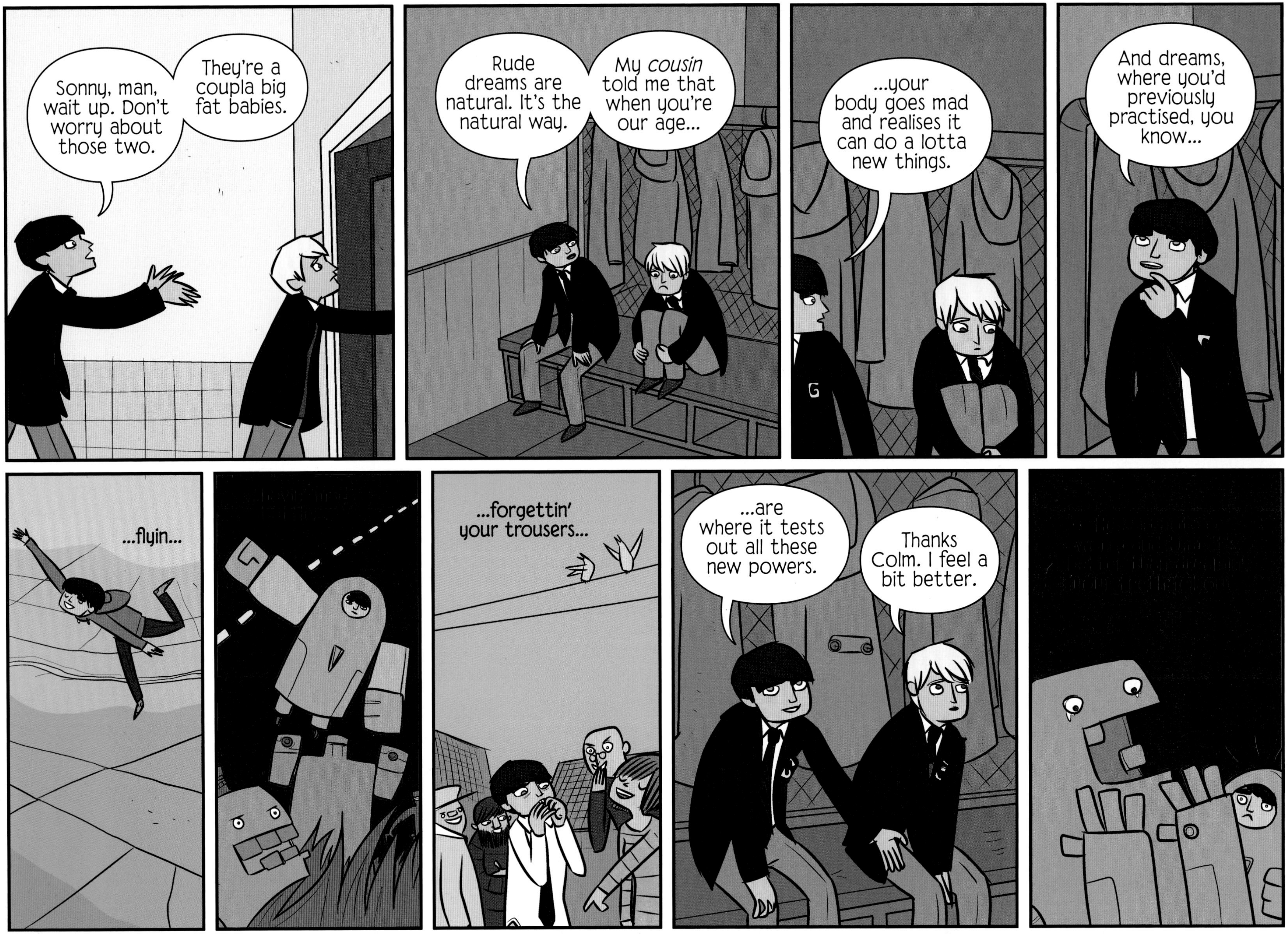
Sonny, man, wait up. Don't worry about those two.
They're a coupla big fat babies.
Rude dreams are natural. It's the natural way.
My *cousin* told me that when you're our age...
...your body goes mad and realises it can do a lotta new things.
And dreams, where you'd previously practised, you know...
...flyin...
...forgettin' your trousers...
...are where it tests out all these new powers.
Thanks Colm. I feel a bit better.

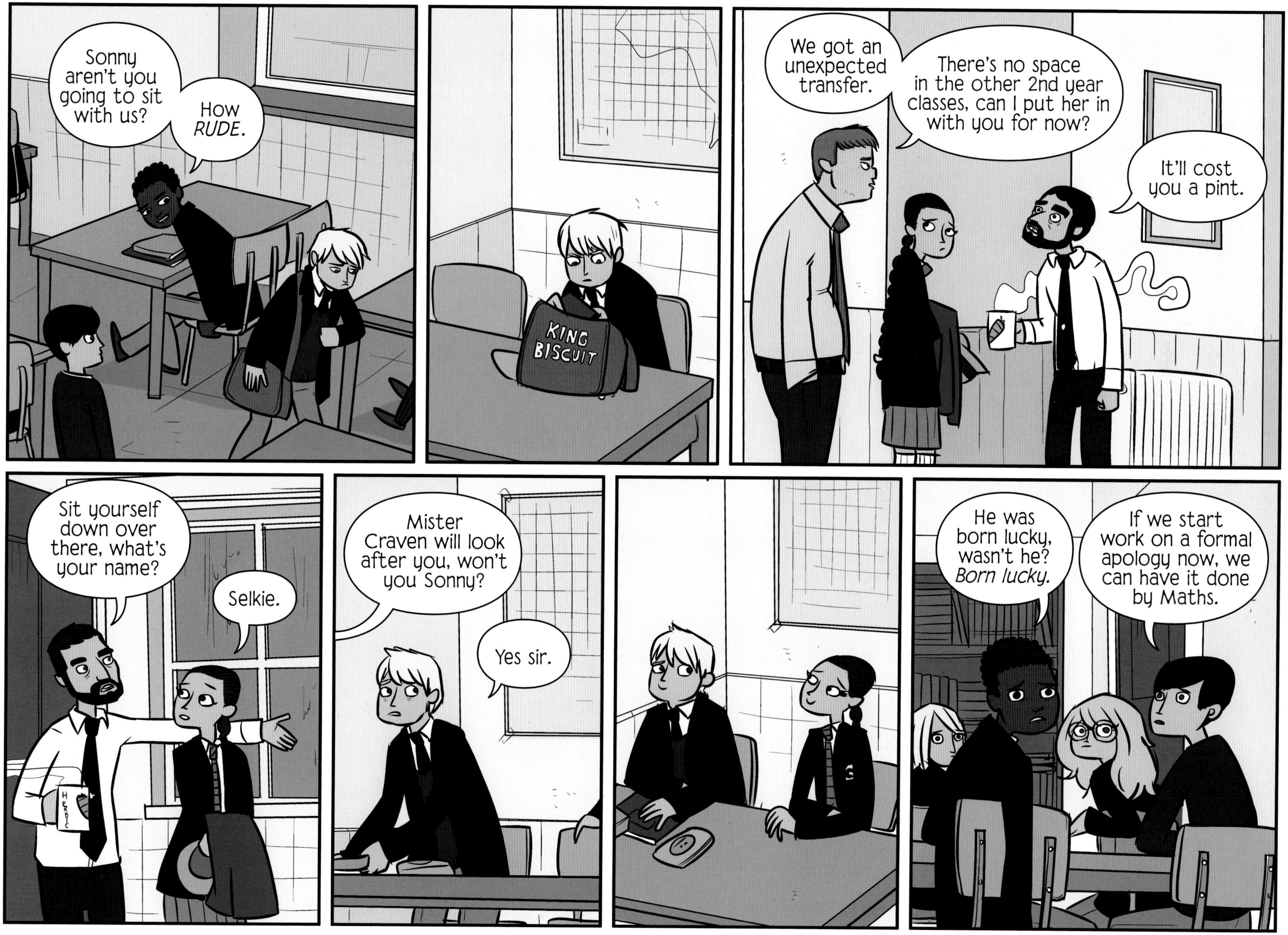
Sonny aren't you going to sit with us?
How *RUDE*.
KING BISCUIT
We got an unexpected transfer.
There's no space in the other 2nd year classes, can I put her in with you for now?
It'll cost you a pint.
Sit yourself down over there, what's your name?
Selkie.
HEROIC
Mister Craven will look after you, won't you Sonny?
Yes sir.
He was born lucky, wasn't he? *Born lucky.*
If we start work on a formal apology now, we can have it done by Maths.

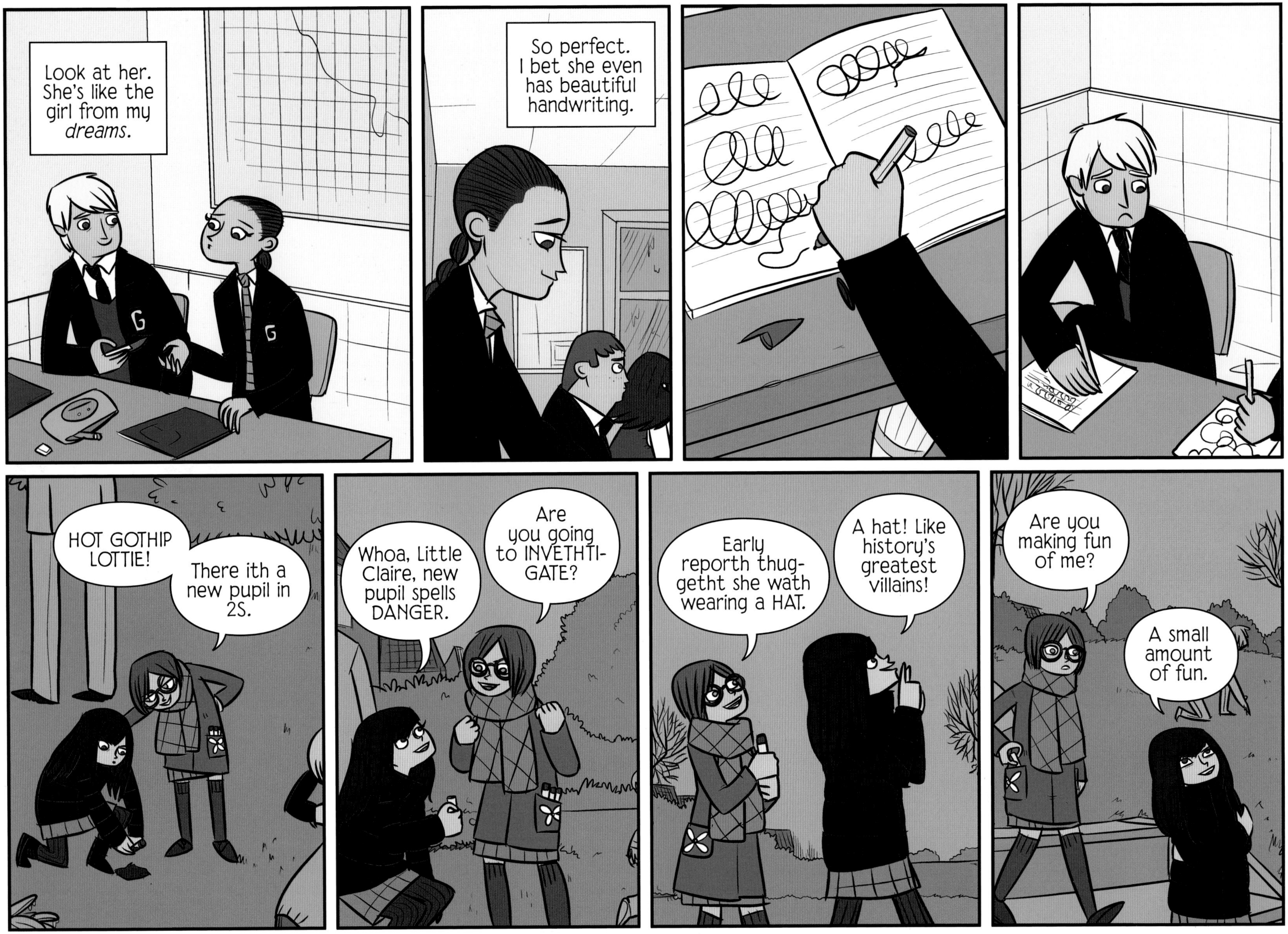

Look at her. She's like the girl from my *dreams*.
So perfect. I bet she even has beautiful handwriting.
HOT GOTHIP LOTTIE!
There ith a new pupil in 2S.
Whoa, Little Claire, new pupil spells DANGER.
Are you going to INVETHTI-GATE?
Early reporth thug-getht she wath wearing a HAT.
A hat! Like history's greatest villains!
Are you making fun of me?
A small amount of fun.

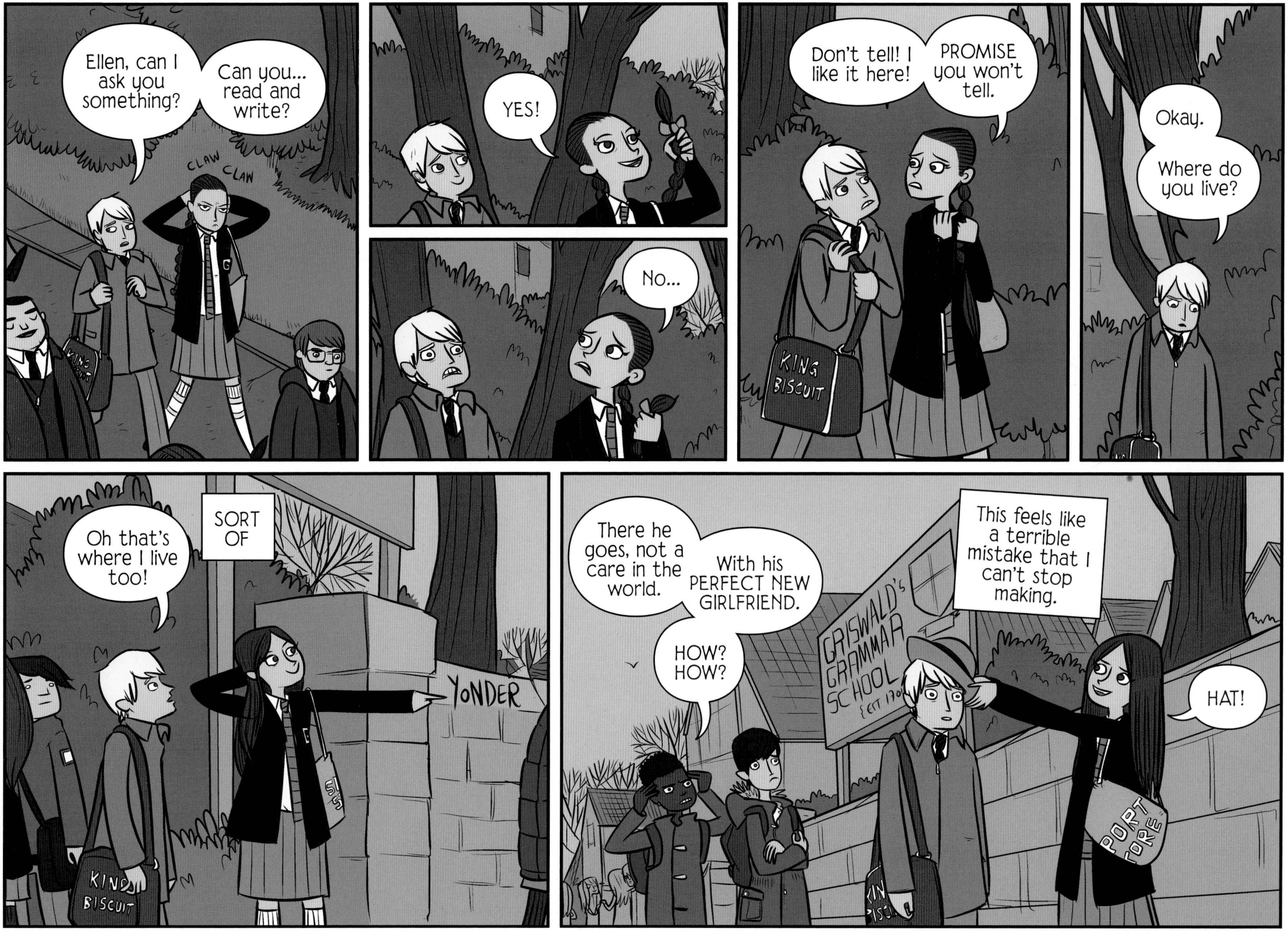
Ellen, can I ask you something?
Can you... read and write?
CLAW CLAW
KING BISCUIT
YES!
No...
Don't tell! I like it here!
PROMISE you won't tell.
KING BISCUIT
Okay.
Where do you live?
Oh that's where I live too!
SORT OF
YONDER
KING BISCUIT
There he goes, not a care in the world.
With his PERFECT NEW GIRLFRIEND.
HOW? HOW?
This feels like a terrible mistake that I can't stop making.
GRISWALD'S GRAMMAR SCHOOL
HAT!

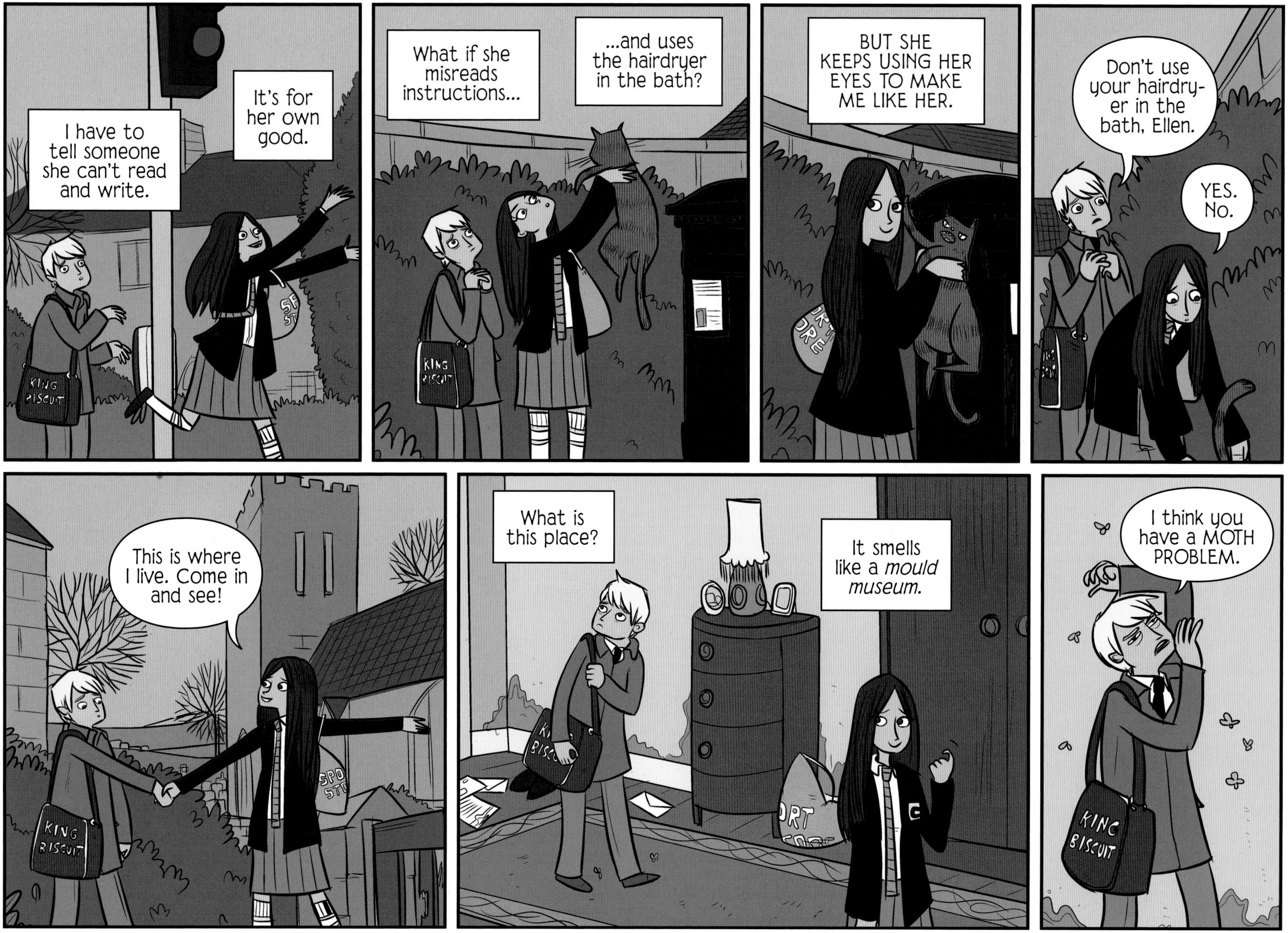
I have to tell someone she can't read and write.
It's for her own good.
What if she misreads instructions...
...and uses the hairdryer in the bath?
BUT SHE KEEPS USING HER EYES TO MAKE ME LIKE HER.
Don't use your hairdry-er in the bath, Ellen.
YES. No.
This is where I live. Come in and see!
What is this place?
It smells like a *mould museum.*
I think you have a MOTH PROBLEM.

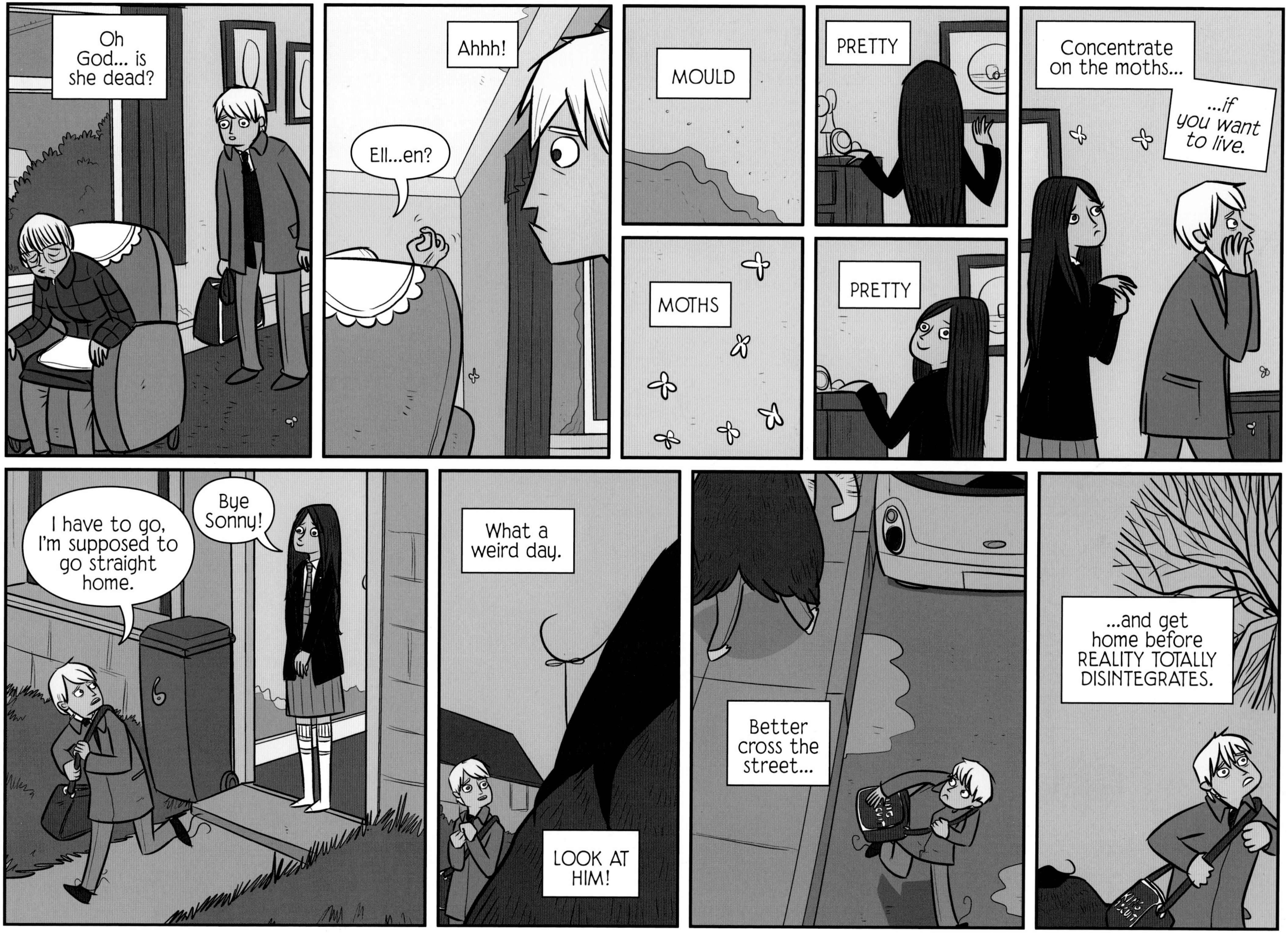
Oh God... is she dead?
Ahhh!
Ell...en?
MOULD
MOTHS
PRETTY
PRETTY
Concentrate on the moths...
...if you want to live.
I have to go, I'm supposed to go straight home.
Bye Sonny!
What a weird day.
LOOK AT HIM!
Better cross the street...
...and get home before REALITY TOTALLY DISINTEGRATES.

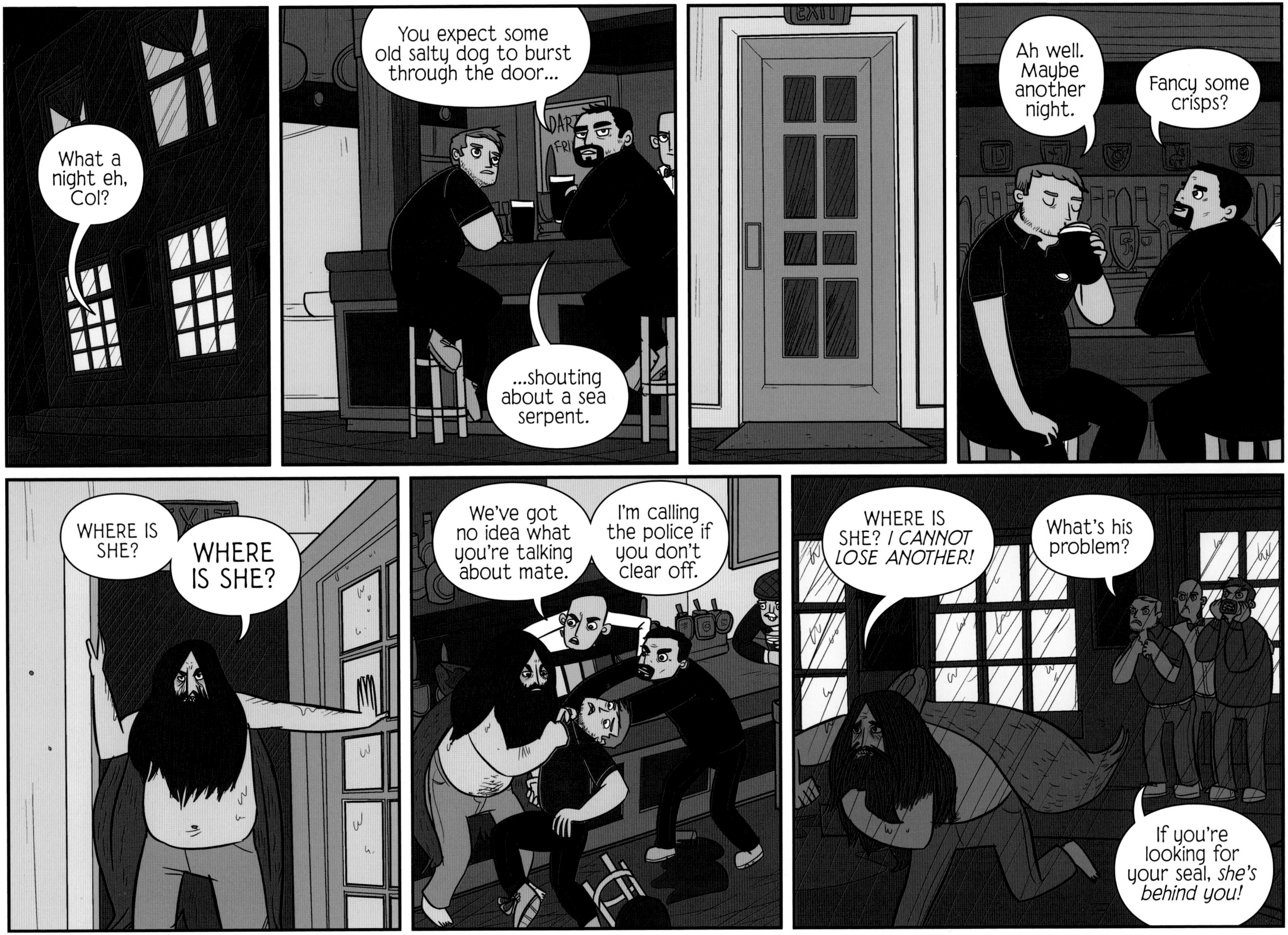
What a night eh, Col?
You expect some old salty dog to burst through the door...
...shouting about a sea serpent.
EXIT
Ah well. Maybe another night.
Fancy some crisps?
WHERE IS SHE?
WHERE IS SHE?
We've got no idea what you're talking about mate.
I'm calling the police if you don't clear off.
WHERE IS SHE? *I CANNOT LOSE ANOTHER!*
What's his problem?
If you're looking for your seal, *she's behind you!*

The Case of the Fire Inside

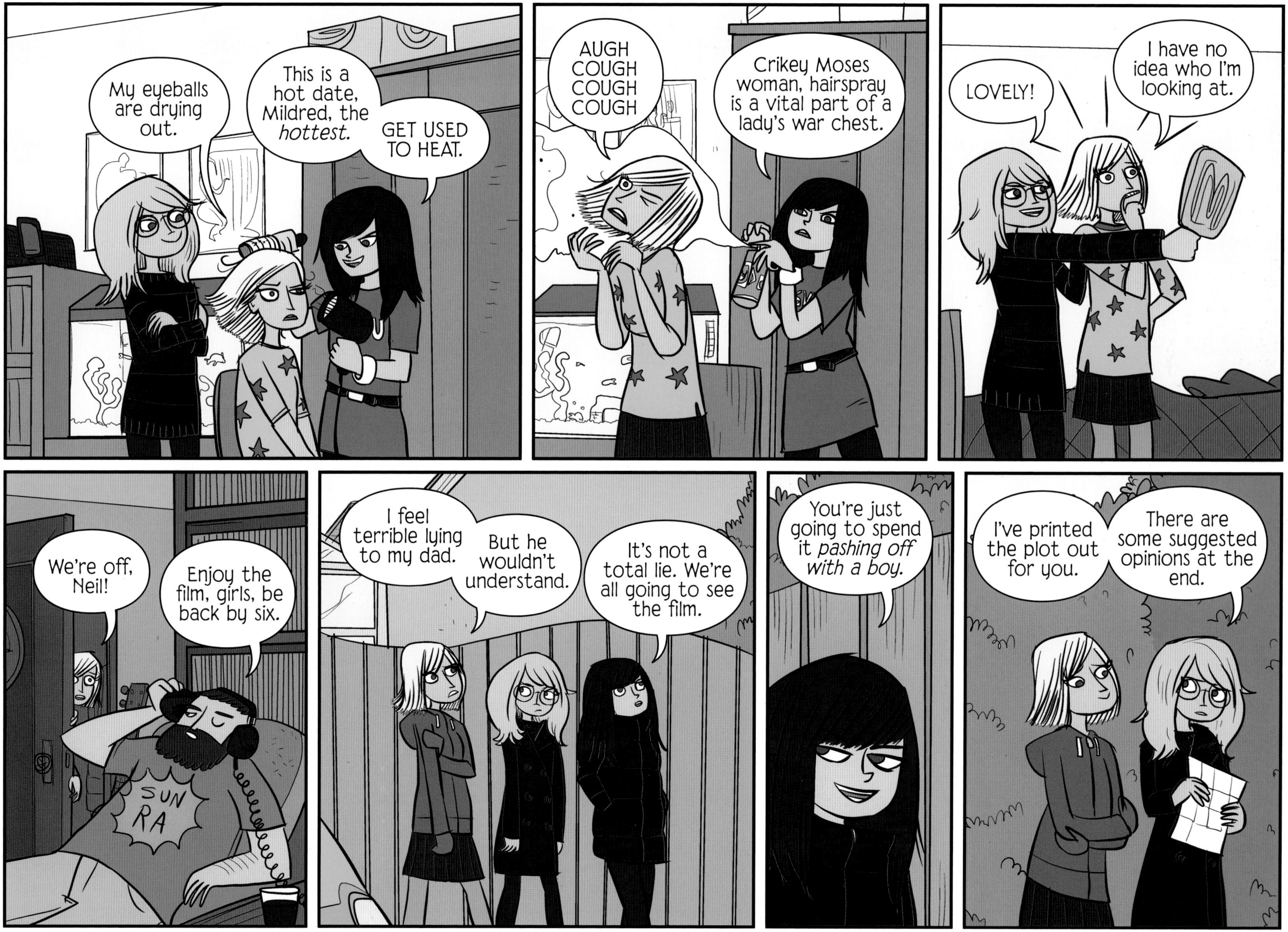
My eyeballs are drying out.
This is a hot date, Mildred, the *hottest*.
GET USED TO HEAT.
AUGH COUGH COUGH COUGH
Crikey Moses woman, hairspray is a vital part of a lady's war chest.
LOVELY!
I have no idea who I'm looking at.
We're off, Neil!
Enjoy the film, girls, be back by six.
SUN RA
I feel terrible lying to my dad.
But he wouldn't understand.
It's not a total lie. We're all going to see the film.
You're just going to spend it *pashing off with a boy.*
I've printed the plot out for you.
There are some suggested opinions at the end.

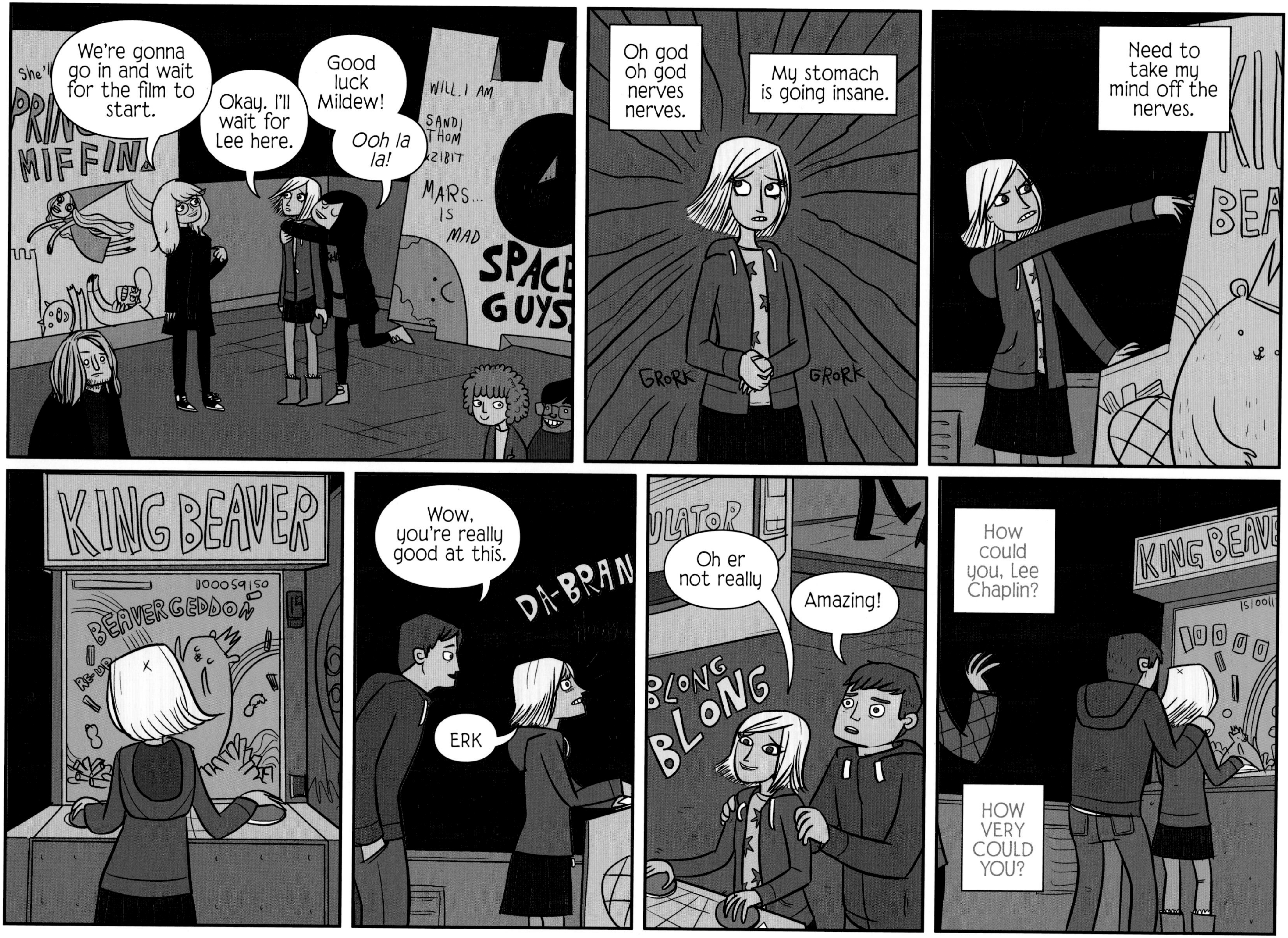
She'll
PRIN
MIFFIN
We're gonna go in and wait for the film to start.
Okay. I'll wait for Lee here.
Good luck Mildew!
Ooh la la!
WILL.I.AM
SANDI
THOM
MARS... IS MAD
SPACE GUYS
Oh god oh god nerves nerves.
My stomach is going insane.
GRORK
GRORK
Need to take my mind off the nerves.
KING BEAVER
10005950
BEAVERGEDDON
Wow, you're really good at this.
DA-BRAN
ERK
ULATOR
Oh er not really
Amazing!
BLONG BLONG
How could you, Lee Chaplin?
KING BEAVE
HOW VERY COULD YOU?

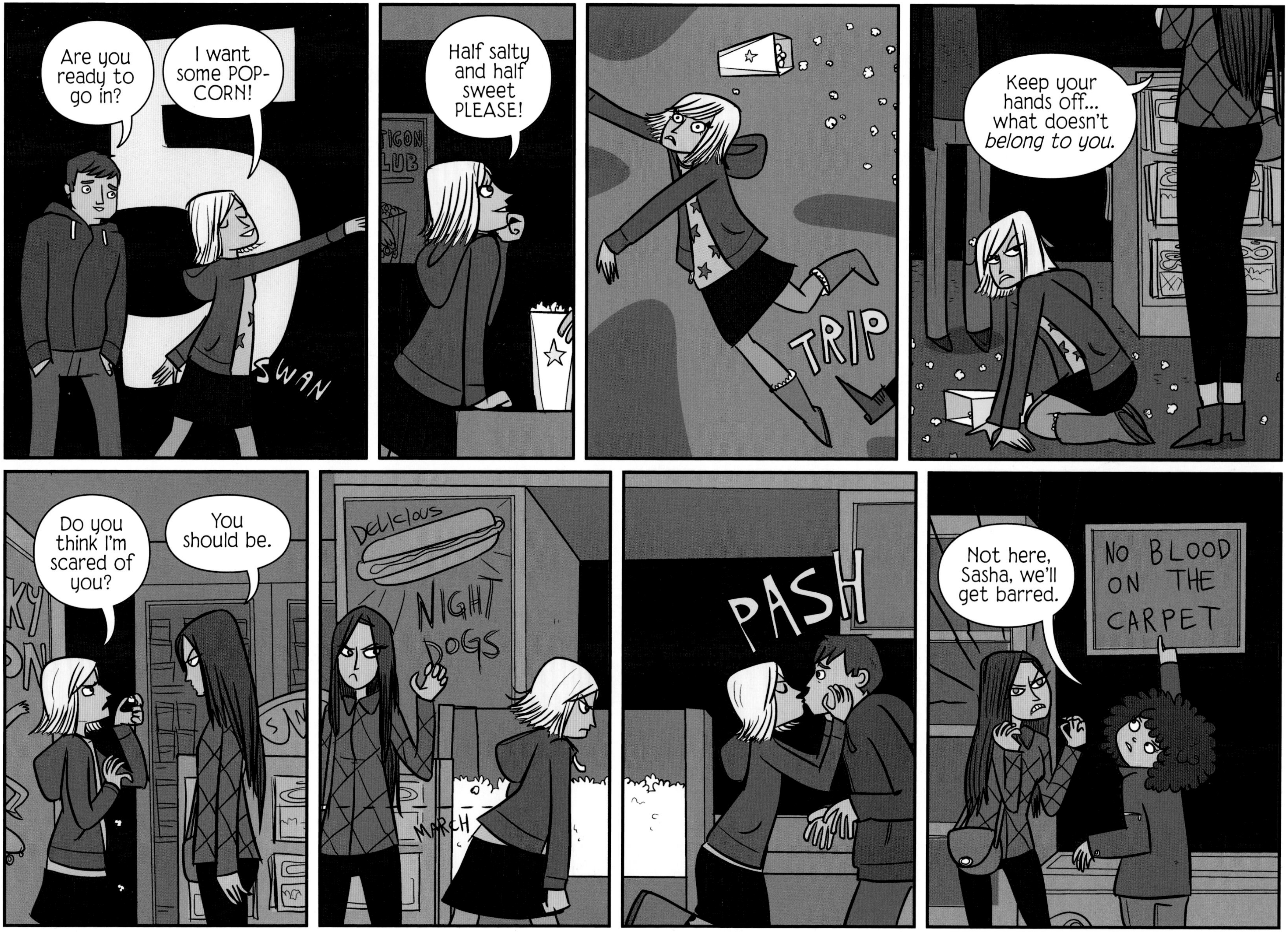

Are you ready to go in?
I want some POP-CORN!
SWAN
Half salty and half sweet PLEASE!
TRIP
Keep your hands off... what doesn't *belong to you.*
Do you think I'm scared of you?
You should be.
DELICIOUS
NIGHT DOGS
MARCH
PASH
Not here, Sasha, we'll get barred.
NO BLOOD ON THE CARPET

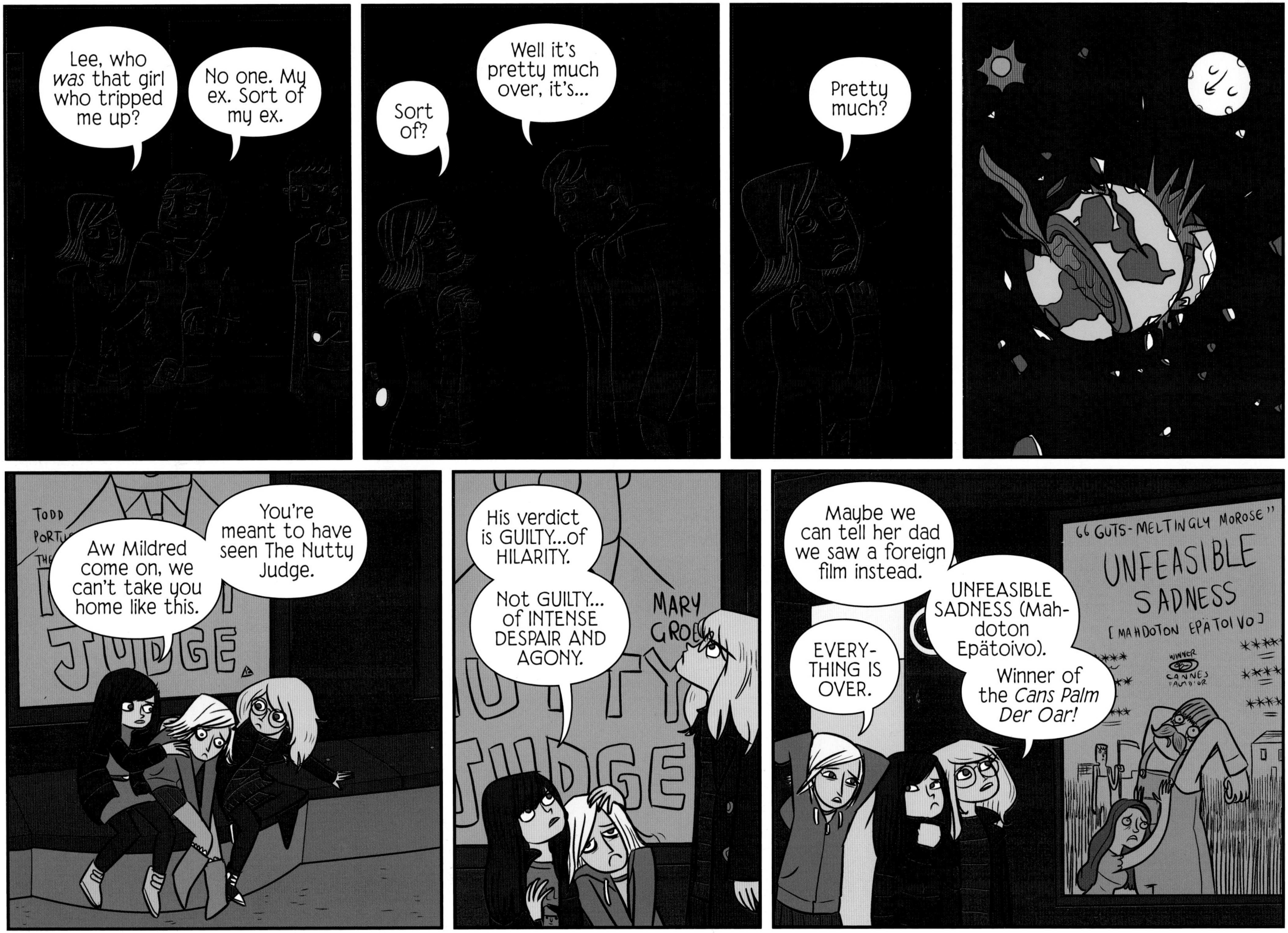
Lee, who *was* that girl who tripped me up?
No one. My ex. Sort of my ex.
Sort of?
Well it's pretty much over, it's...
Pretty much?
JUDGE
Aw Mildred come on, we can't take you home like this.
You're meant to have seen The Nutty Judge.
His verdict is GUILTY...of HILARITY.
Not GUILTY... of INTENSE DESPAIR AND AGONY.
Maybe we can tell her dad we saw a foreign film instead.
EVERYTHING IS OVER.
"GUTS-MELTINGLY MOROSE"
UNFEASIBLE SADNESS
[MAHDOTON EPÄTOIVO]
UNFEASIBLE SADNESS (Mahdoton Epätoivo).
Winner of the *Cans Palm Der Oar!*

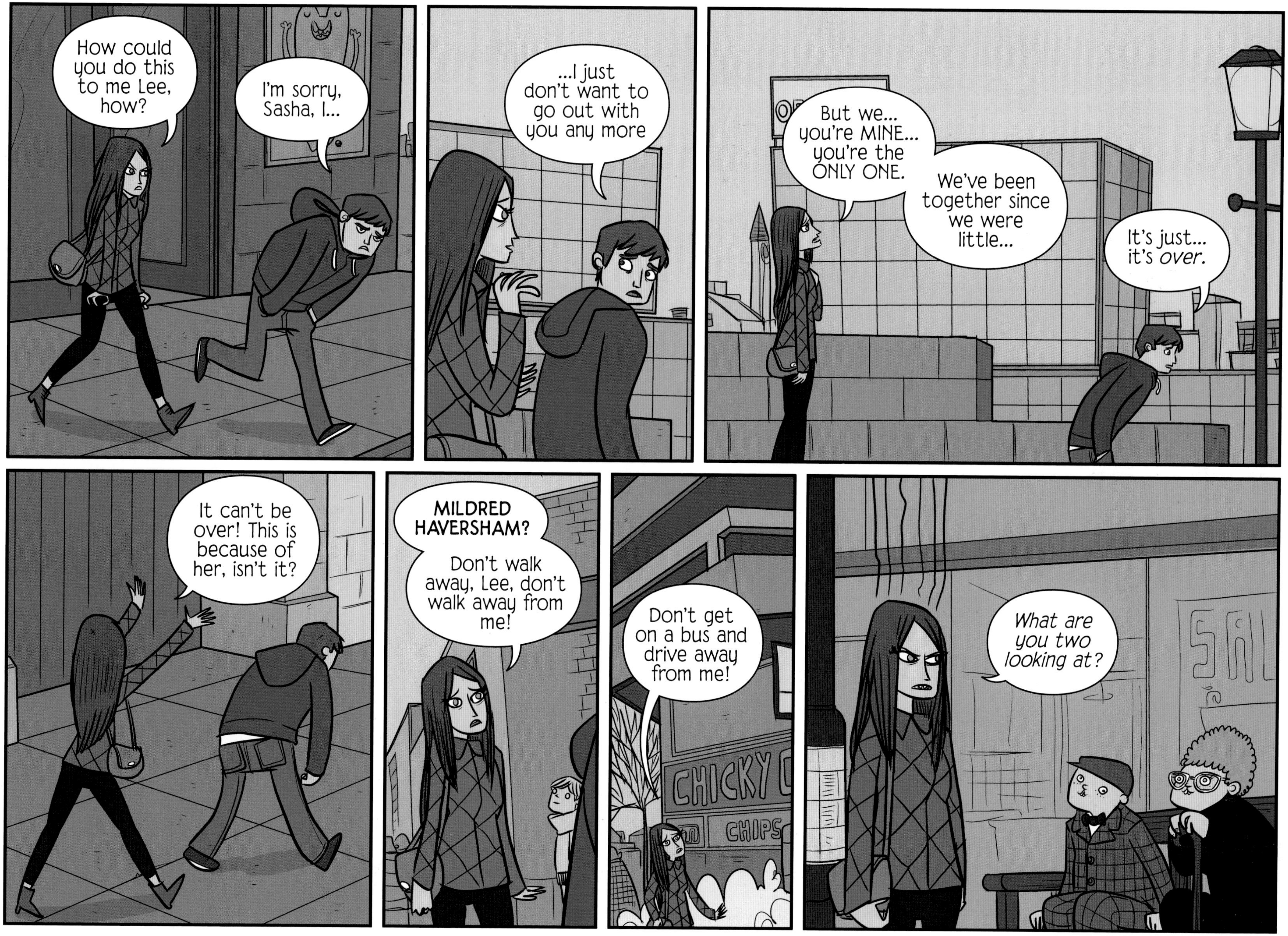
How could you do this to me Lee, how?
I'm sorry, Sasha, I...
...I just don't want to go out with you any more
But we... you're MINE... you're the ONLY ONE.
We've been together since we were little...
It's just... it's *over*.
It can't be over! This is because of her, isn't it?
MILDRED HAVERSHAM?
Don't walk away, Lee, don't walk away from me!
Don't get on a bus and drive away from me!
CHIPS
What are you two looking at?

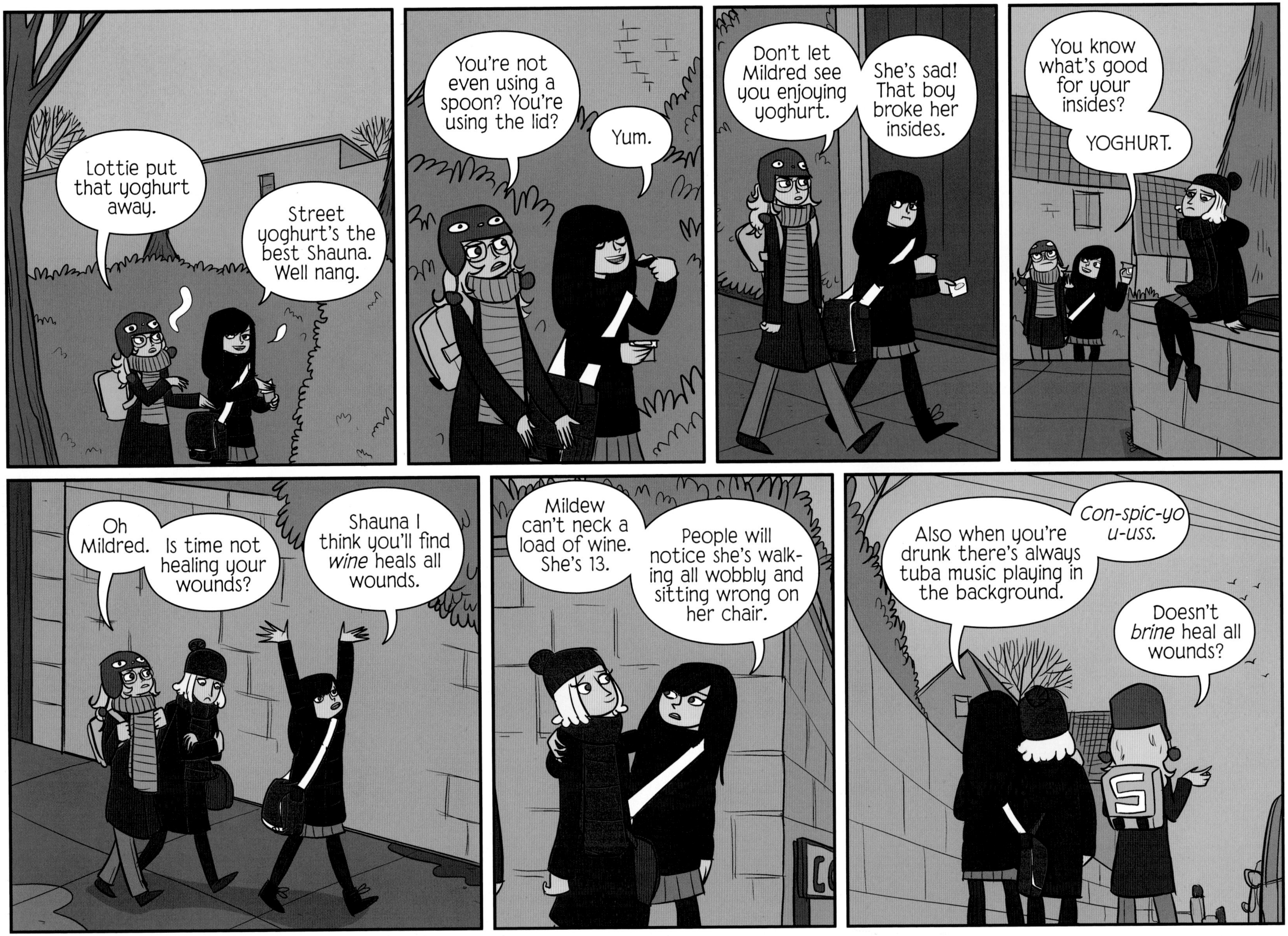
Lottie put that yoghurt away.
Street yoghurt's the best Shauna. Well nang.
You're not even using a spoon? You're using the lid?
Yum.
Don't let Mildred see you enjoying yoghurt.
She's sad! That boy broke her insides.
You know what's good for your insides?
YOGHURT.
Oh Mildred.
Is time not healing your wounds?
Shauna I think you'll find *wine* heals all wounds.
Mildew can't neck a load of wine. She's 13.
People will notice she's walking all wobbly and sitting wrong on her chair.
Also when you're drunk there's always tuba music playing in the background.
Con-spic-yo u-uss.
Doesn't *brine* heal all wounds?

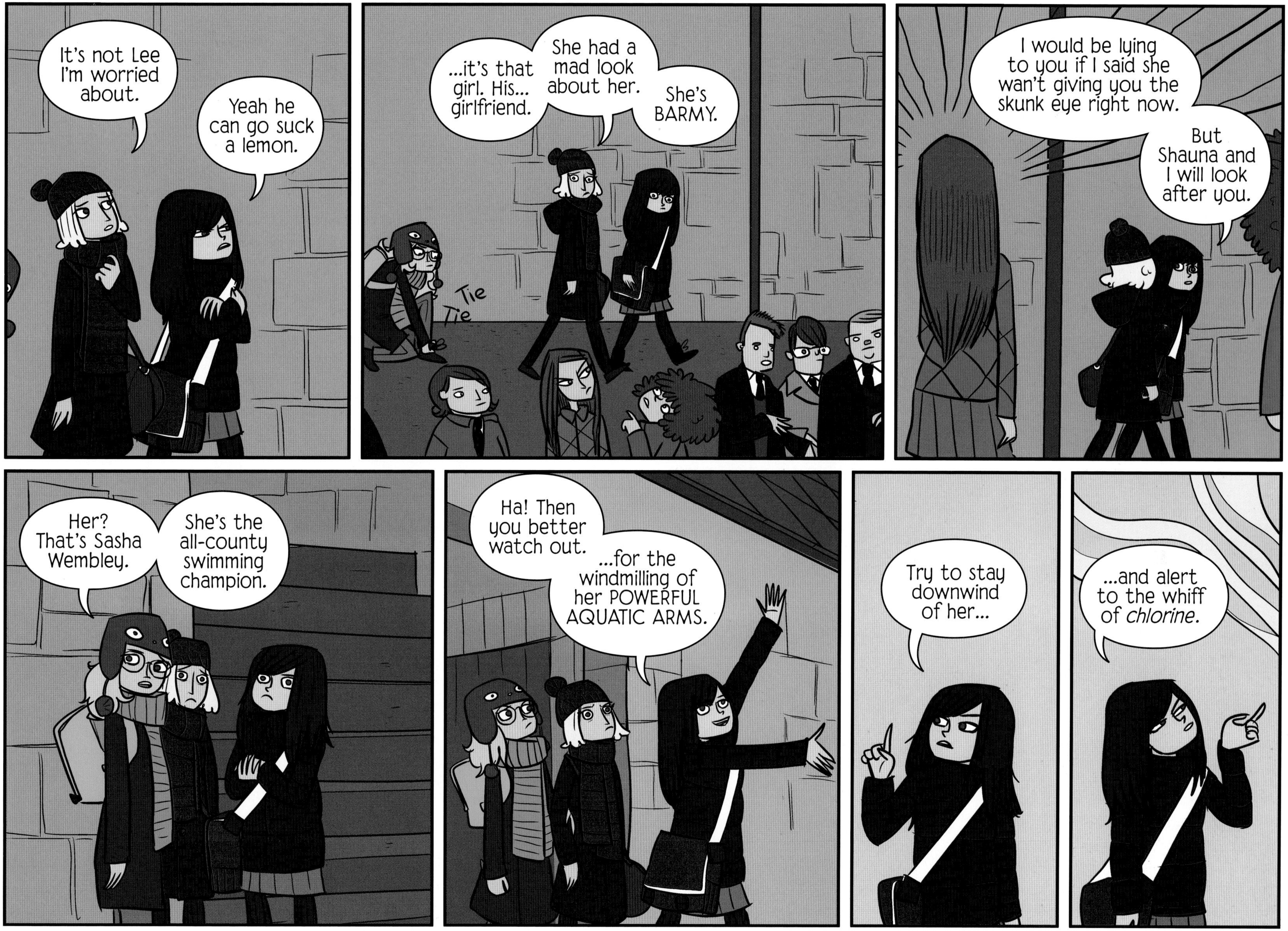
It's not Lee I'm worried about.
Yeah he can go suck a lemon.
...it's that girl. His... girlfriend.
She had a mad look about her.
She's BARMY.
Tie
Tie
I would be lying to you if I said she wan't giving you the skunk eye right now.
But Shauna and I will look after you.
Her? That's Sasha Wembley.
She's the all-county swimming champion.
Ha! Then you better watch out.
...for the windmilling of her POWERFUL AQUATIC ARMS.
Try to stay downwind of her...
...and alert to the whiff of *chlorine*.

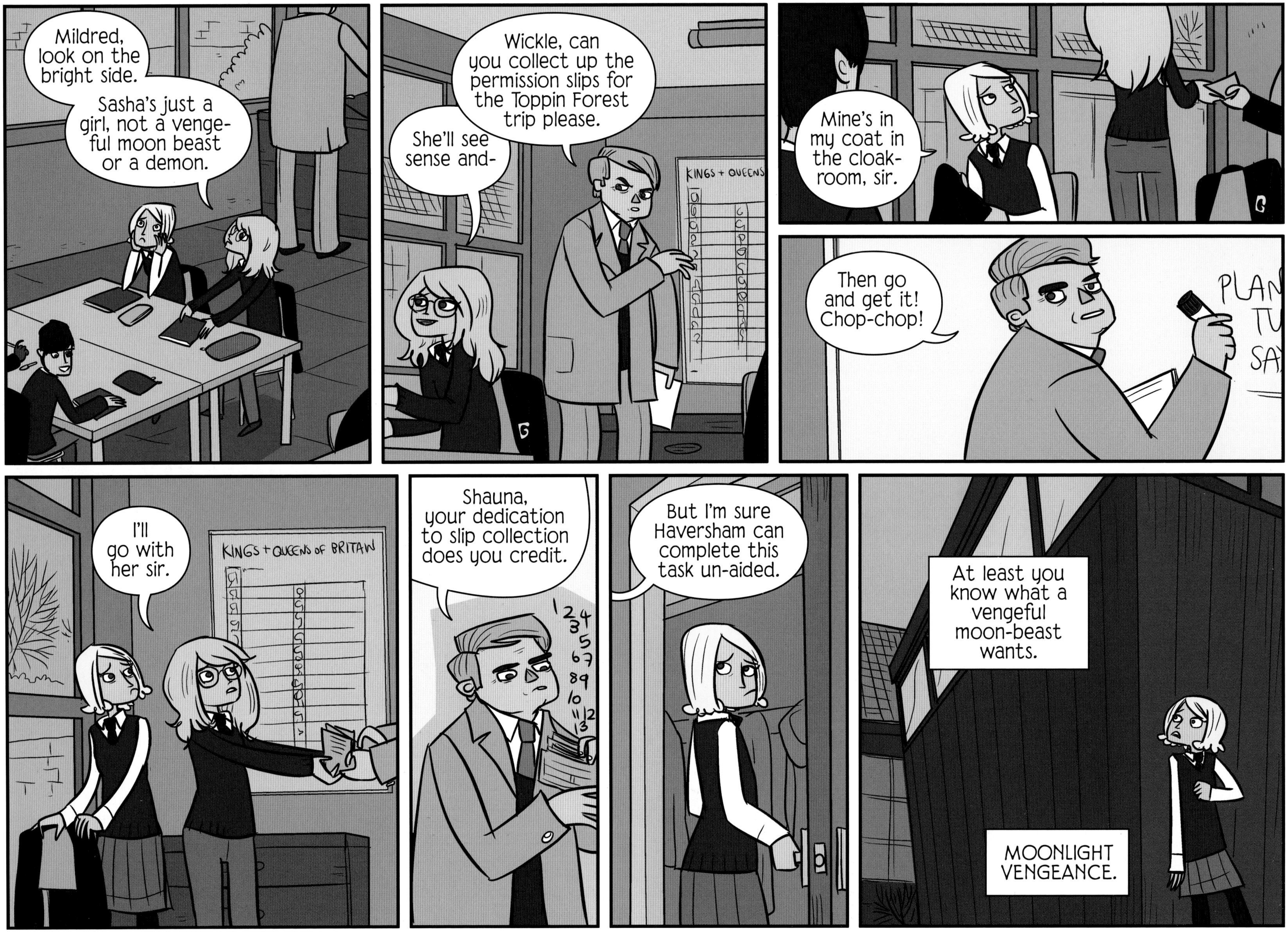
Mildred, look on the bright side.
Sasha's just a girl, not a vengeful moon beast or a demon.
She'll see sense and-
Wickle, can you collect up the permission slips for the Toppin Forest trip please.
KINGS + QUEENS
Mine's in my coat in the cloak-room, sir.
Then go and get it! Chop-chop!
I'll go with her sir.
KINGS + QUEENS OF BRITAIN
Shauna, your dedication to slip collection does you credit.
But I'm sure Haversham can complete this task un-aided.
At least you know what a vengeful moon-beast wants.
MOONLIGHT VENGEANCE.

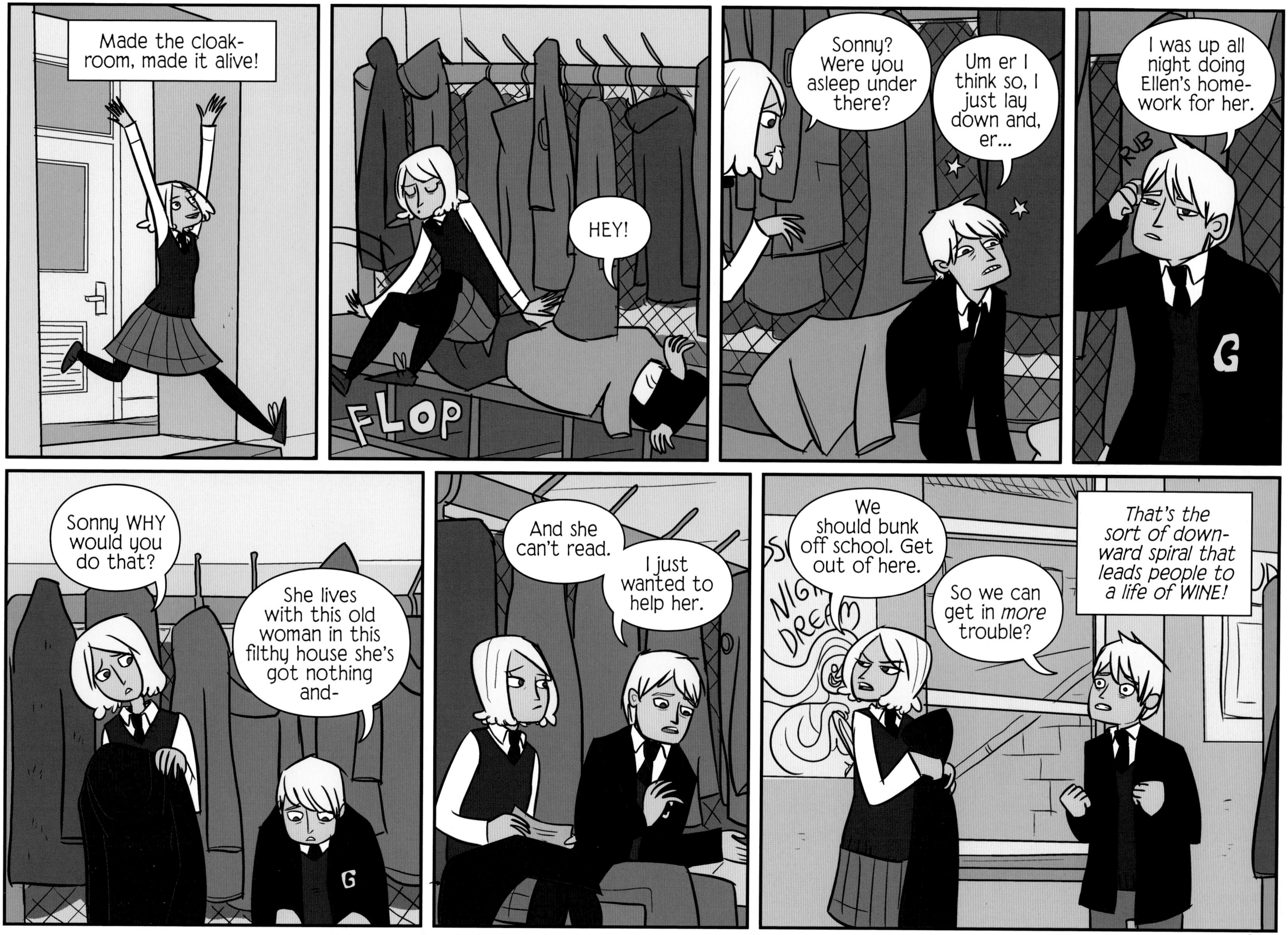
Made the cloak-room, made it alive!
HEY!
FLOP
Sonny? Were you asleep under there?
Um er I think so, I just lay down and, er...
RUB
I was up all night doing Ellen's home-work for her.
Sonny WHY would you do that?
She lives with this old woman in this filthy house she's got nothing and-
And she can't read.
I just wanted to help her.
We should bunk off school. Get out of here.
So we can get in *more* trouble?
That's the sort of down-ward spiral that leads people to a life of WINE!

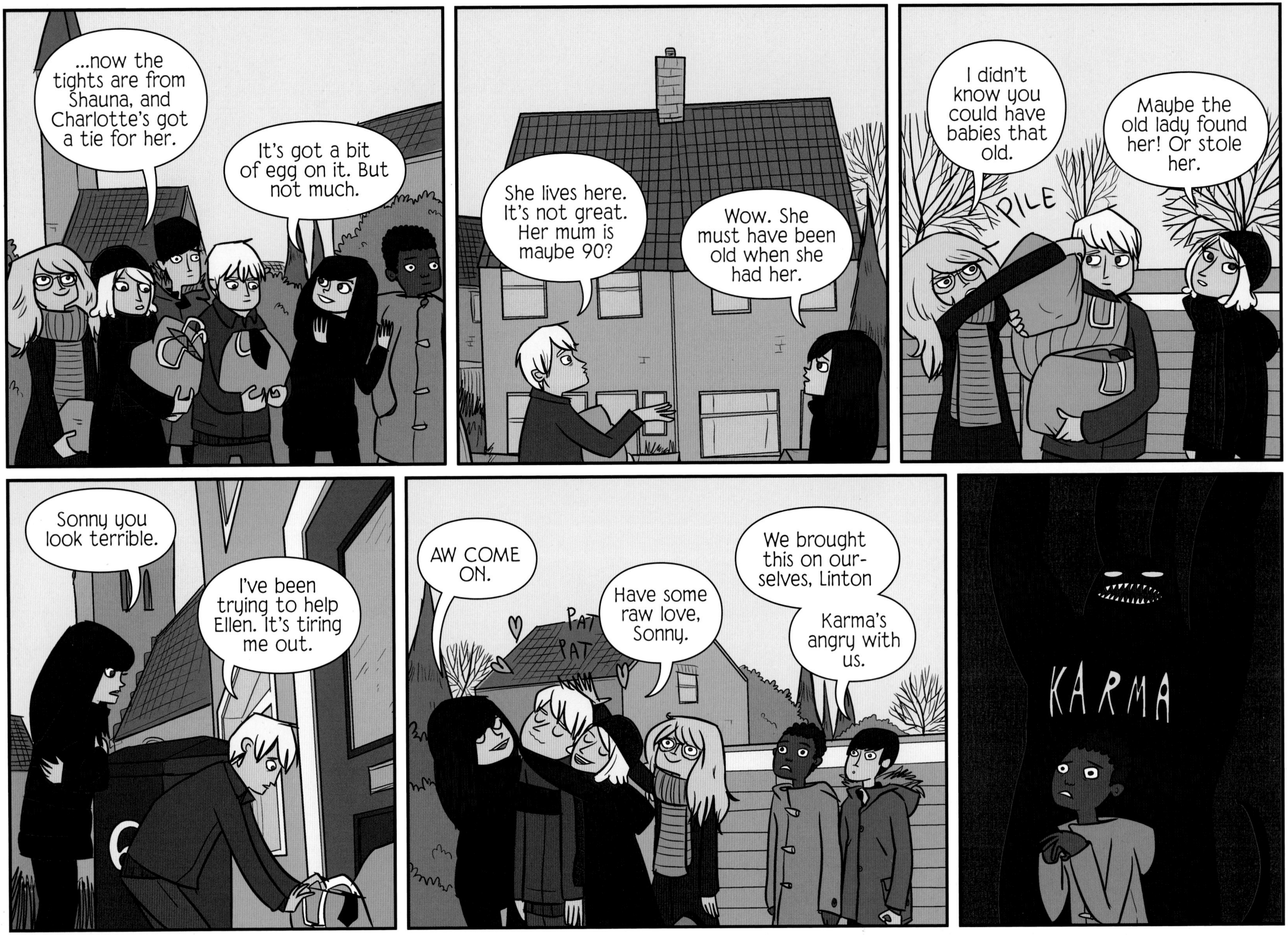
...now the tights are from Shauna, and Charlotte's got a tie for her.
It's got a bit of egg on it. But not much.
She lives here. It's not great. Her mum is maybe 90?
Wow. She must have been old when she had her.
I didn't know you could have babies that old.
PILE
Maybe the old lady found her! Or stole her.
Sonny you look terrible.
I've been trying to help Ellen. It's tiring me out.
AW COME ON.
PAT PAT
Have some raw love, Sonny.
We brought this on our-selves, Linton
Karma's angry with us.
KARMA

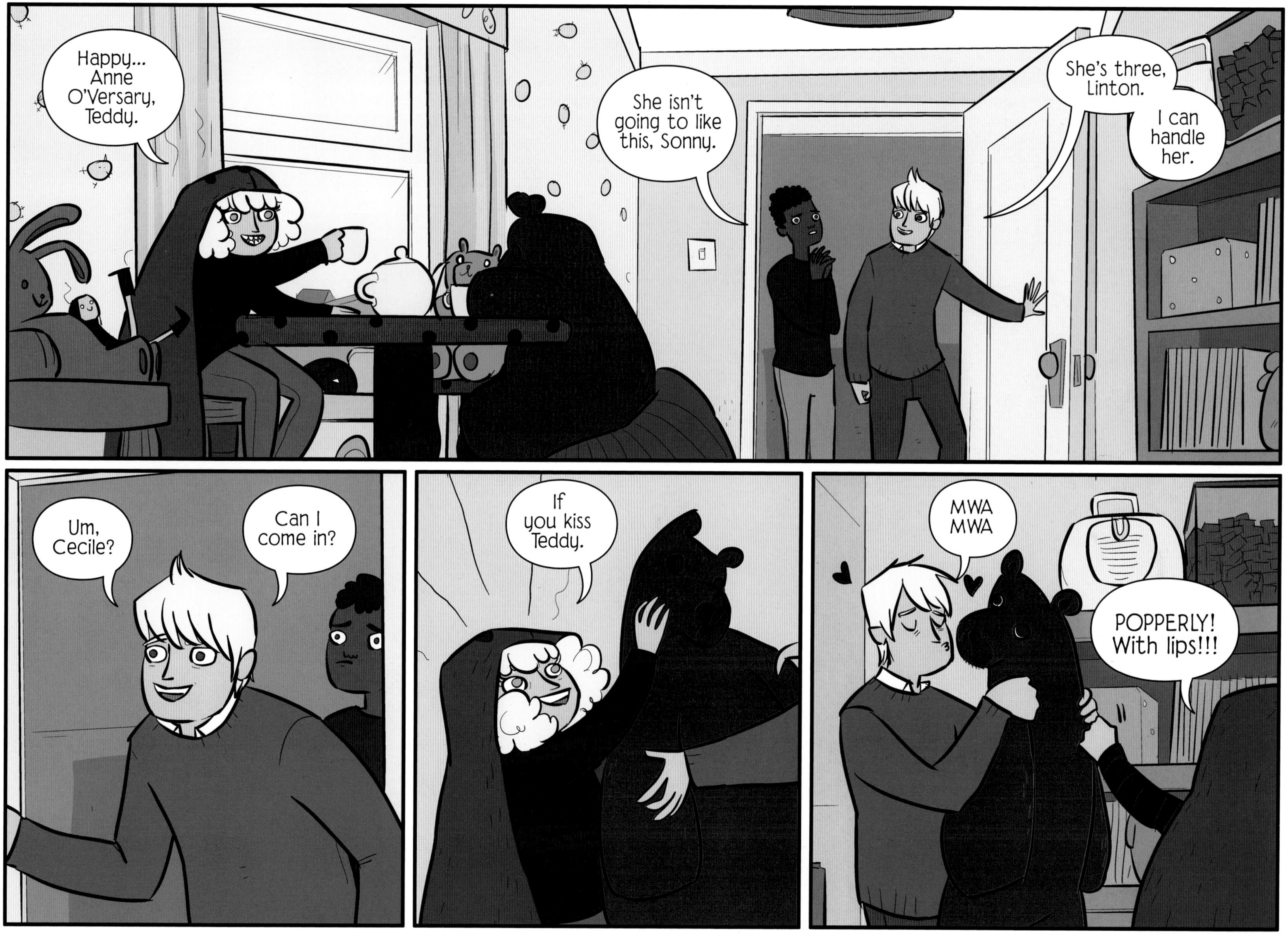
Happy... Anne O'Versary, Teddy.
She isn't going to like this, Sonny.
She's three, Linton.
I can handle her.
Um, Cecile?
Can I come in?
If you kiss Teddy.
MWA MWA
POPPERLY! With lips!!!

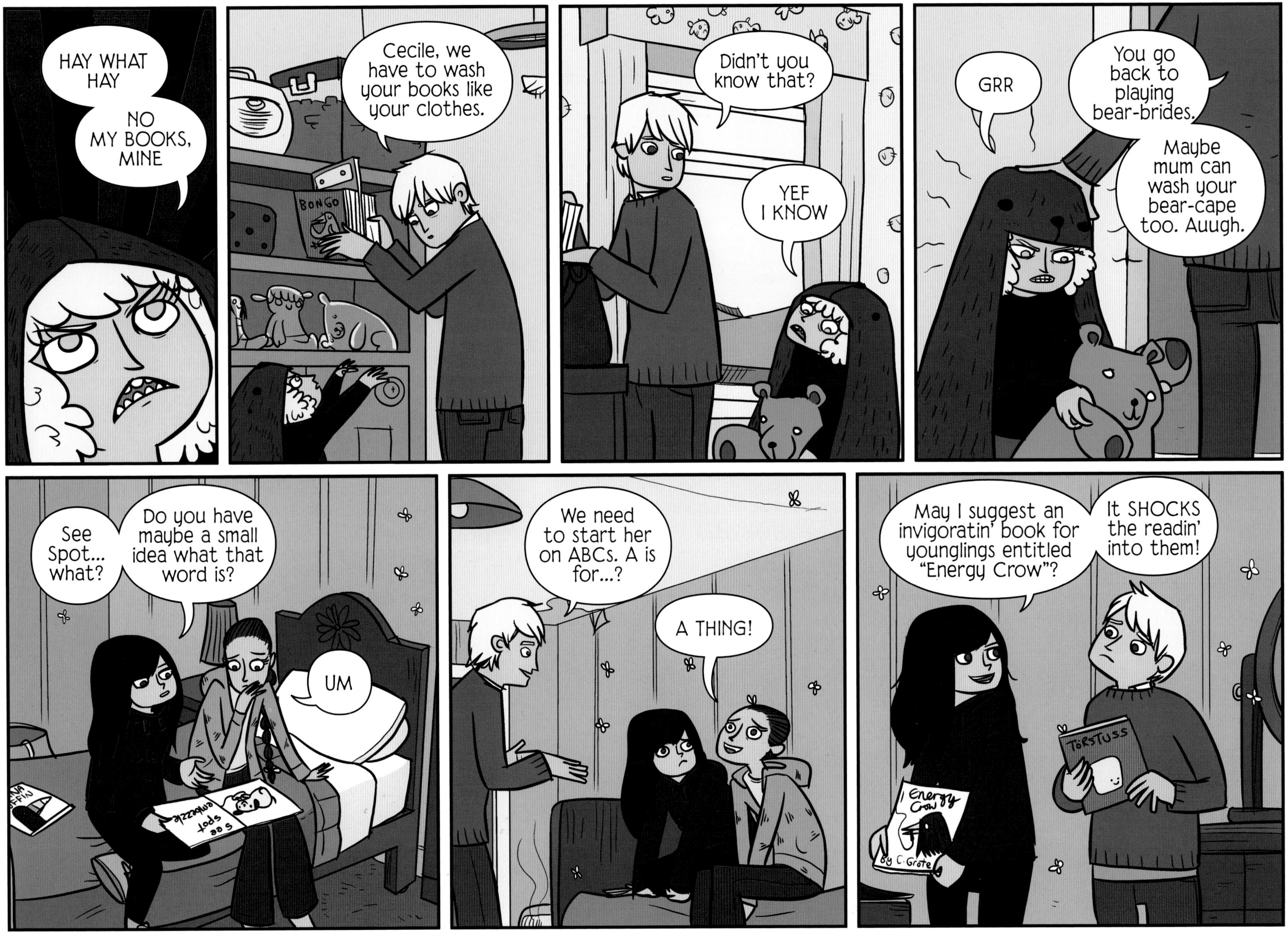
HAY WHAT HAY
NO MY BOOKS, MINE
Cecile, we have to wash your books like your clothes.
BONGO
Didn't you know that?
YEF I KNOW
GRR
You go back to playing bear-brides.
Maybe mum can wash your bear-cape too. Auugh.
See Spot... what?
Do you have maybe a small idea what that word is?
UM
We need to start her on ABCs. A is for...?
A THING!
May I suggest an invigoratin' book for younglings entitled "Energy Crow"?
It SHOCKS the readin' into them!
Energy Crow
By C. Grote
TÖRSTUSS

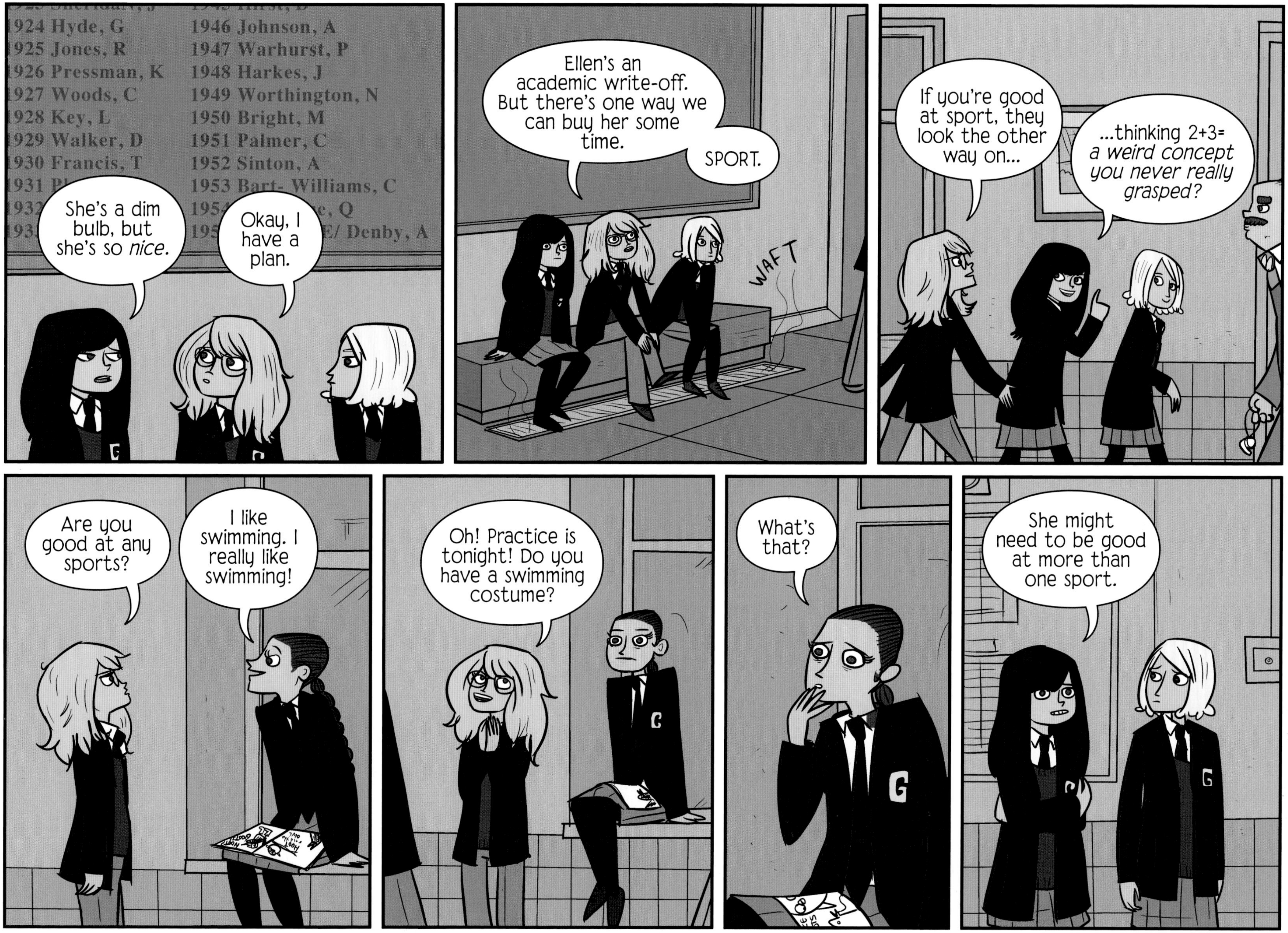
1924 Hyde, G
1925 Jones, R
1926 Pressman, K
1927 Woods, C
1928 Key, L
1929 Walker, D
1930 Francis, T
1946 Johnson, A
1947 Warhurst, P
1948 Harkes, J
1949 Worthington, N
1950 Bright, M
1951 Palmer, C
1952 Sinton, A
1953 Bart- Williams, C
She's a dim bulb, but she's so *nice*.
Okay, I have a plan.
Ellen's an academic write-off. But there's one way we can buy her some time.
SPORT.
WAFT
If you're good at sport, they look the other way on...
...thinking 2+3= *a weird concept you never really grasped?*
Are you good at any sports?
I like swimming. I really like swimming!
Oh! Practice is tonight! Do you have a swimming costume?
What's that?
She might need to be good at more than one sport.

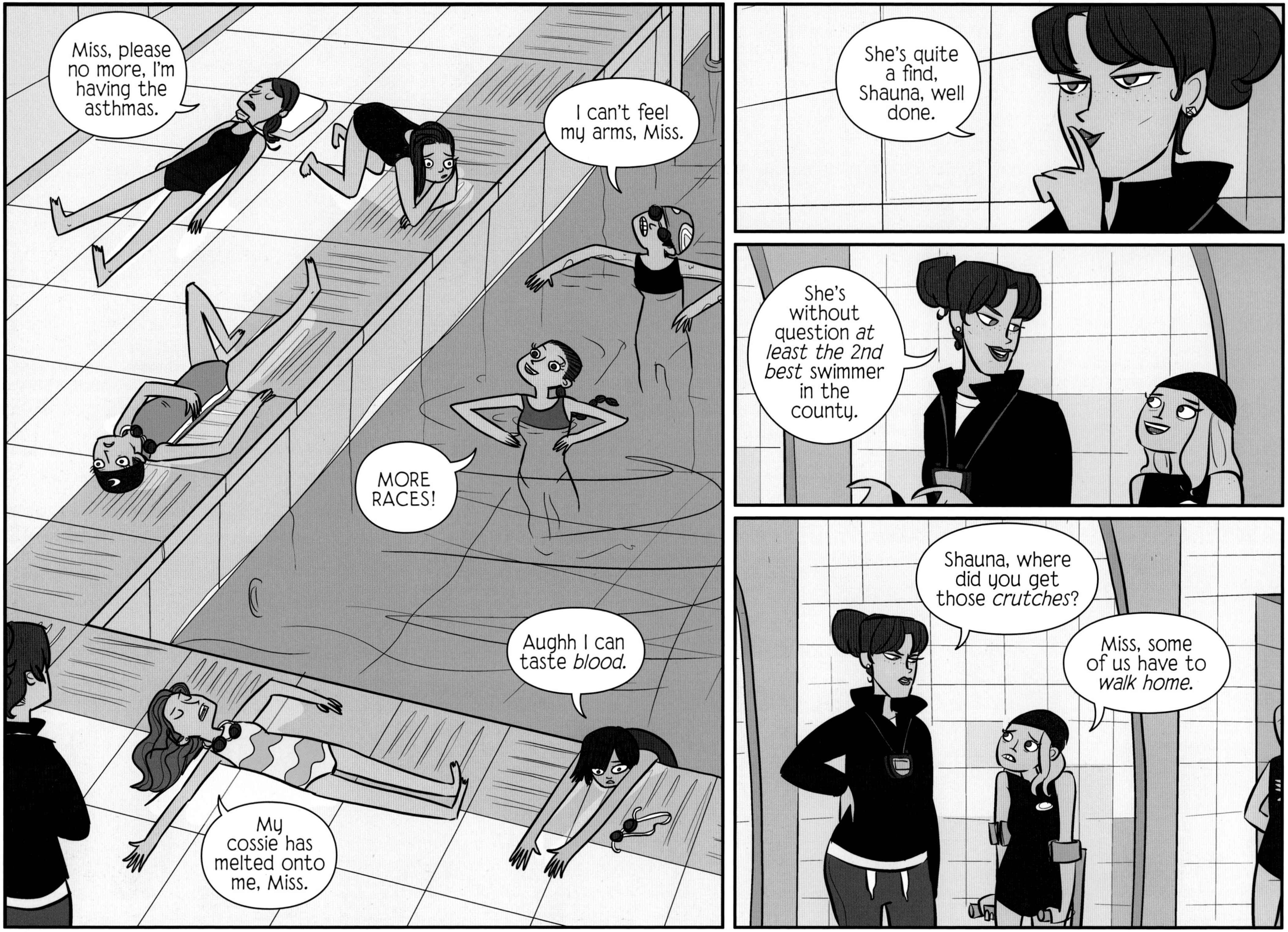
Miss, please no more, I'm having the asthmas.
I can't feel my arms, Miss.
MORE RACES!
Augh I can taste *blood.*
My cossie has melted onto me, Miss.
She's quite a find, Shauna, well done.
She's without question *at least the 2nd best* swimmer in the county.
Shauna, where did you get those *crutches*?
Miss, some of us have to *walk home.*

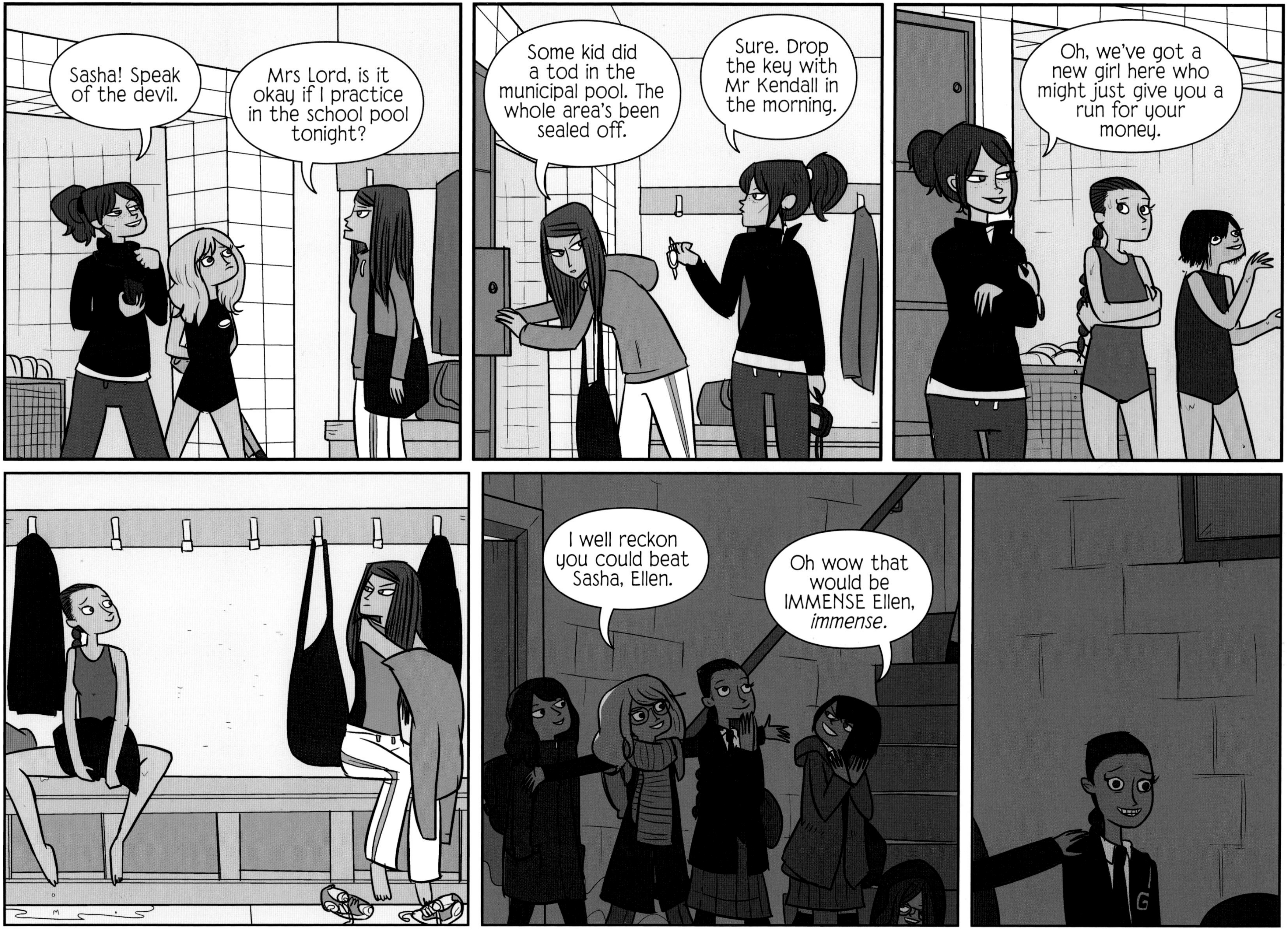
Sasha! Speak of the devil.
Mrs Lord, is it okay if I practice in the school pool tonight?
Some kid did a tod in the municipal pool. The whole area's been sealed off.
Sure. Drop the key with Mr Kendall in the morning.
Oh, we've got a new girl here who might just give you a run for your money.
I well reckon you could beat Sasha, Ellen.
Oh wow that would be IMMENSE Ellen, *immense.*

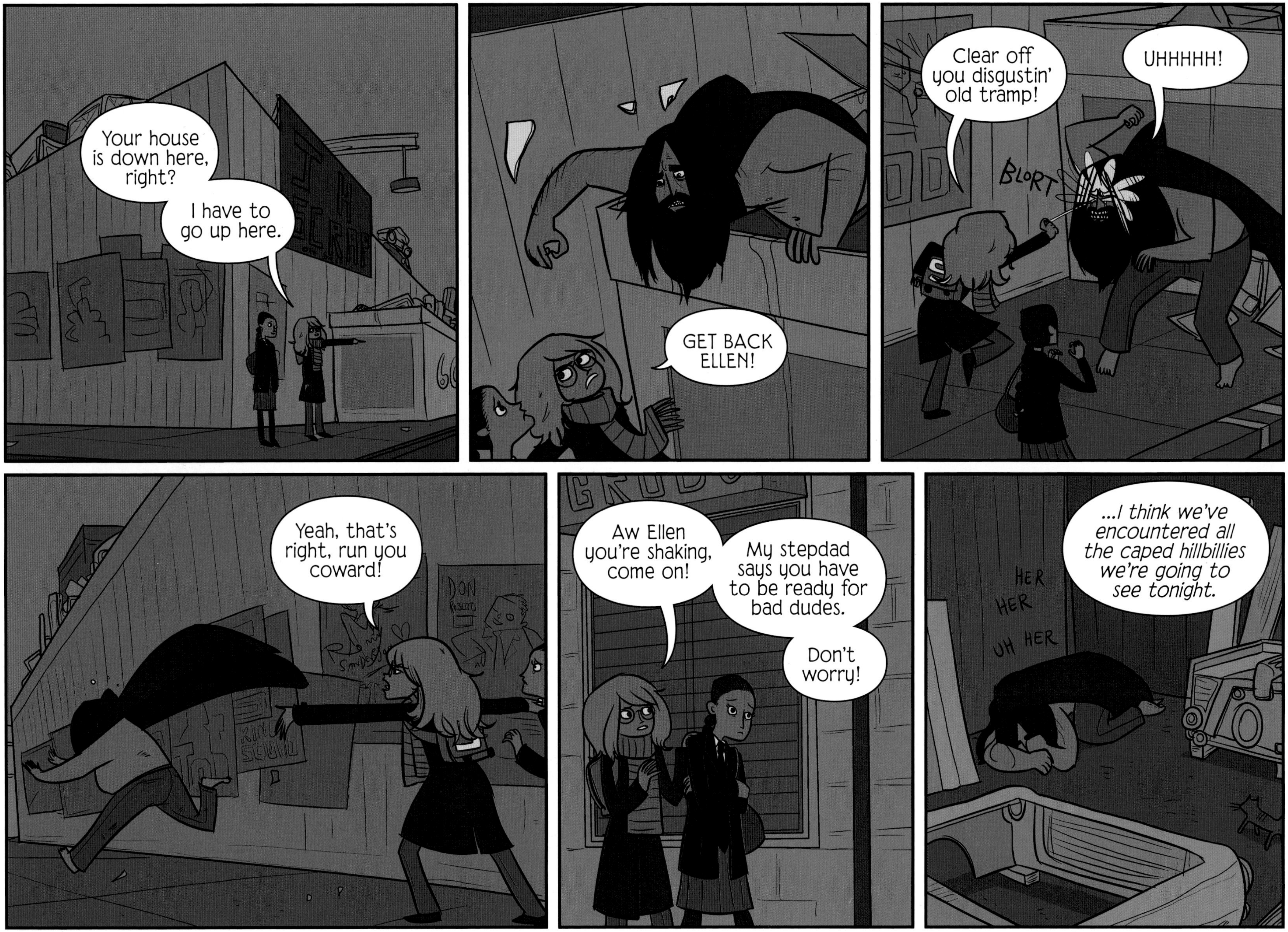
Your house is down here, right?
I have to go up here.
GET BACK ELLEN!
Clear off you disgustin' old tramp!
UHHHHH!
BLORT
Yeah, that's right, run you coward!
Aw Ellen you're shaking, come on!
My stepdad says you have to be ready for bad dudes.
Don't worry!
HER
HER
UH HER
...I think we've encountered all the caped hillbillies we're going to see tonight.

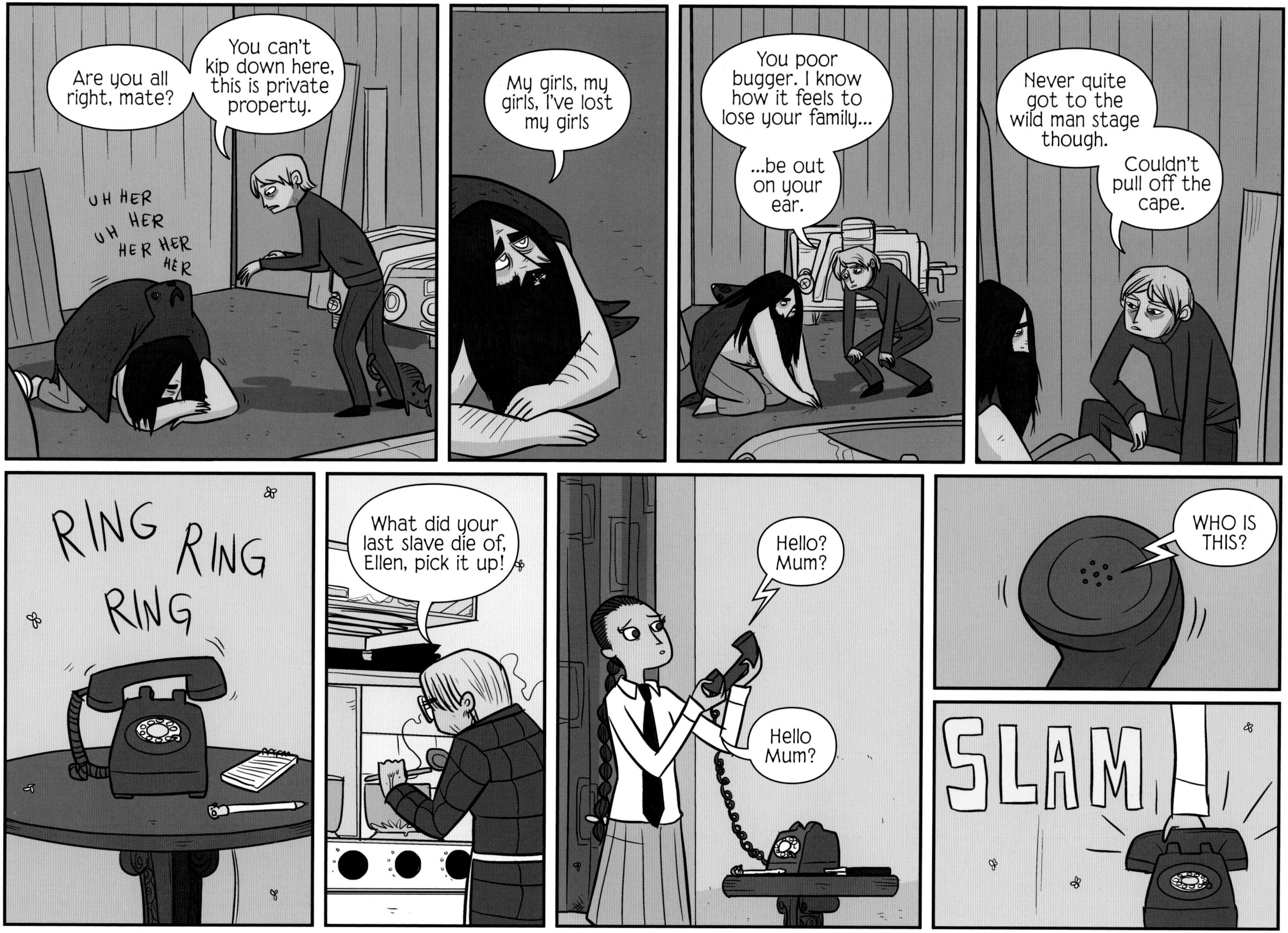
Are you all right, mate?
You can't kip down here, this is private property.
UH HER UH HER HER HER HER HER
My girls, my girls, I've lost my girls
You poor bugger. I know how it feels to lose your family...
...be out on your ear.
Never quite got to the wild man stage though.
Couldn't pull off the cape.
RING RING RING
What did your last slave die of, Ellen, pick it up!
Hello? Mum?
Hello Mum?
WHO IS THIS?
SLAM

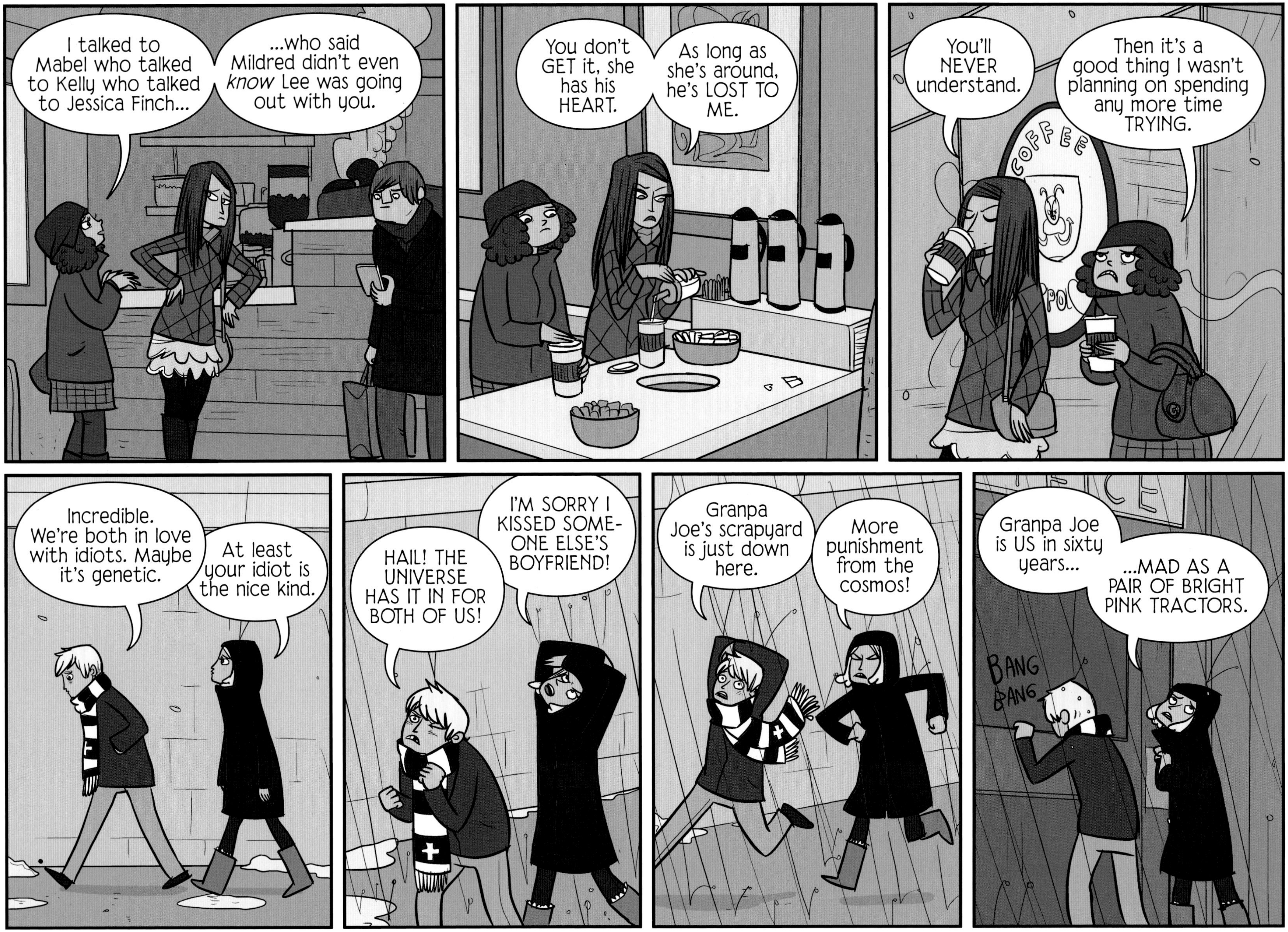
I talked to Mabel who talked to Kelly who talked to Jessica Finch...
...who said Mildred didn't even *know* Lee was going out with you.
You don't GET it, she has his HEART.
As long as she's around, he's LOST TO ME.
You'll NEVER understand.
Then it's a good thing I wasn't planning on spending any more time TRYING.
COFFEE
Incredible. We're both in love with idiots. Maybe it's genetic.
At least your idiot is the nice kind.
HAIL! THE UNIVERSE HAS IT IN FOR BOTH OF US!
I'M SORRY I KISSED SOME-ONE ELSE'S BOYFRIEND!
Granpa Joe's scrapyard is just down here.
More punishment from the cosmos!
Granpa Joe is US in sixty years...
...MAD AS A PAIR OF BRIGHT PINK TRACTORS.
BANG
BANG

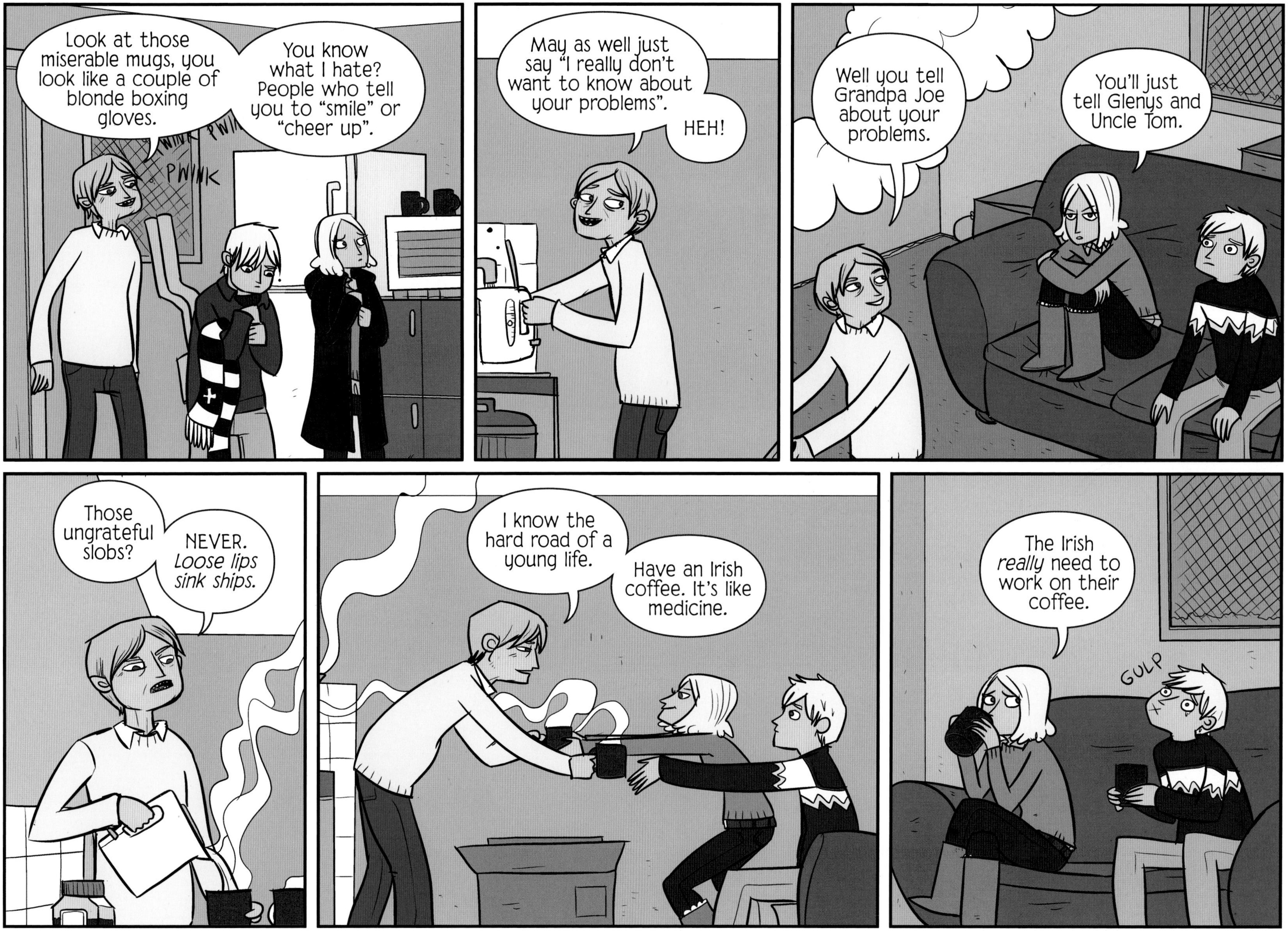
Look at those miserable mugs, you look like a couple of blonde boxing gloves.
PWINK PWINK
PWINK
You know what I hate? People who tell you to "smile" or "cheer up".
May as well just say "I really don't want to know about your problems".
HEH!
Well you tell Grandpa Joe about your problems.
You'll just tell Glenys and Uncle Tom.
Those ungrateful slobs?
NEVER. *Loose lips sink ships.*
I know the hard road of a young life.
Have an Irish coffee. It's like medicine.
The Irish *really* need to work on their coffee.
GULP

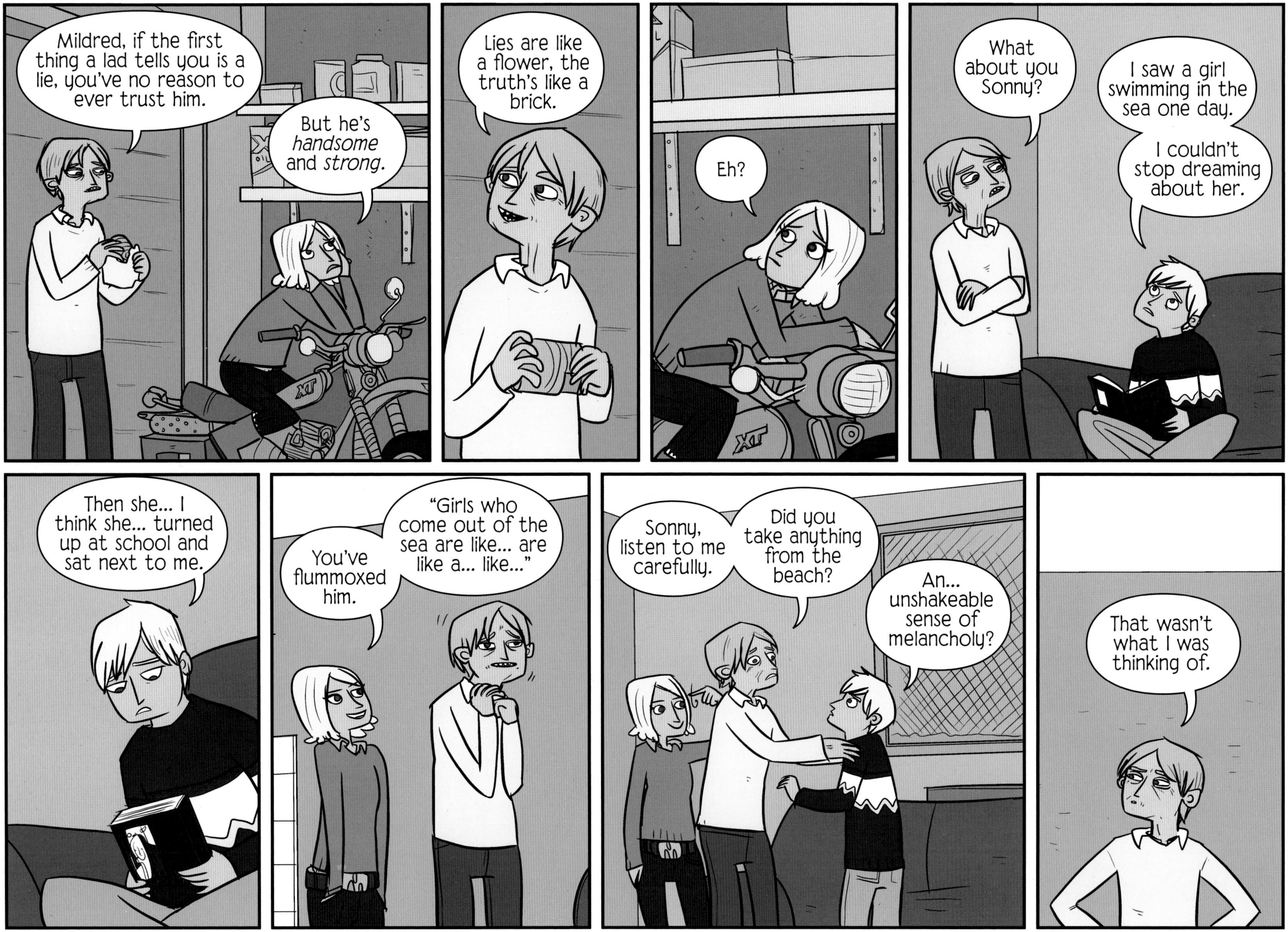
Mildred, if the first thing a lad tells you is a lie, you've no reason to ever trust him.
But he's *handsome* and *strong*.
Lies are like a flower, the truth's like a brick.
Eh?
What about you Sonny?
I saw a girl swimming in the sea one day.
I couldn't stop dreaming about her.
Then she... I think she... turned up at school and sat next to me.
You've flummoxed him.
"Girls who come out of the sea are like... are like a... like..."
Sonny, listen to me carefully.
Did you take anything from the beach?
An... unshakeable sense of melancholy?
That wasn't what I was thinking of.

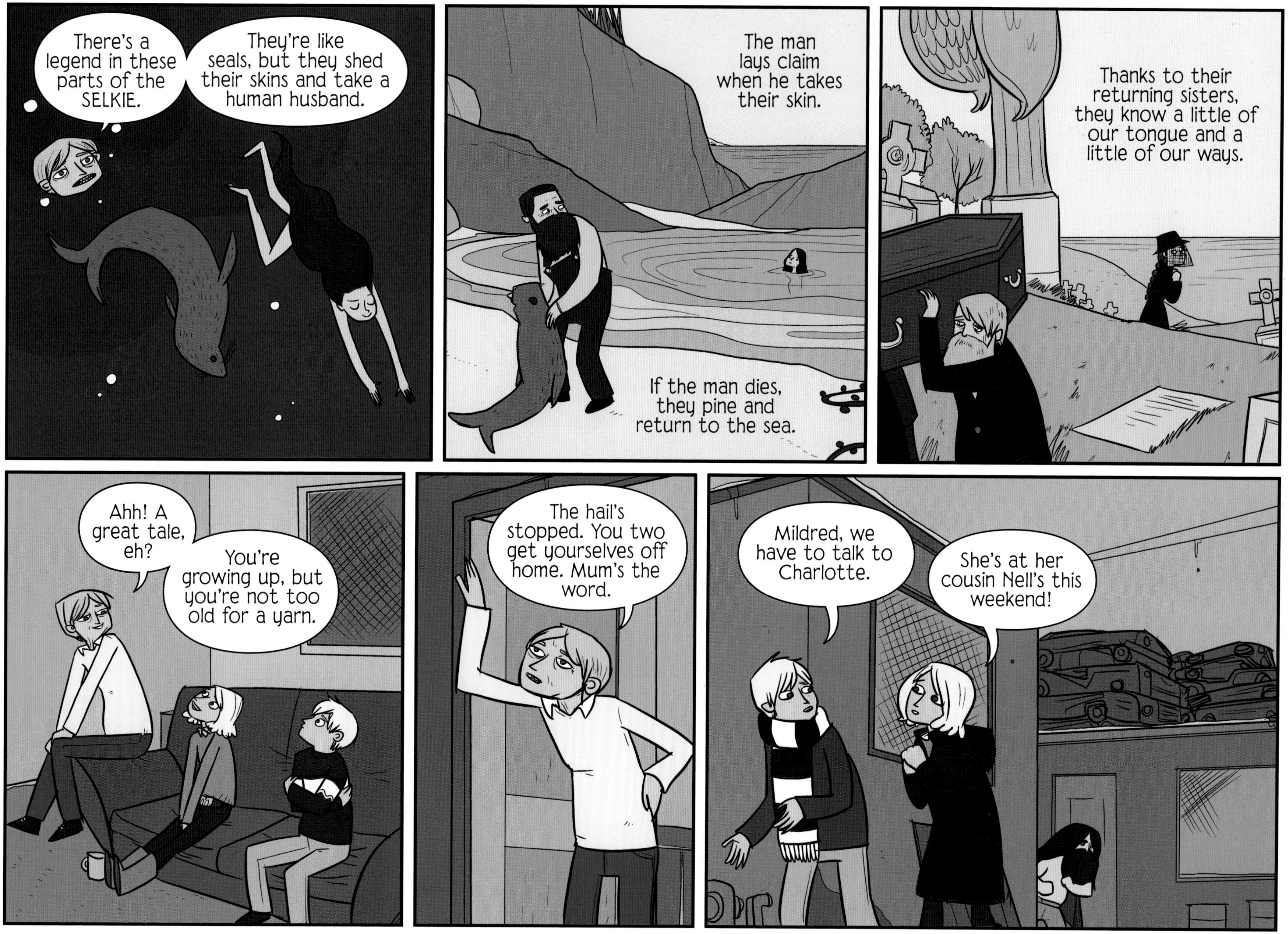
There's a legend in these parts of the SELKIE.
They're like seals, but they shed their skins and take a human husband.
The man lays claim when he takes their skin.
If the man dies, they pine and return to the sea.
Thanks to their returning sisters, they know a little of our tongue and a little of our ways.
Ahh! A great tale, eh?
You're growing up, but you're not too old for a yarn.
The hail's stopped. You two get yourselves off home. Mum's the word.
Mildred, we have to talk to Charlotte.
She's at her cousin Nell's this weekend!

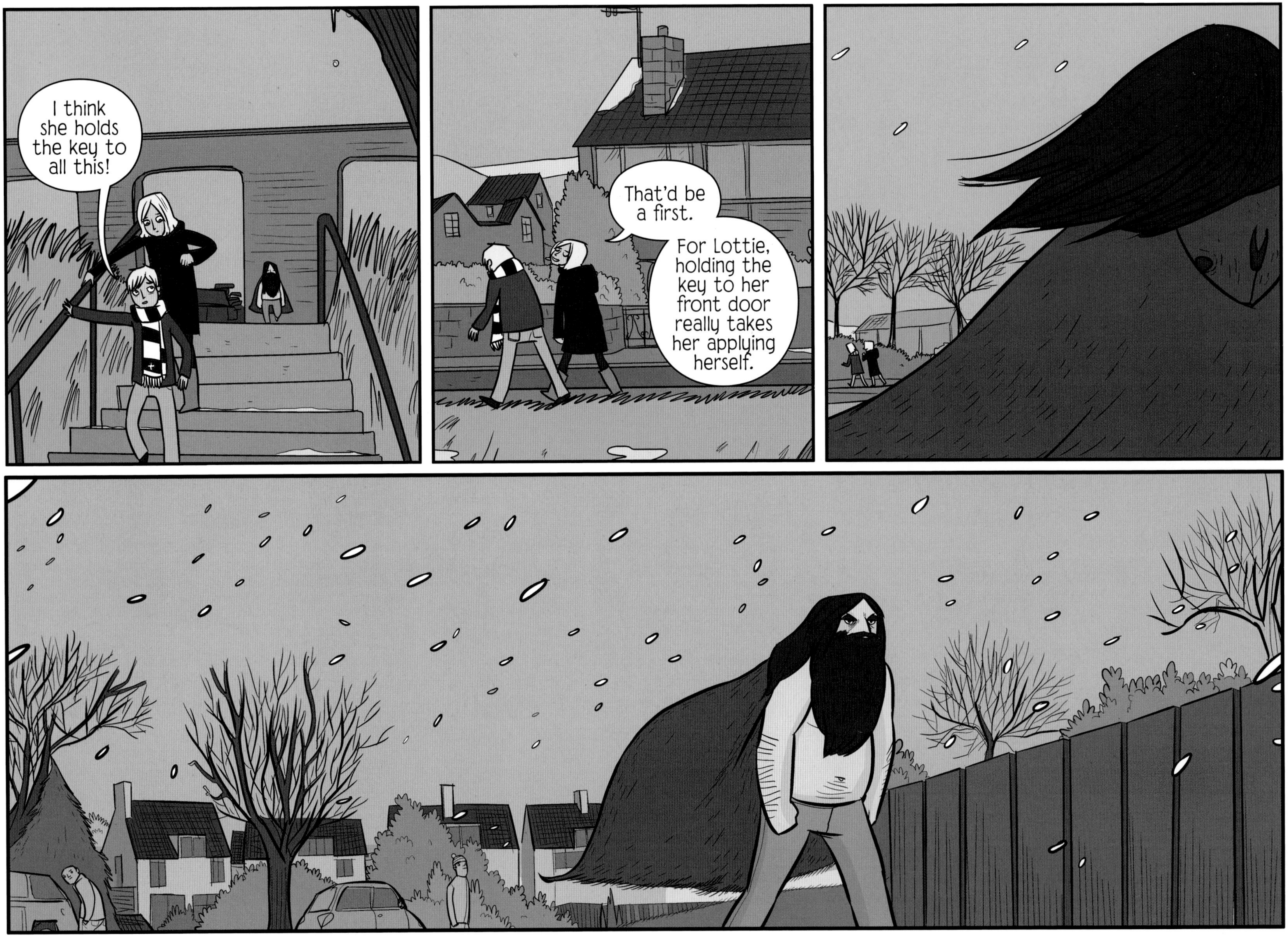
I think she holds the key to all this!
That'd be a first.
For Lottie, holding the key to her front door really takes her applying herself.

3

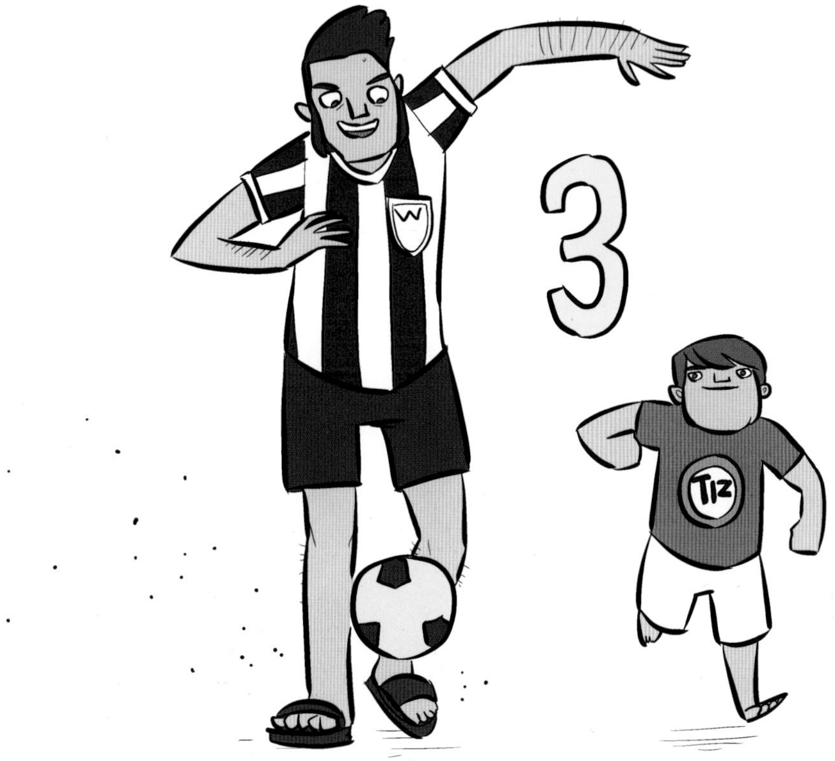
TIZ

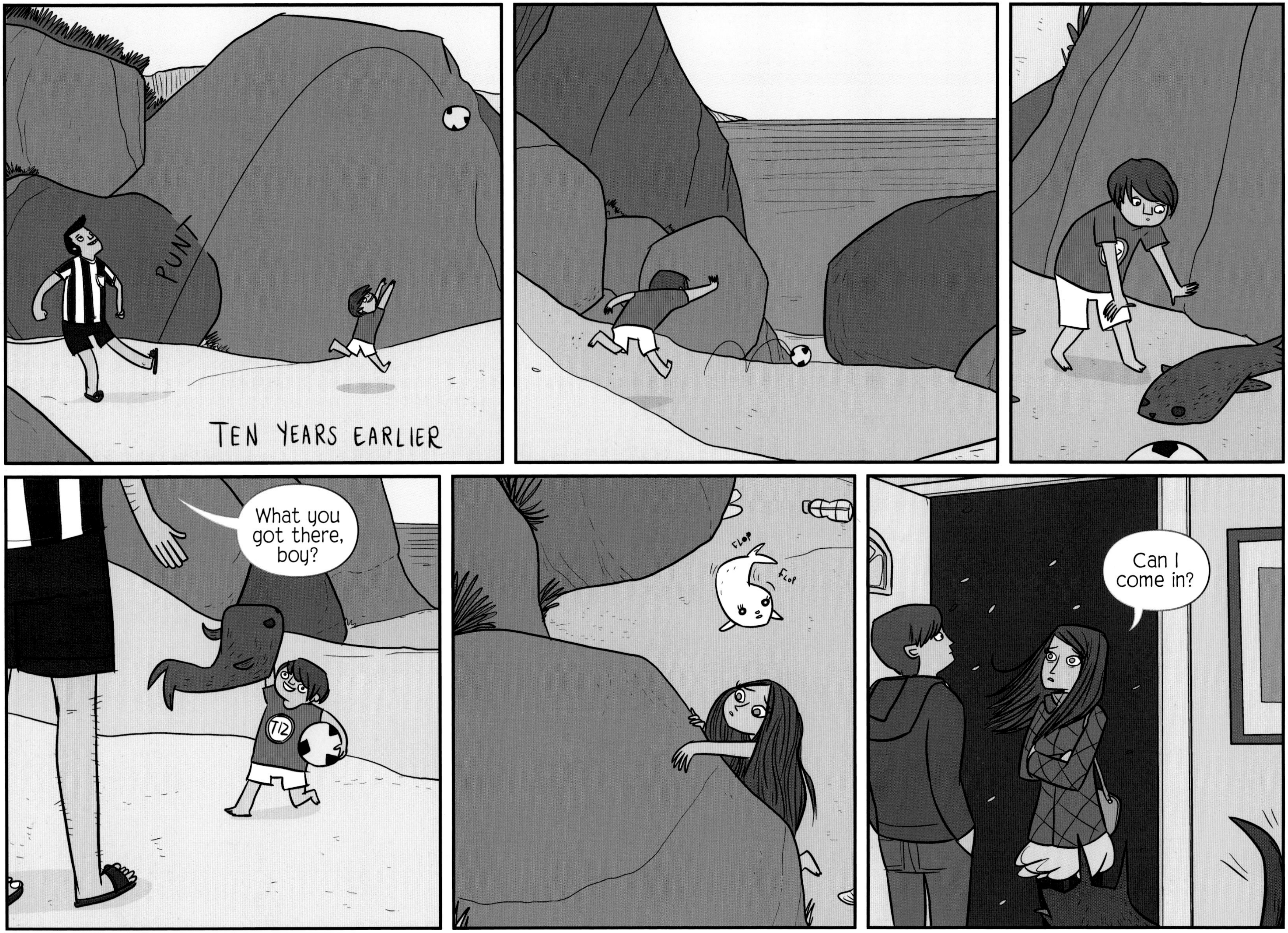
PUNT
TEN YEARS EARLIER
What you got there, boy?
FLOP
FLOP
Can I come in?

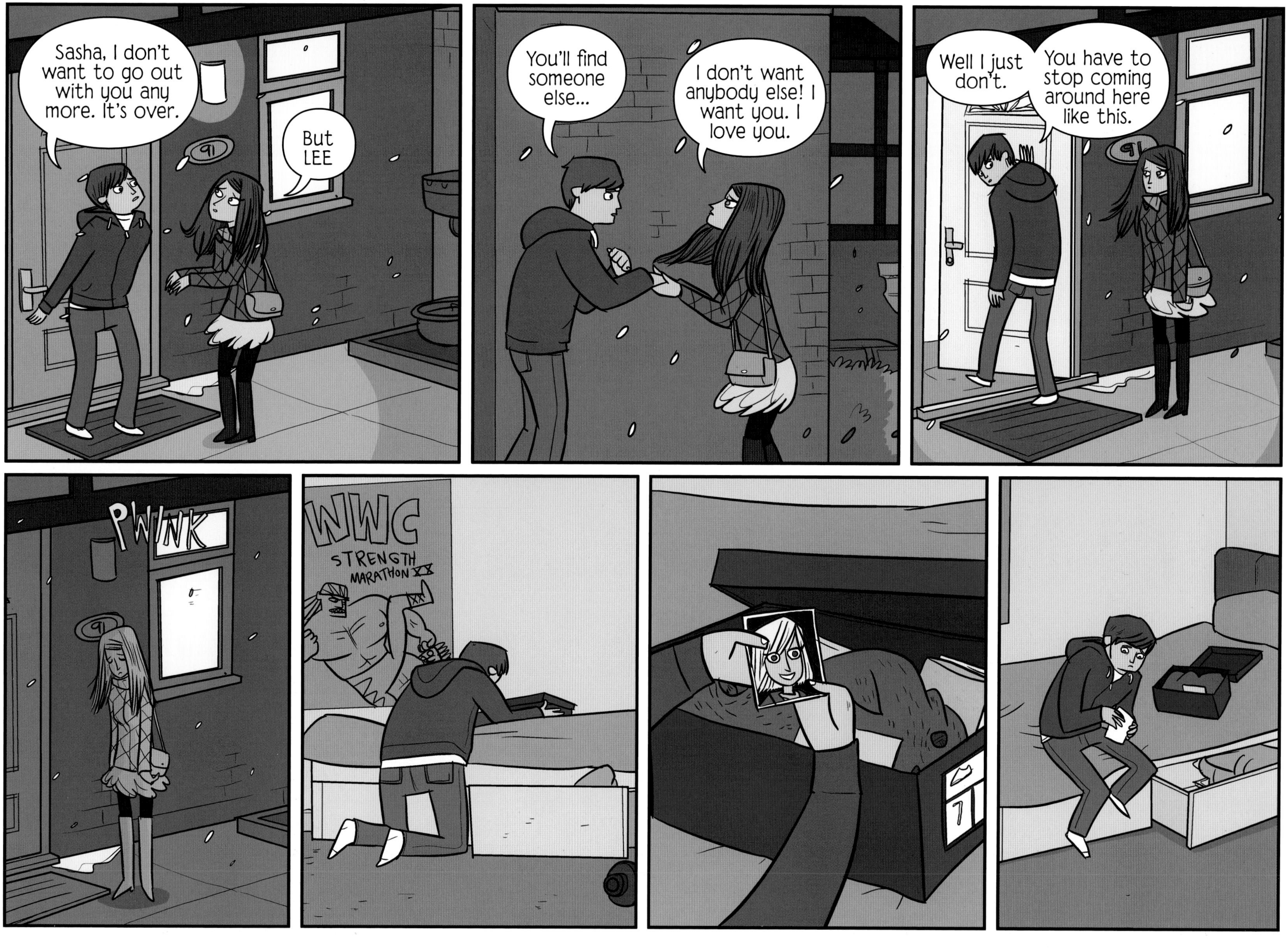
Sasha, I don't want to go out with you any more. It's over.
But LEE
You'll find someone else...
I don't want anybody else! I want you. I love you.
Well I just don't.
You have to stop coming around here like this.
PWINK
WWC
STRENGTH MARATHON XX

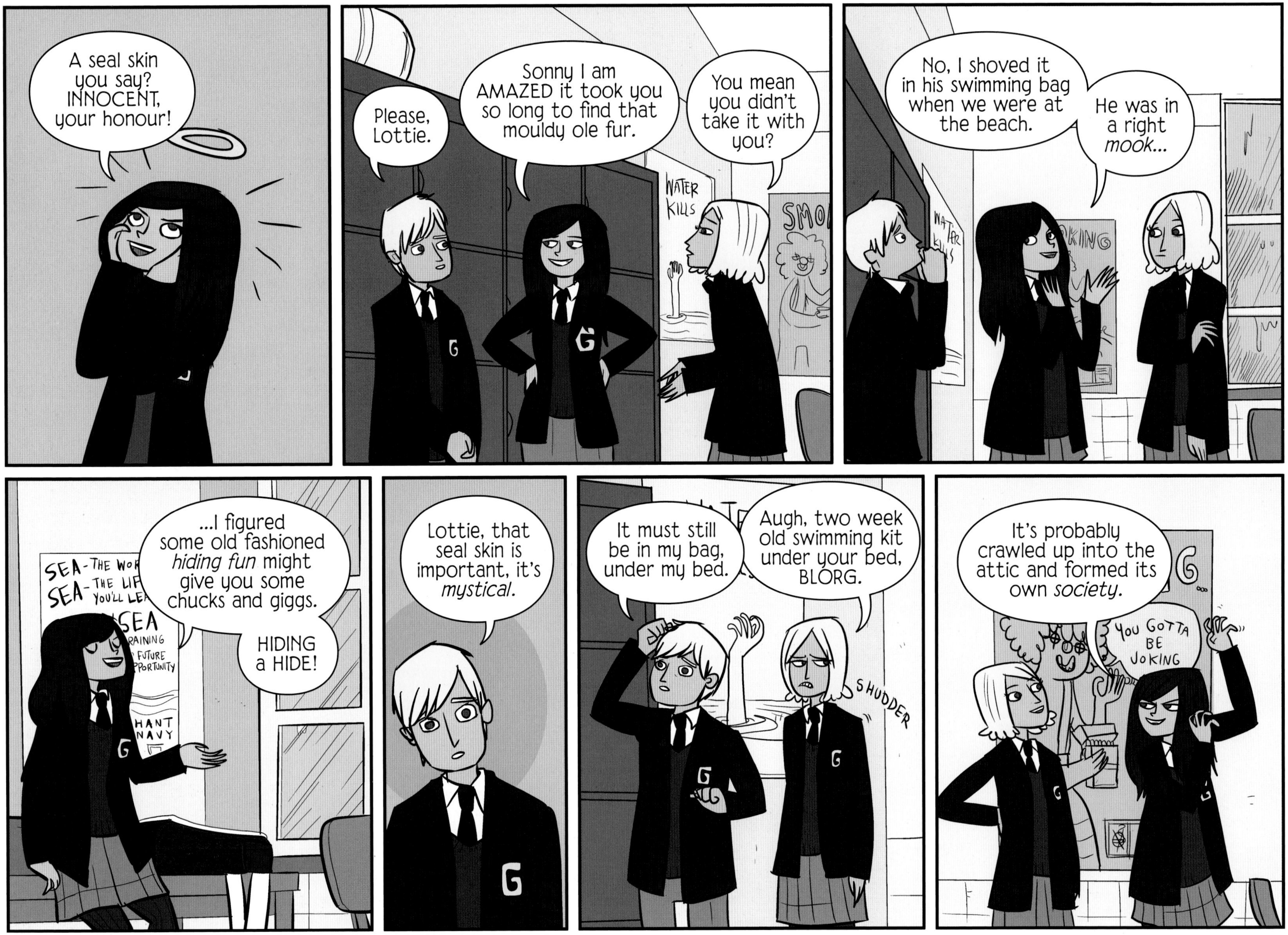
A seal skin you say? INNOCENT, your honour!
Please, Lottie.
Sonny I am AMAZED it took you so long to find that mouldy ole fur.
WATER KILLS
You mean you didn't take it with you?
No, I shoved it in his swimming bag when we were at the beach.
He was in a right *mook*...
...I figured some old fashioned *hiding fun* might give you some chucks and giggs.
HIDING a HIDE!
Lottie, that seal skin is important, it's *mystical*.
It must still be in my bag, under my bed.
Augh, two week old swimming kit under your bed, BLORG.
SHUDDER
It's probably crawled up into the attic and formed its own *society*.
YOU GOTTA BE JOKING

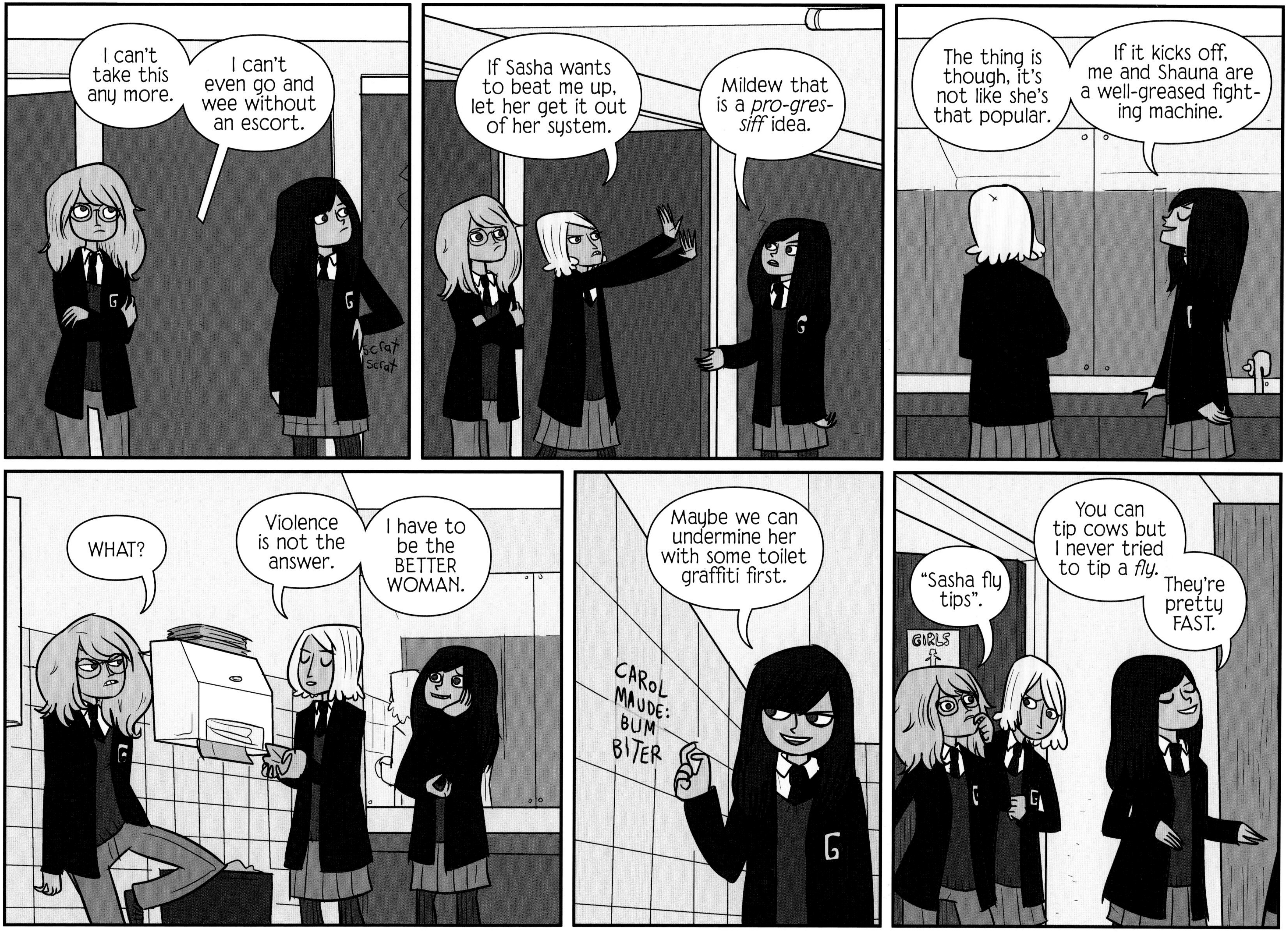
I can't take this any more.
I can't even go and wee without an escort.
scrat scrat
If Sasha wants to beat me up, let her get it out of her system.
Mildew that is a *pro-gres-siff* idea.
The thing is though, it's not like she's that popular.
If it kicks off, me and Shauna are a well-greased fight-ing machine.
WHAT?
Violence is not the answer.
I have to be the BETTER WOMAN.
Maybe we can undermine her with some toilet graffiti first.
CAROL MAUDE: BUM BITER
"Sasha fly tips".
You can tip cows but I never tried to tip a *fly*.
They're pretty FAST.
GIRLS

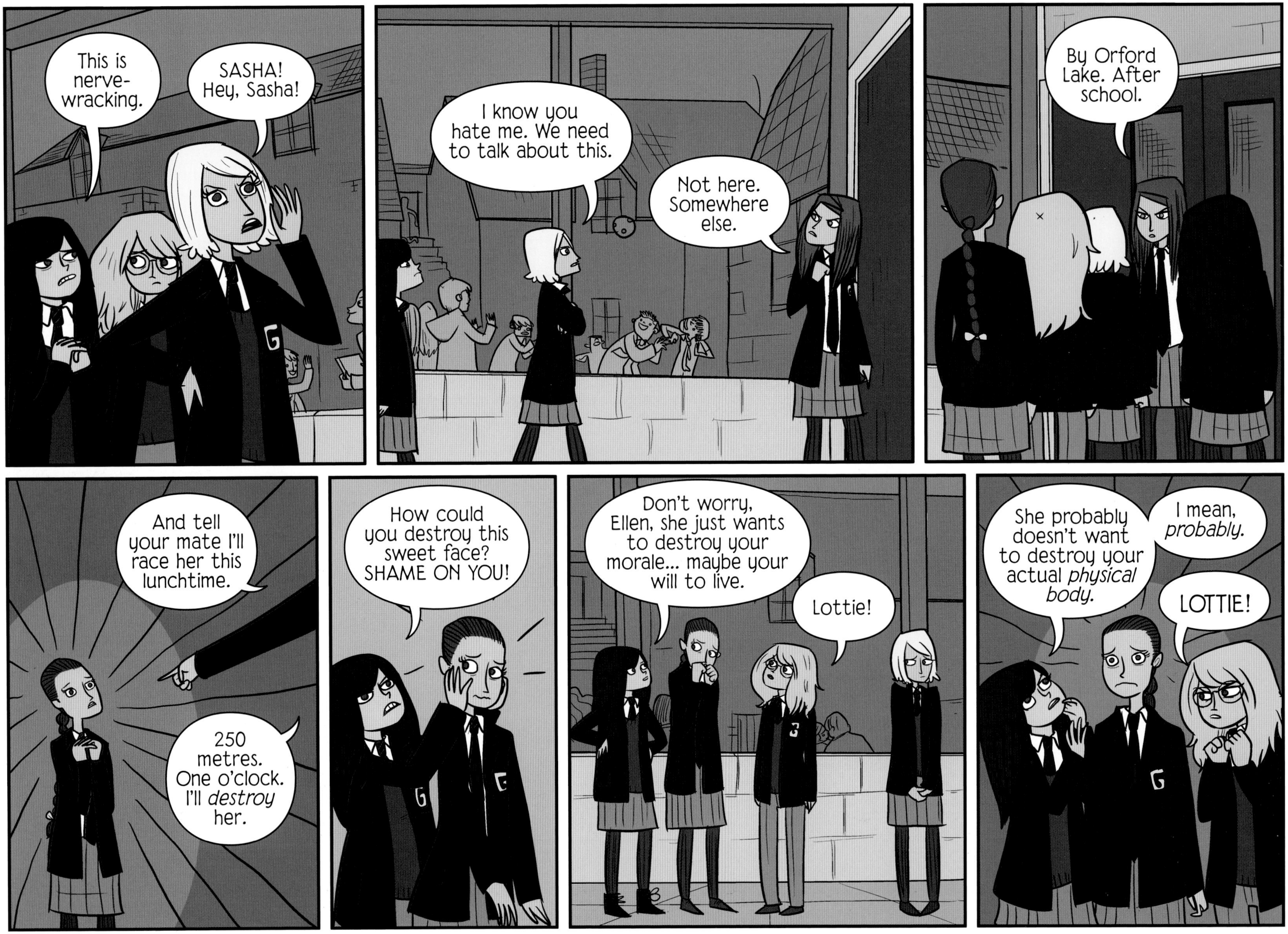
This is nerve-wracking.
SASHA! Hey, Sasha!
I know you hate me. We need to talk about this.
Not here. Somewhere else.
By Orford Lake. After school.
And tell your mate I'll race her this lunchtime.
250 metres. One o'clock. I'll *destroy* her.
How could you destroy this sweet face? SHAME ON YOU!
Don't worry, Ellen, she just wants to destroy your morale... maybe your will to live.
Lottie!
She probably doesn't want to destroy your actual *physical body*.
I mean, *probably*.
LOTTIE!

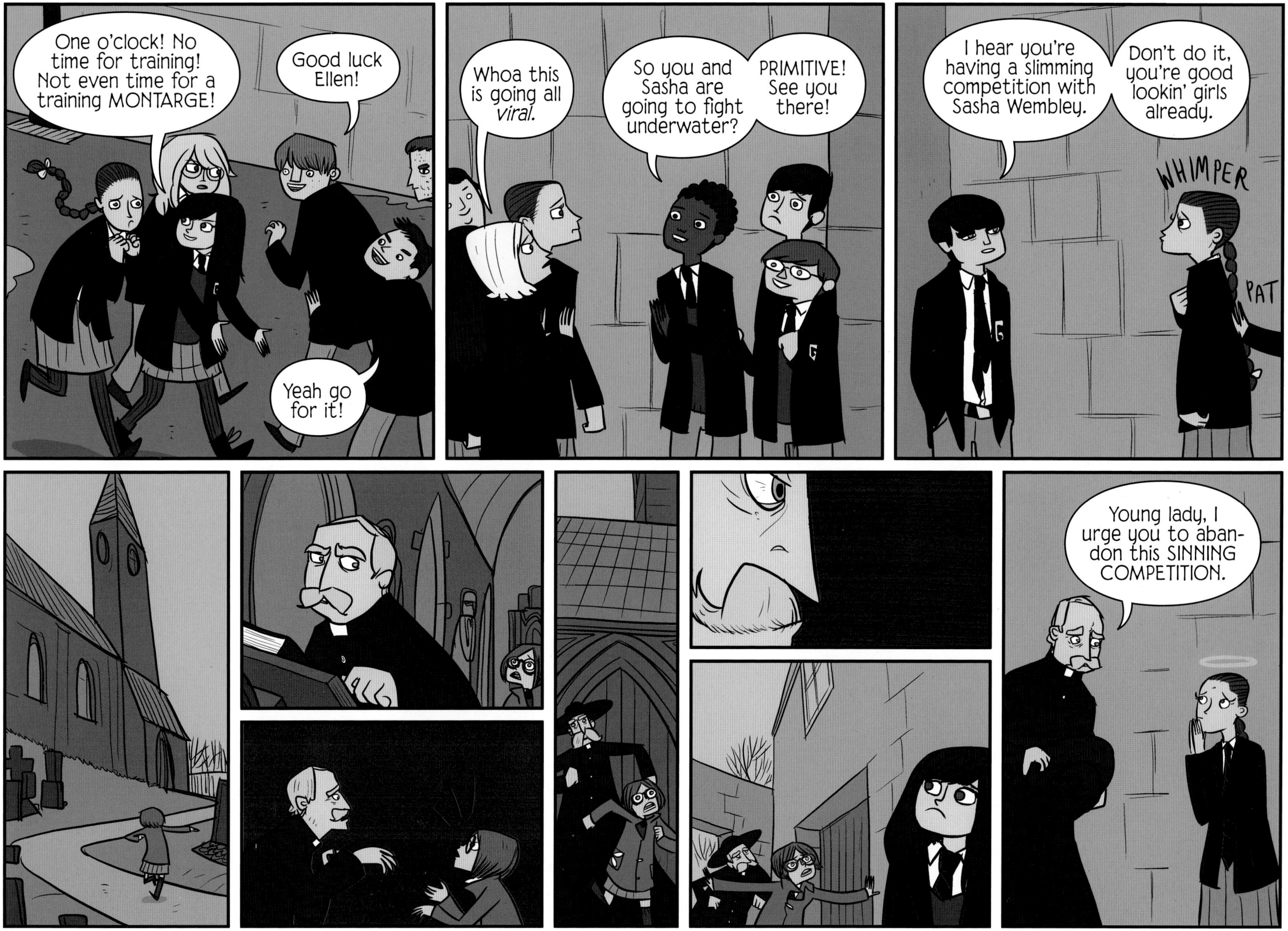
One o'clock! No time for training! Not even time for a training MONTARGE!
Good luck Ellen!
Yeah go for it!
Whoa this is going all *viral.*
So you and Sasha are going to fight underwater?
PRIMITIVE! See you there!
I hear you're having a slimming competition with Sasha Wembley.
Don't do it, you're good lookin' girls already.
WHIMPER
PAT
Young lady, I urge you to abandon this SINNING COMPETITION.

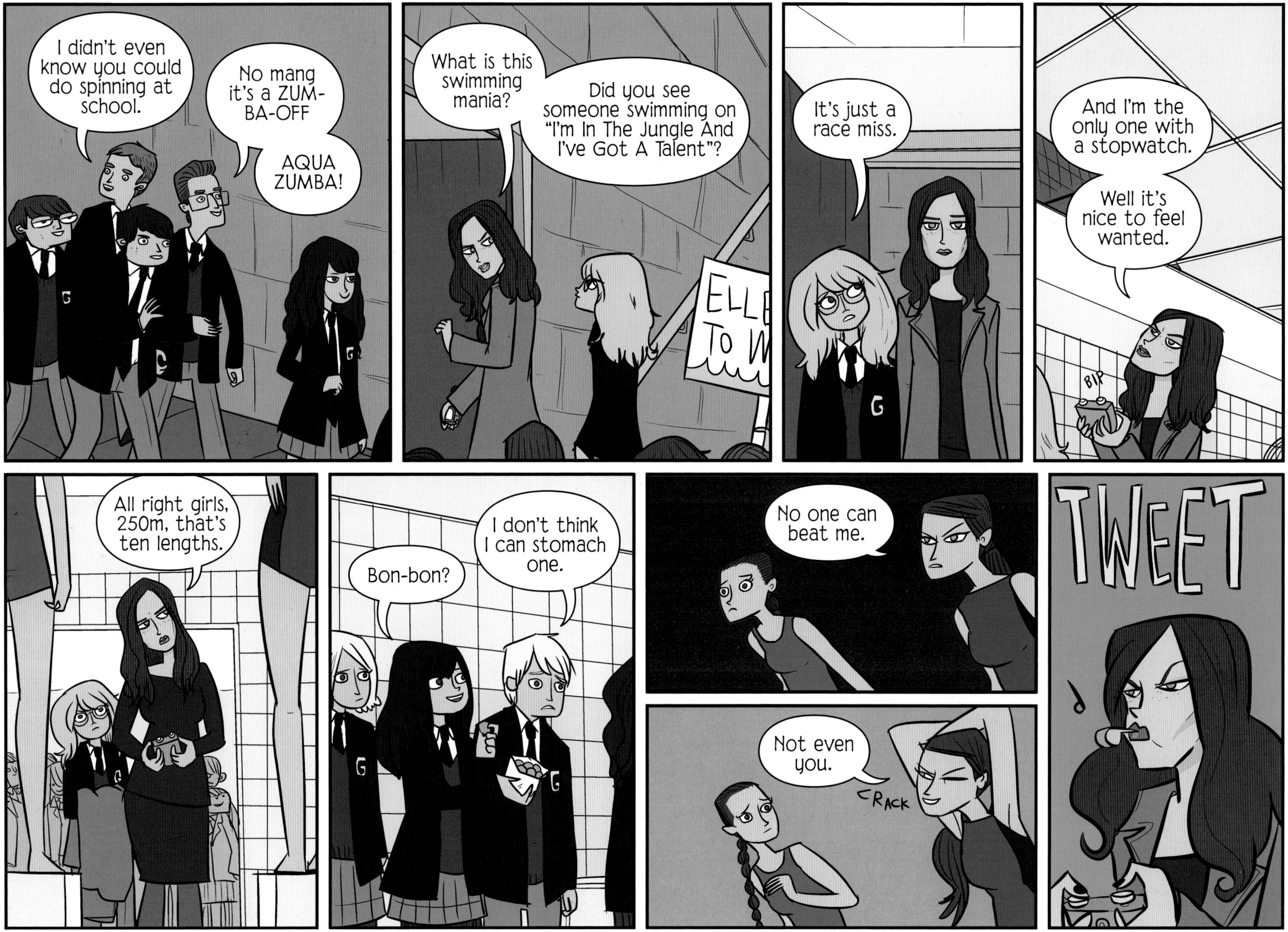
I didn't even know you could do spinning at school.
No mang it's a ZUM-BA-OFF
AQUA ZUMBA!
What is this swimming mania?
Did you see someone swimming on "I'm In The Jungle And I've Got A Talent"?
It's just a race miss.
And I'm the only one with a stopwatch.
Well it's nice to feel wanted.
BIP
All right girls, 250m, that's ten lengths.
Bon-bon?
I don't think I can stomach one.
No one can beat me.
Not even you.
CRACK
TWEET

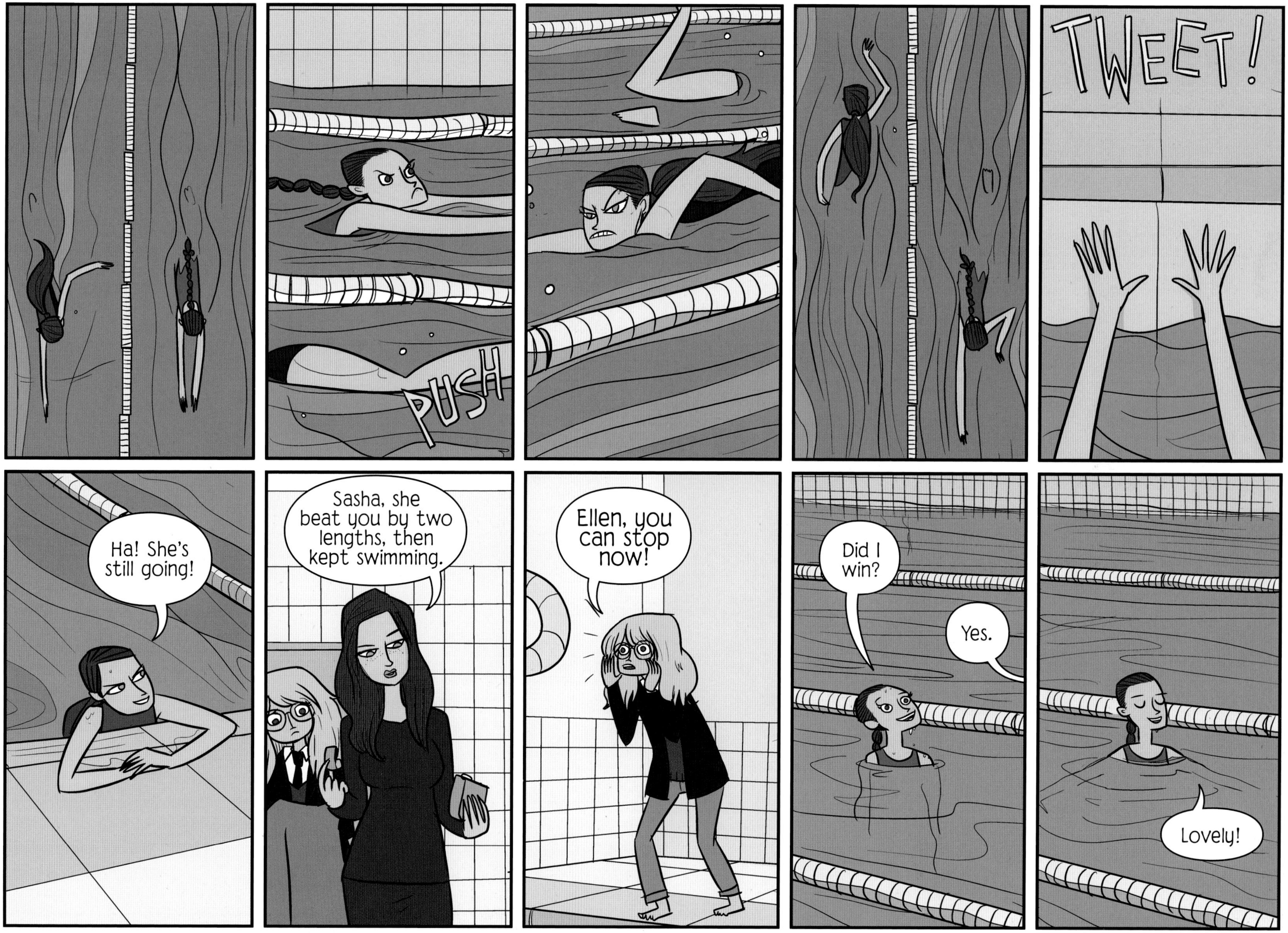
PUSH
TWEET!
Ha! She's still going!
Sasha, she beat you by two lengths, then kept swimming.
Ellen, you can stop now!
Did I win?
Yes.
Lovely!

Bad Machinery, Volume Five

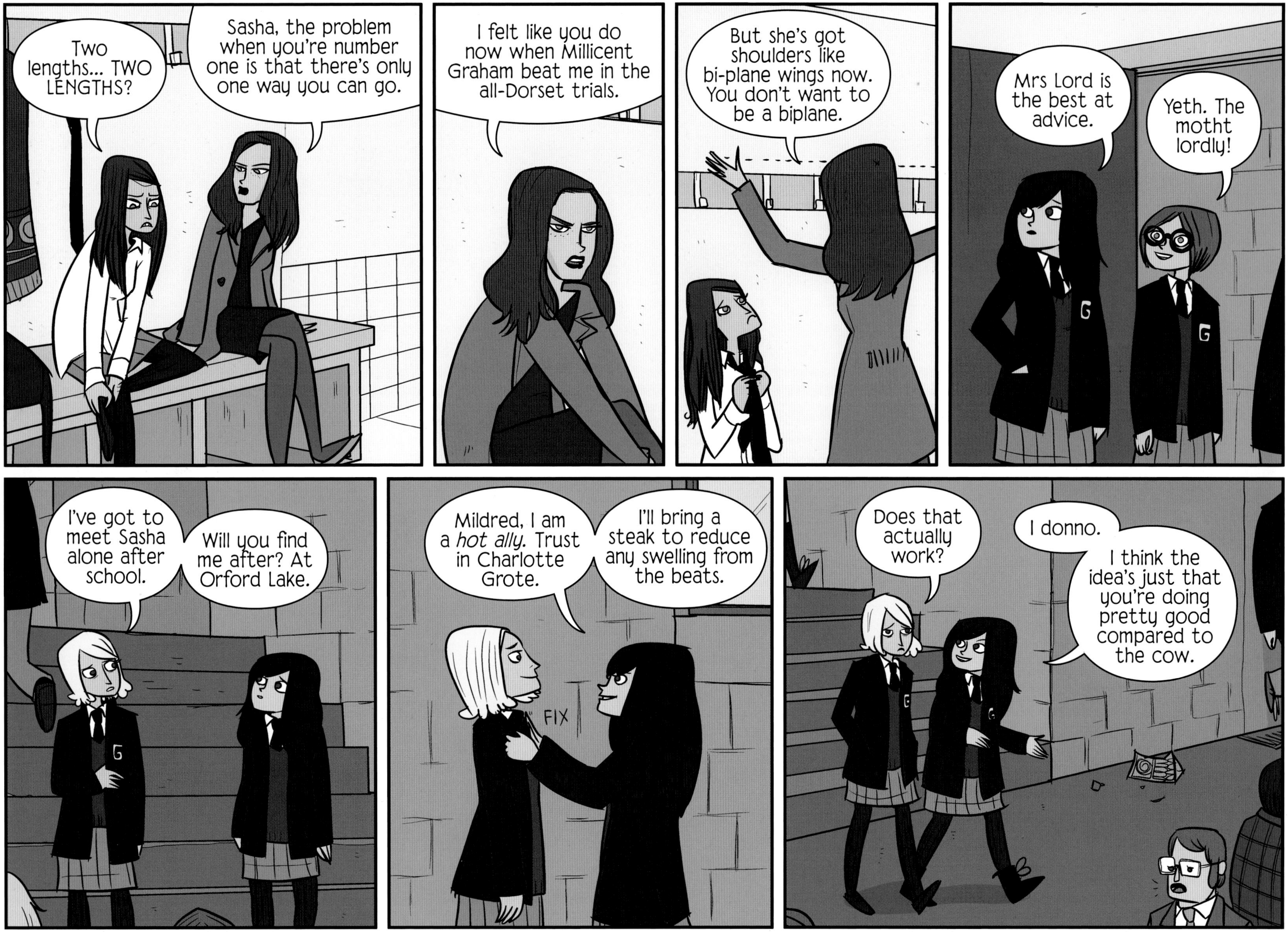
Two lengths... TWO LENGTHS?
Sasha, the problem when you're number one is that there's only one way you can go.
I felt like you do now when Millicent Graham beat me in the all-Dorset trials.
But she's got shoulders like bi-plane wings now. You don't want to be a biplane.
Mrs Lord is the best at advice.
Yeth. The motht lordly!
I've got to meet Sasha alone after school.
Will you find me after? At Orford Lake.
Mildred, I am a *hot ally*. Trust in Charlotte Grote.
I'll bring a steak to reduce any swelling from the beats.
FIX
Does that actually work?
I donno.
I think the idea's just that you're doing pretty good compared to the cow.

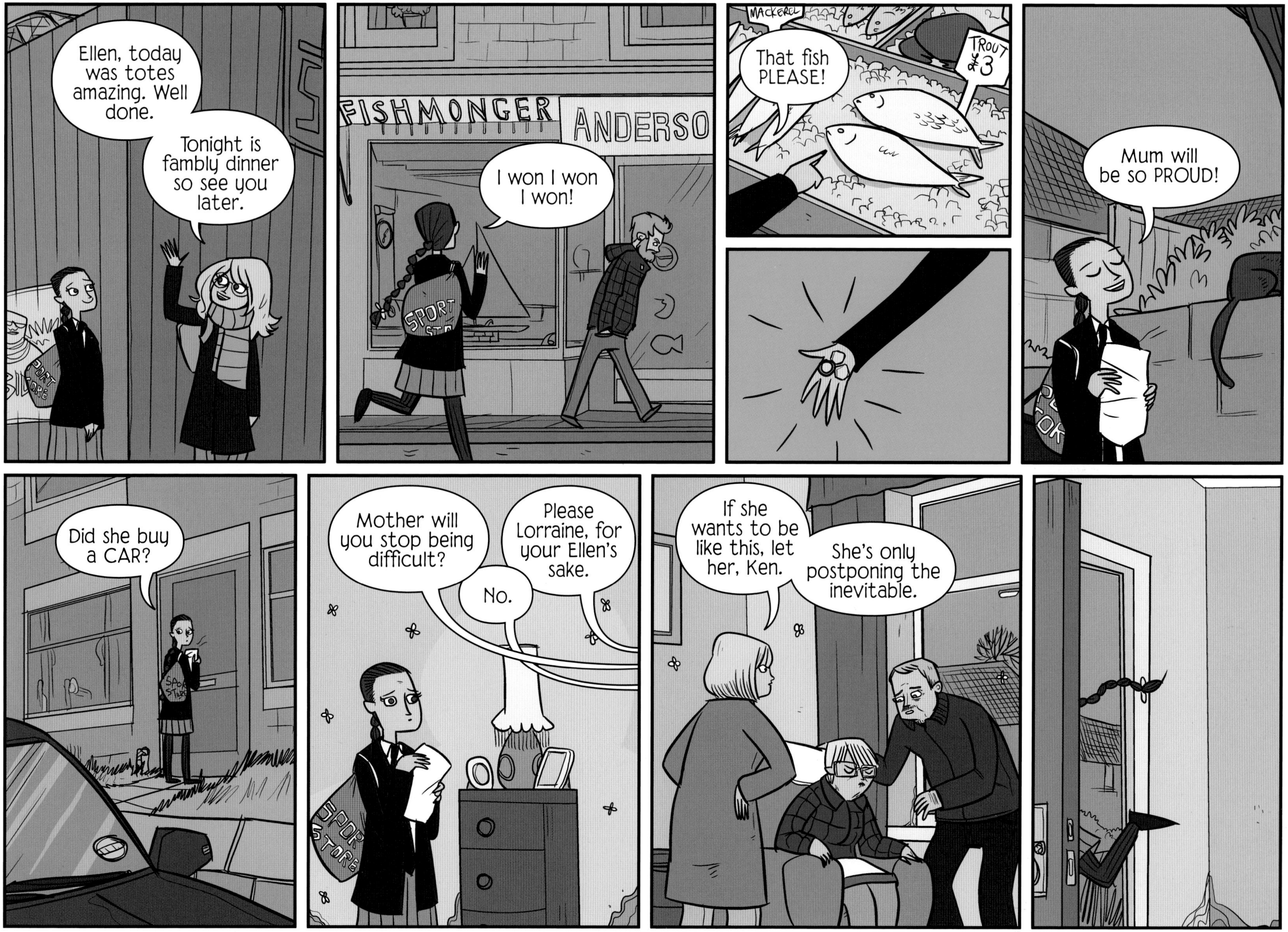
Ellen, today was totes amazing. Well done.
Tonight is fambly dinner so see you later.
FISHMONGER
ANDERSO
I won I won I won!
MACKEREL
That fish PLEASE!
TROUT £3
Mum will be so PROUD!
Did she buy a CAR?
Mother will you stop being difficult?
No.
Please Lorraine, for your Ellen's sake.
If she wants to be like this, let her, Ken.
She's only postponing the inevitable.

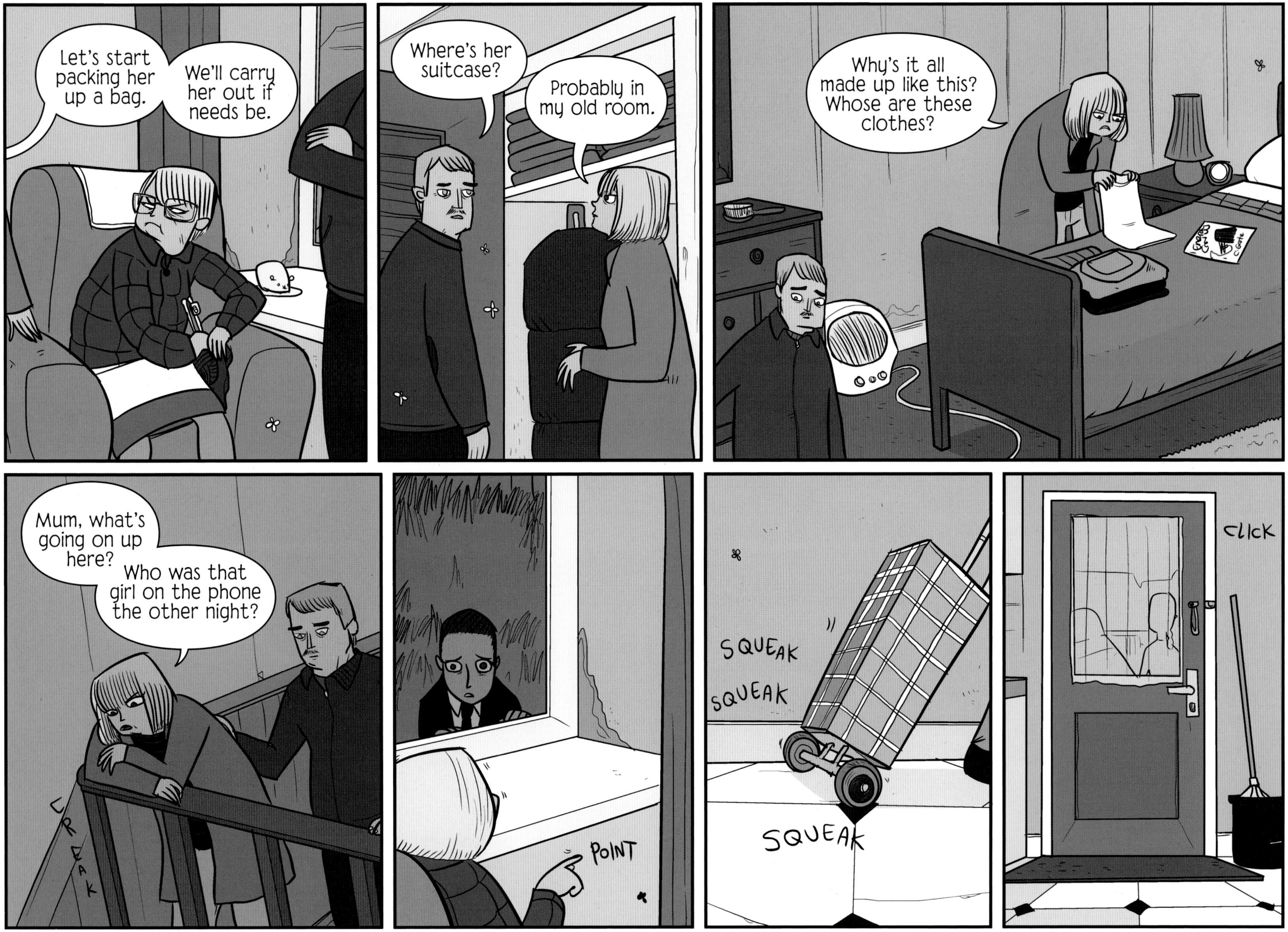
Let's start packing her up a bag.
We'll carry her out if needs be.
Where's her suitcase?
Probably in my old room.
Why's it all made up like this? Whose are these clothes?
Mum, what's going on up here?
Who was that girl on the phone the other night?
CREAK
POINT
SQUEAK
SQUEAK
SQUEAK
CLICK

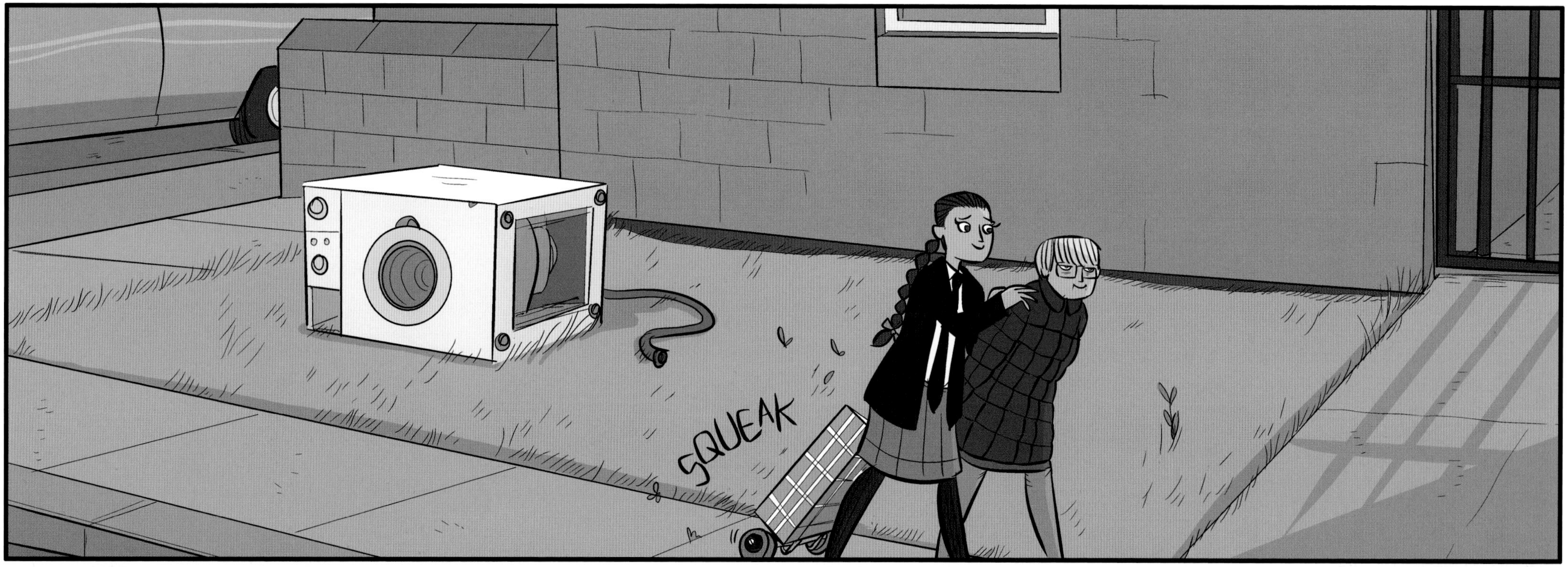
SQUEAK

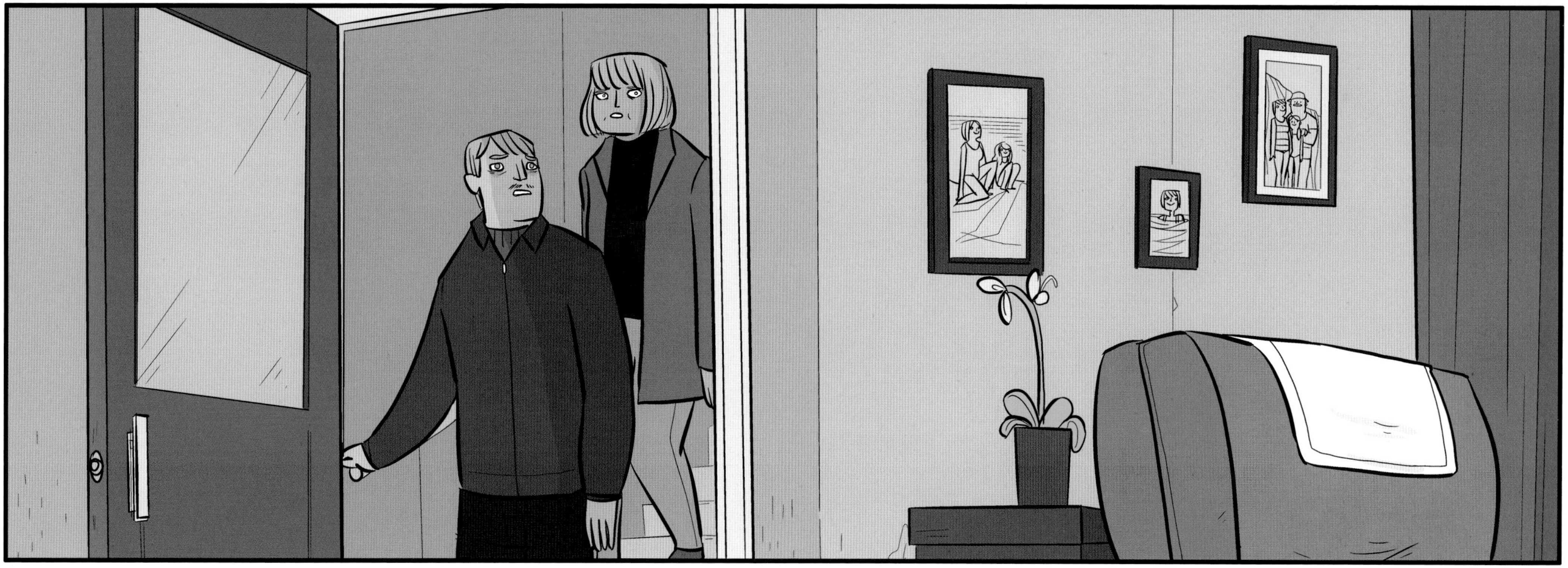

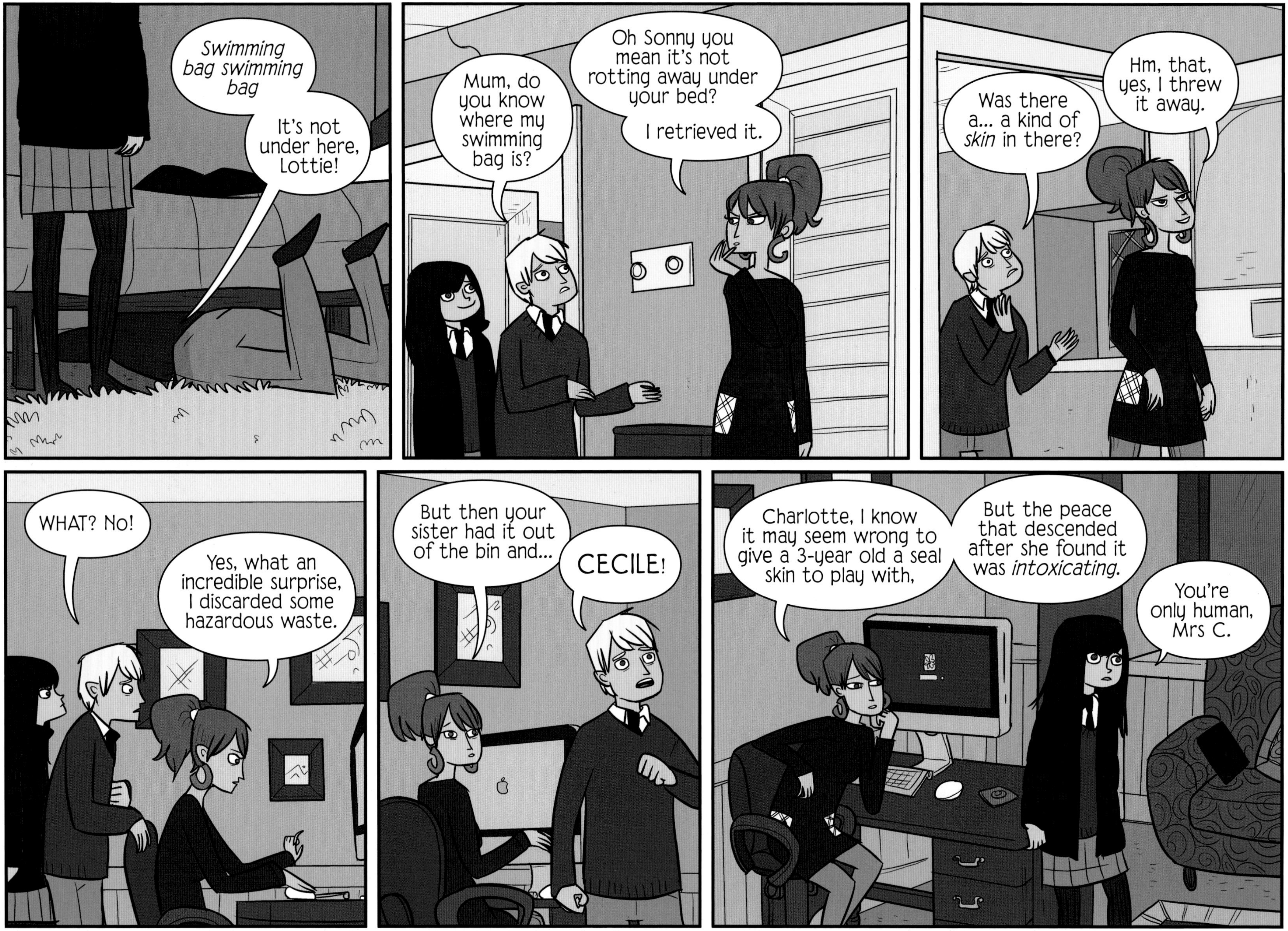
Swimming bag swimming bag
It's not under here, Lottie!
Mum, do you know where my swimming bag is?
Oh Sonny you mean it's not rotting away under your bed?
I retrieved it.
Was there a... a kind of *skin* in there?
Hm, that, yes, I threw it away.
WHAT? No!
Yes, what an incredible surprise, I discarded some hazardous waste.
But then your sister had it out of the bin and...
CECILE!
Charlotte, I know it may seem wrong to give a 3-year old a seal skin to play with,
But the peace that descended after she found it was *intoxicating.*
You're only human, Mrs C.

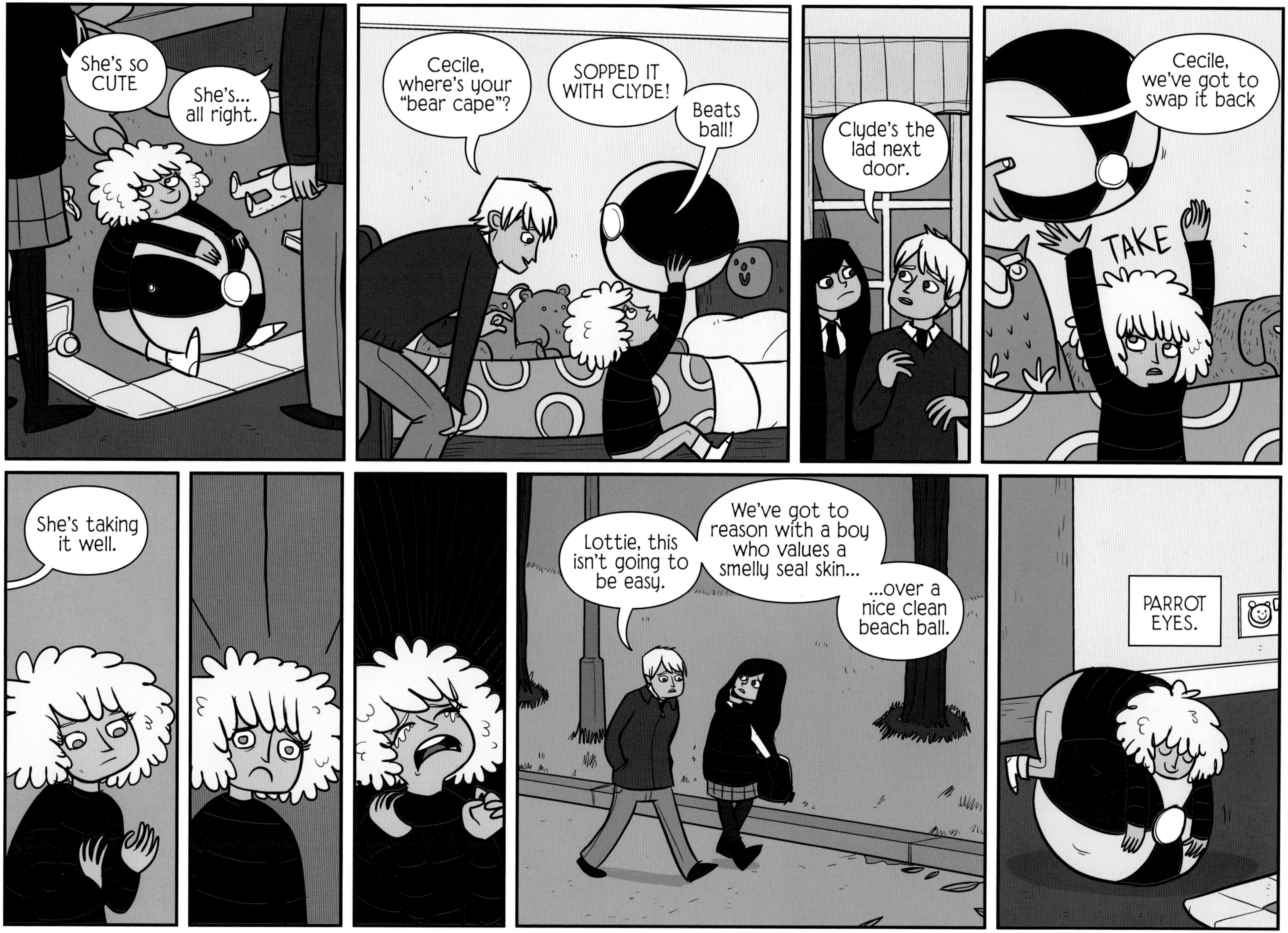
She's so CUTE
She's... all right.
Cecile, where's your "bear cape"?
SOPPED IT WITH CLYDE!
Beats ball!
Clyde's the lad next door.
Cecile, we've got to swap it back
TAKE
She's taking it well.
Lottie, this isn't going to be easy.
We've got to reason with a boy who values a smelly seal skin...
...over a nice clean beach ball.
PARROT EYES.

Bad Machinery, Volume Five

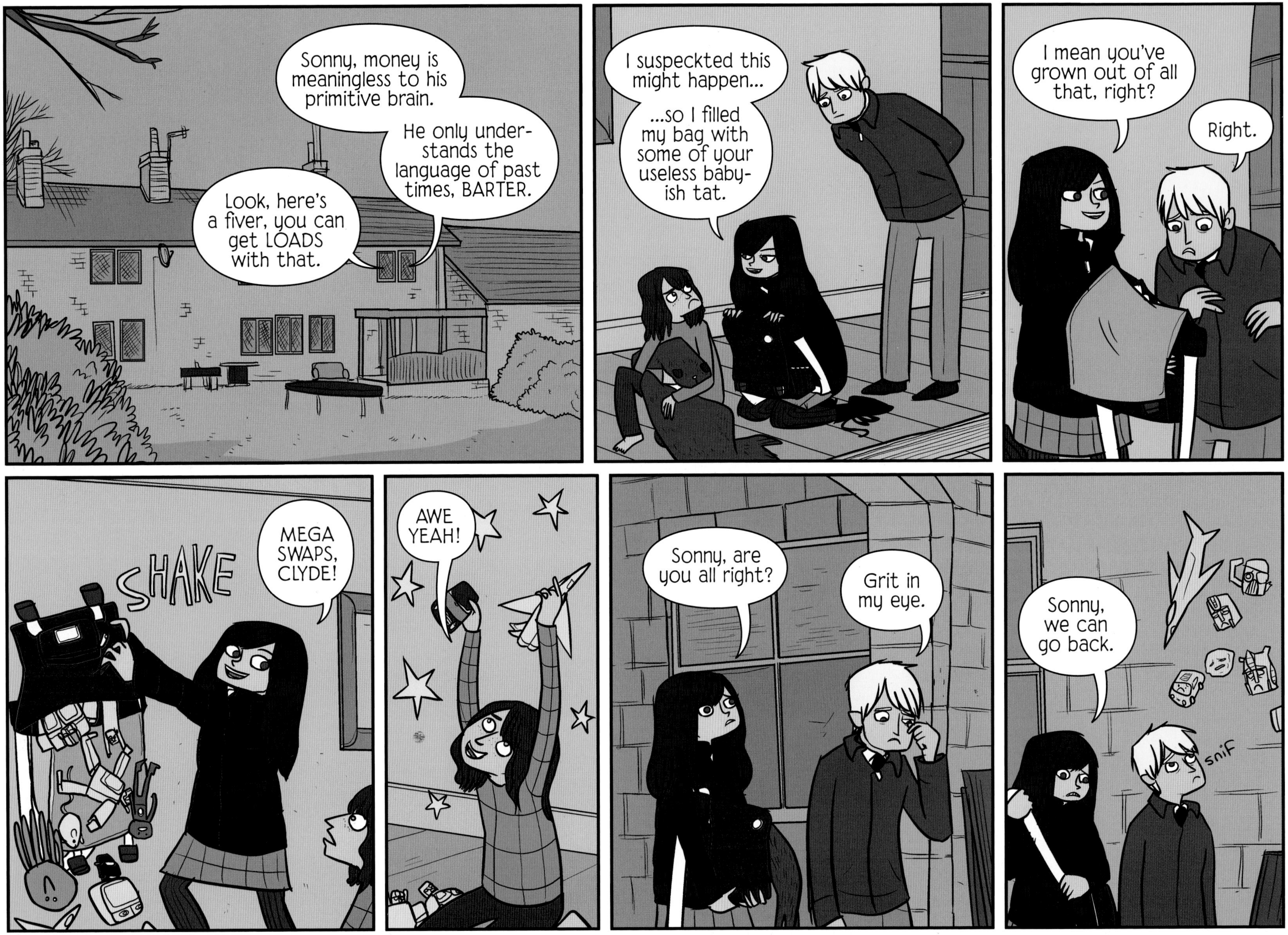
Sonny, money is meaningless to his primitive brain.
He only under-stands the language of past times, BARTER.
Look, here's a fiver, you can get LOADS with that.
I suspeckted this might happen...
...so I filled my bag with some of your useless baby-ish tat.
I mean you've grown out of all that, right?
Right.
SHAKE
MEGA SWAPS, CLYDE!
AWE YEAH!
Sonny, are you all right?
Grit in my eye.
Sonny, we can go back.
snif

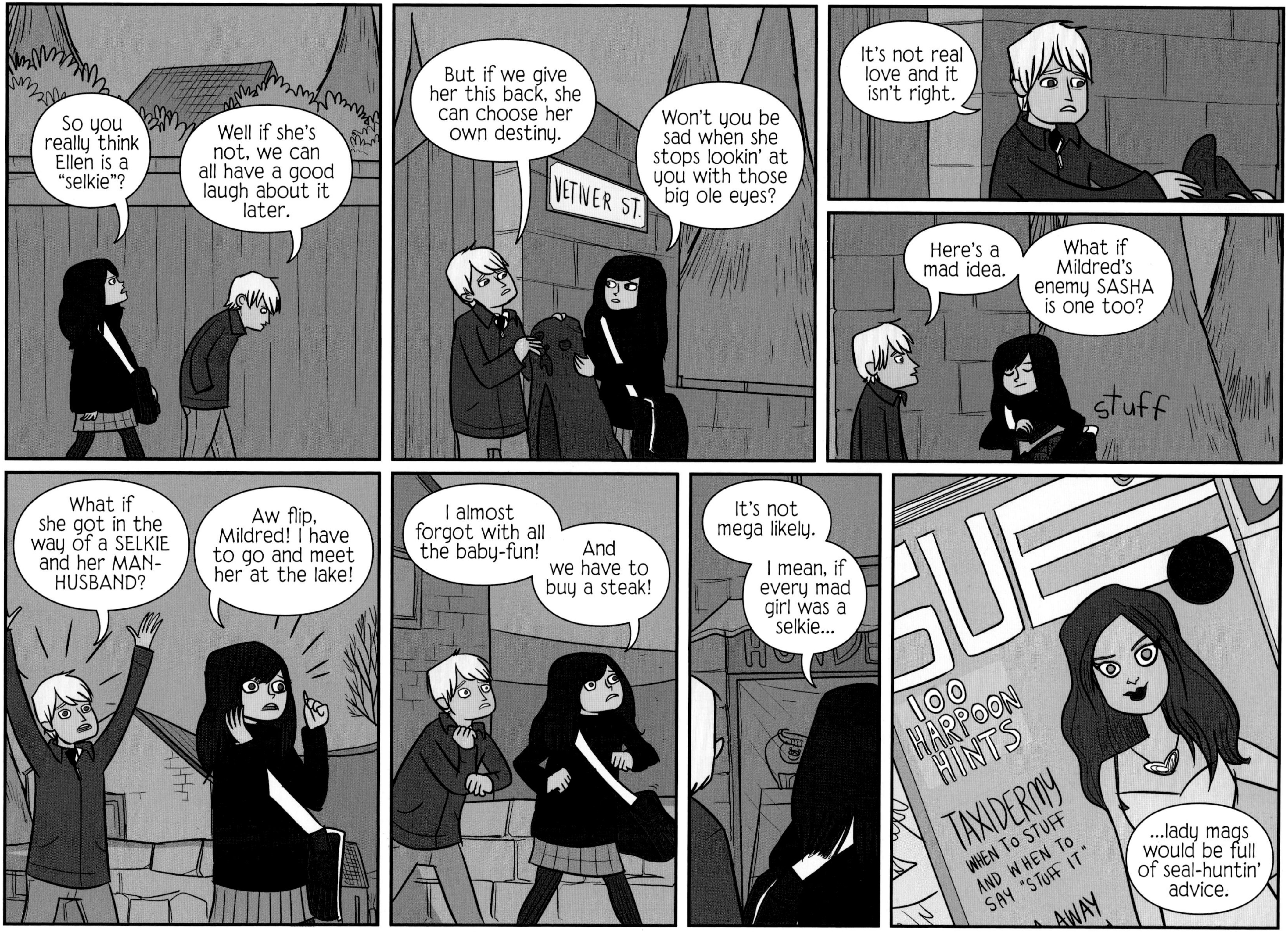
So you really think Ellen is a "selkie"?
Well if she's not, we can all have a good laugh about it later.
But if we give her this back, she can choose her own destiny.
VETIVER ST.
Won't you be sad when she stops lookin' at you with those big ole eyes?
It's not real love and it isn't right.
Here's a mad idea.
What if Mildred's enemy SASHA is one too?
stuff
What if she got in the way of a SELKIE and her MAN-HUSBAND?
Aw flip, Mildred! I have to go and meet her at the lake!
I almost forgot with all the baby-fun!
And we have to buy a steak!
It's not mega likely.
I mean, if every mad girl was a selkie...
100 HARPOON HINTS
TAXIDERMY WHEN TO STUFF AND WHEN TO SAY "STUFF IT"
...lady mags would be full of seal-huntin' advice.

Bad Machinery, Volume Five

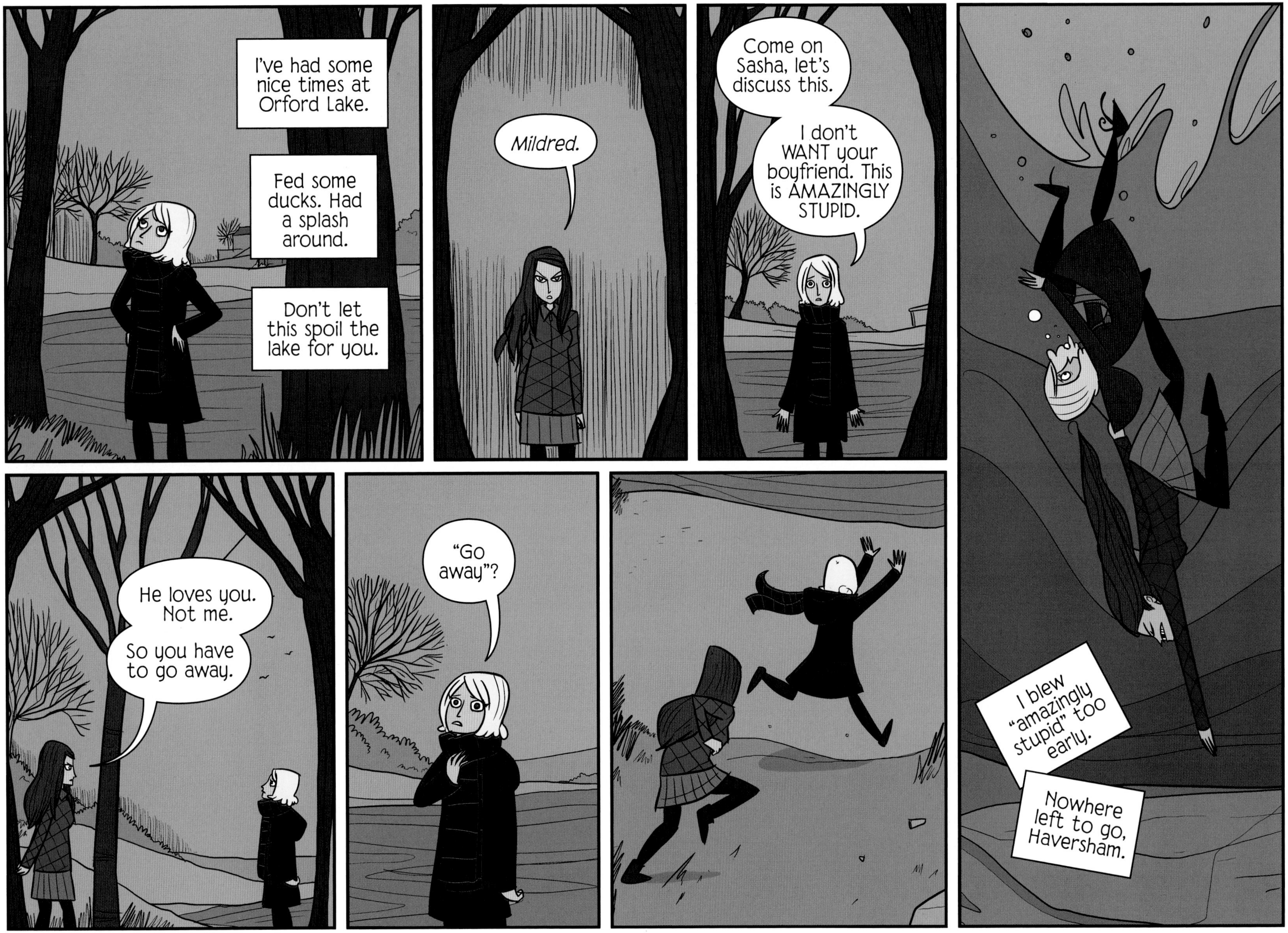

I've had some nice times at Orford Lake.
Fed some ducks. Had a splash around.
Don't let this spoil the lake for you.
Mildred.
Come on Sasha, let's discuss this.
I don't WANT your boyfriend. This is AMAZINGLY STUPID.
He loves you. Not me.
So you have to go away.
"Go away"?
I blew "amazingly stupid" too early.
Nowhere left to go, Haversham.

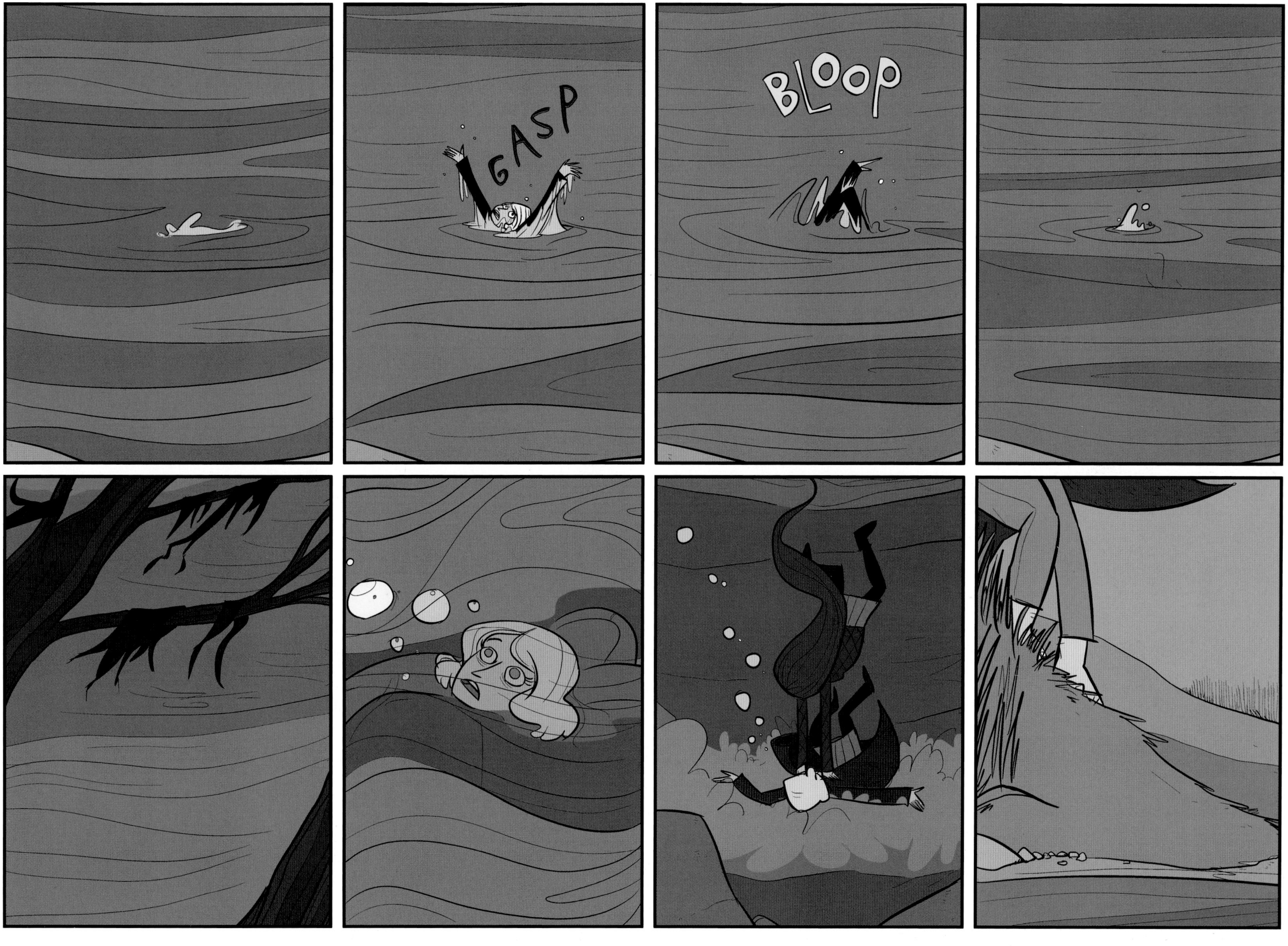
GASP
BLOOP

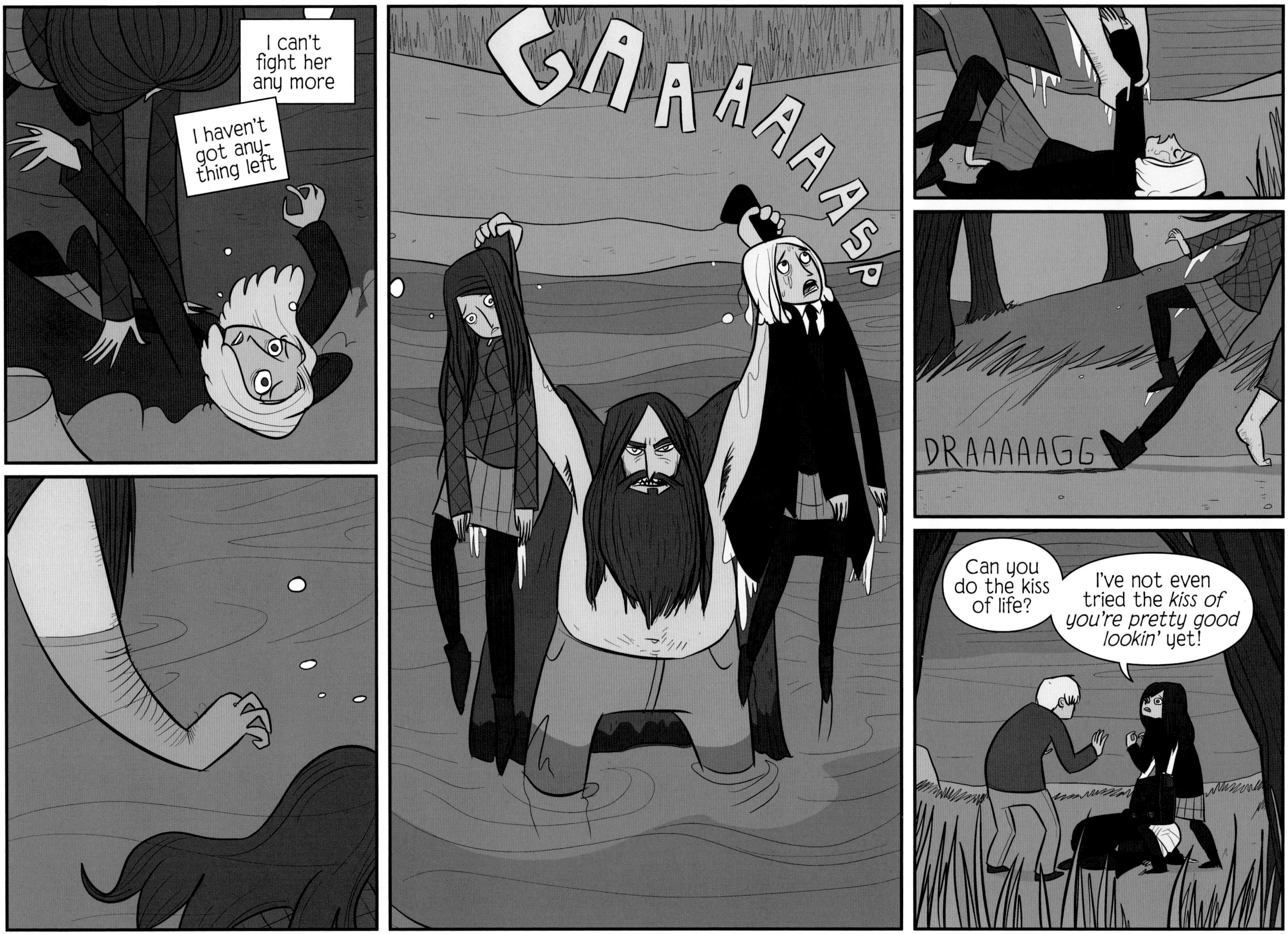
I can't fight her any more
I haven't got any-thing left
GAAAAAASP
DRAAAAAGG
Can you do the kiss of life?
I've not even tried the *kiss of you're pretty good lookin'* yet!

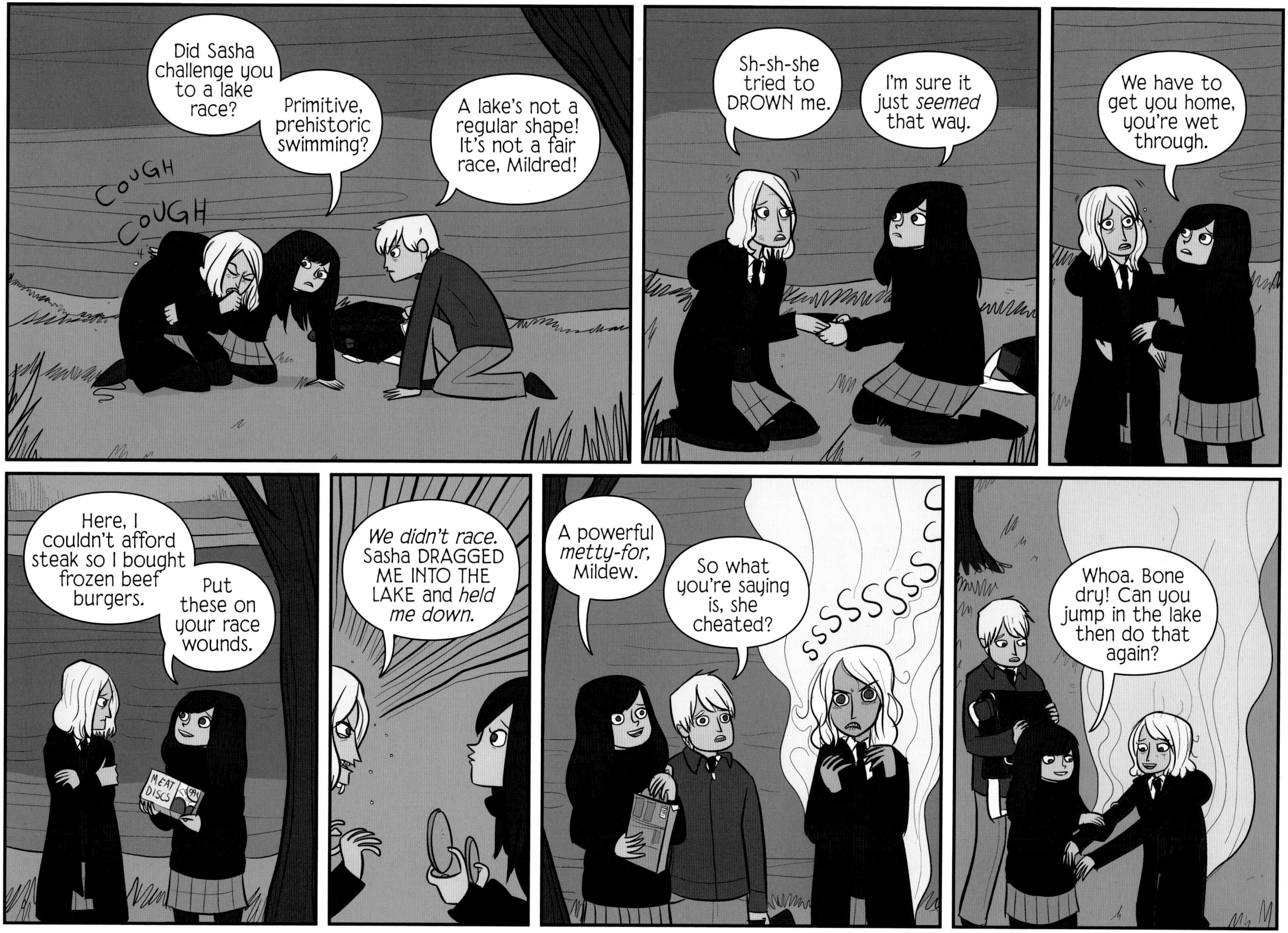
Did Sasha challenge you to a lake race?
Primitive, prehistoric swimming?
A lake's not a regular shape! It's not a fair race, Mildred!
COUGH
COUGH
Sh-sh-she tried to DROWN me.
I'm sure it just *seemed* that way.
We have to get you home, you're wet through.
Here, I couldn't afford steak so I bought frozen beef burgers.
Put these on your race wounds.
MEAT DISCS
We didn't race. Sasha DRAGGED ME INTO THE LAKE and *held me down.*
A powerful *metty-for,* Mildew.
So what you're saying is, she cheated?
SSSSSSSSSS
Whoa. Bone dry! Can you jump in the lake then do that again?

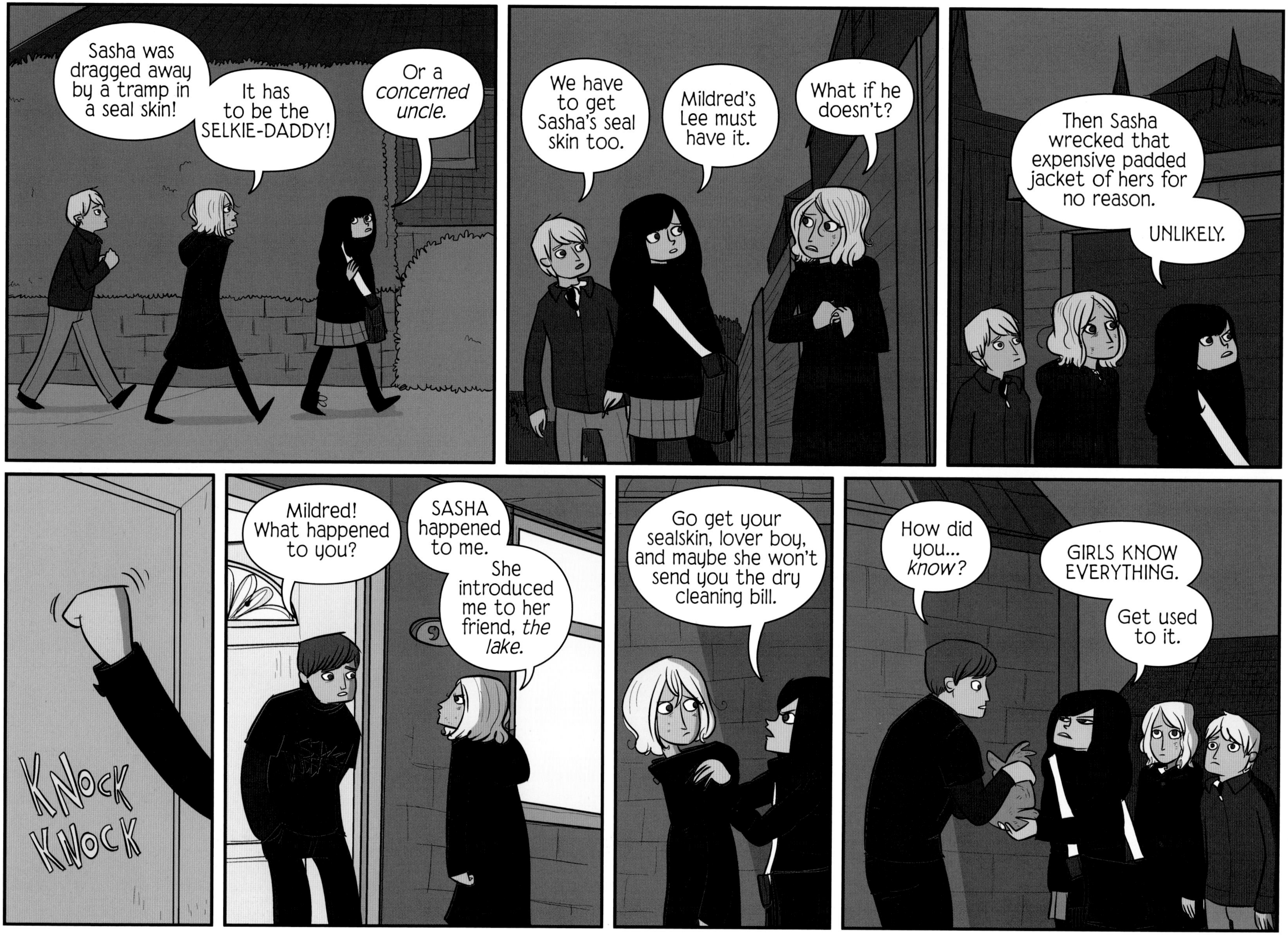

Sasha was dragged away by a tramp in a seal skin!
It has to be the SELKIE-DADDY!
Or a *concerned uncle.*
We have to get Sasha's seal skin too.
Mildred's Lee must have it.
What if he doesn't?
Then Sasha wrecked that expensive padded jacket of hers for no reason.
UNLIKELY.
KNOCK KNOCK
Mildred! What happened to you?
SASHA happened to me.
She introduced me to her friend, *the lake.*
Go get your sealskin, lover boy, and maybe she won't send you the dry cleaning bill.
How did you... *know?*
GIRLS KNOW EVERYTHING.
Get used to it.

The Case of the Fire Inside

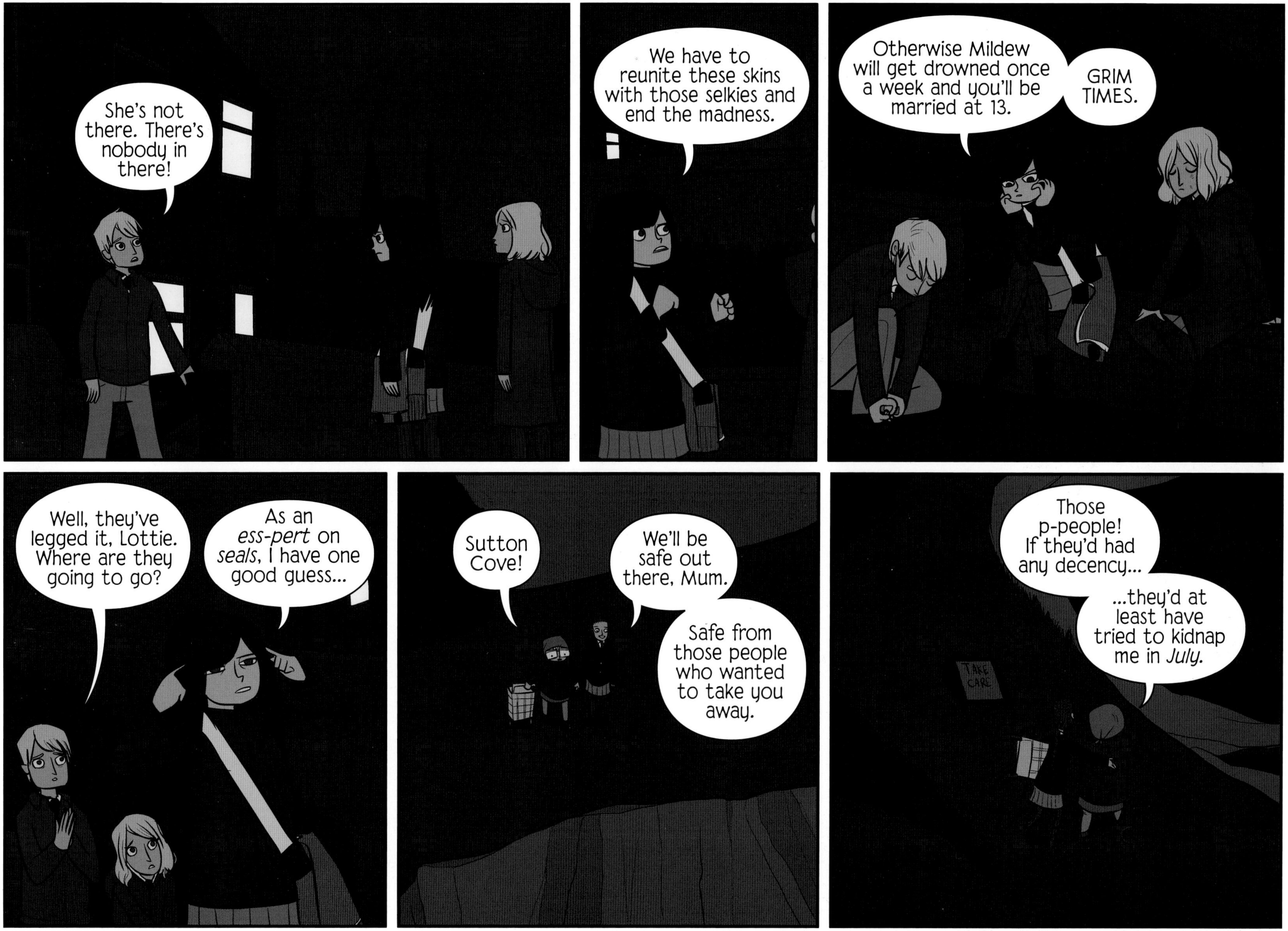
She's not there. There's nobody in there!
We have to reunite these skins with those selkies and end the madness.
Otherwise Mildew will get drowned once a week and you'll be married at 13.
GRIM TIMES.
Well, they've legged it, Lottie. Where are they going to go?
As an *ess-pert* on *seals*, I have one good guess...
Sutton Cove!
We'll be safe out there, Mum.
Safe from those people who wanted to take you away.
TAKE CARE
Those p-people! If they'd had any decency...
...they'd at least have tried to kidnap me in *July*.

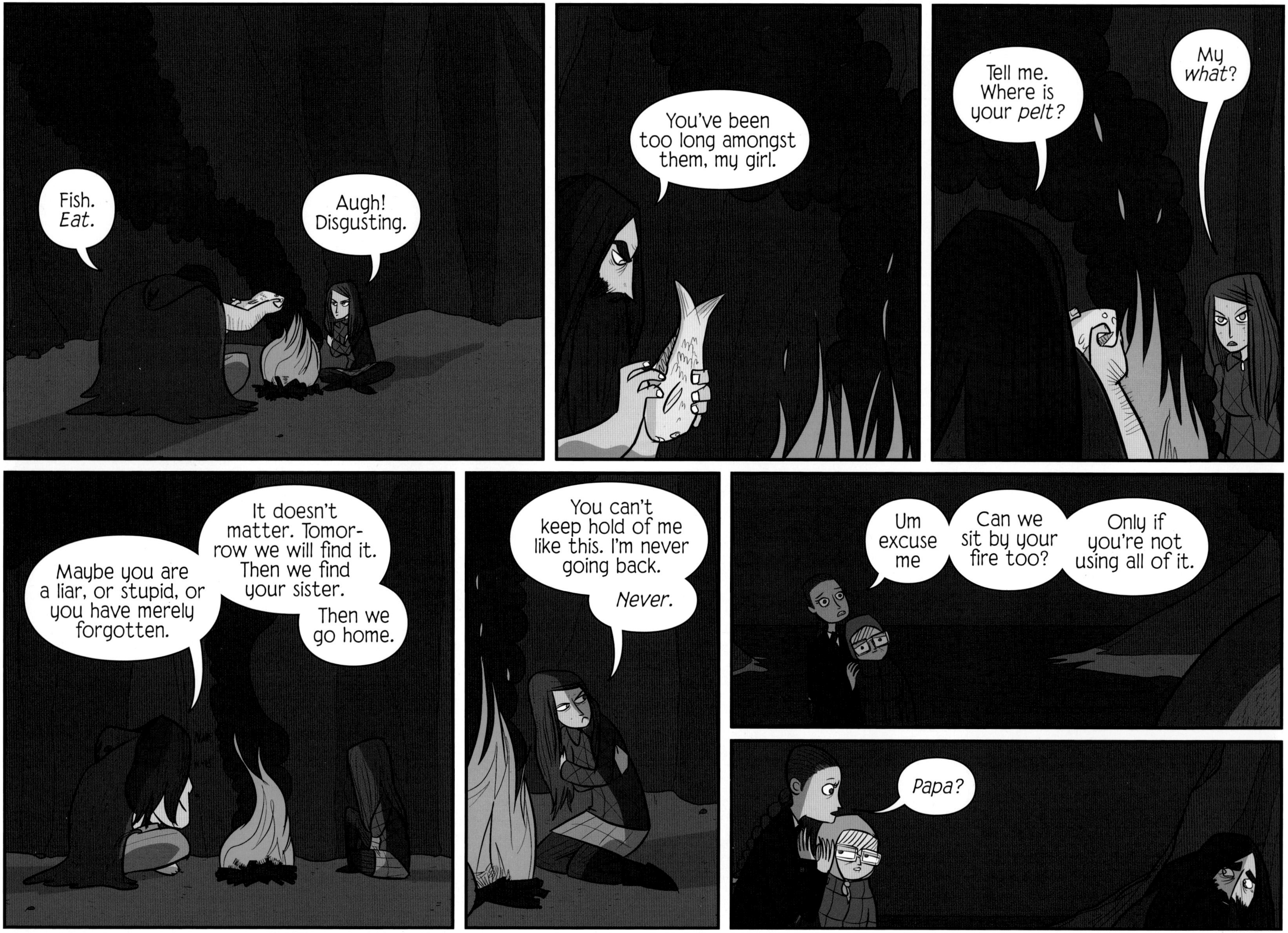
Fish.
Eat.
Augh! Disgusting.
You've been too long amongst them, my girl.
Tell me. Where is your *pelt?*
My *what?*
Maybe you are a liar, or stupid, or you have merely forgotten.
It doesn't matter. Tomorrow we will find it. Then we find your sister.
Then we go home.
You can't keep hold of me like this. I'm never going back.
Never.
Um excuse me
Can we sit by your fire too?
Only if you're not using all of it.
Papa?

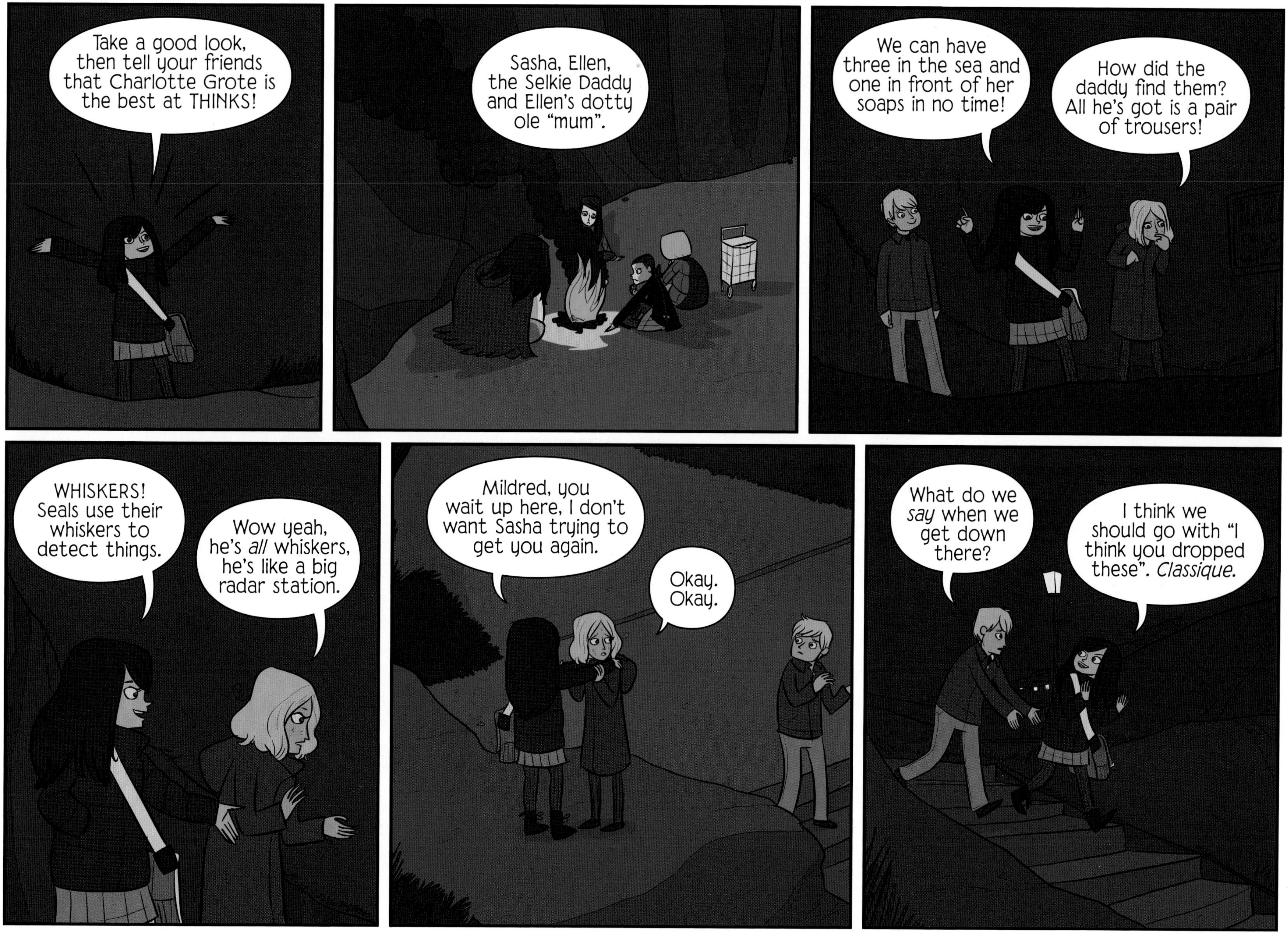

Take a good look, then tell your friends that Charlotte Grote is the best at THINKS!
Sasha, Ellen, the Selkie Daddy and Ellen's dotty ole "mum".
We can have three in the sea and one in front of her soaps in no time!
How did the daddy find them? All he's got is a pair of trousers!
WHISKERS! Seals use their whiskers to detect things.
Wow yeah, he's *all* whiskers, he's like a big radar station.
Mildred, you wait up here, I don't want Sasha trying to get you again.
Okay. Okay.
What do we *say* when we get down there?
I think we should go with "I think you dropped these". *Classique.*

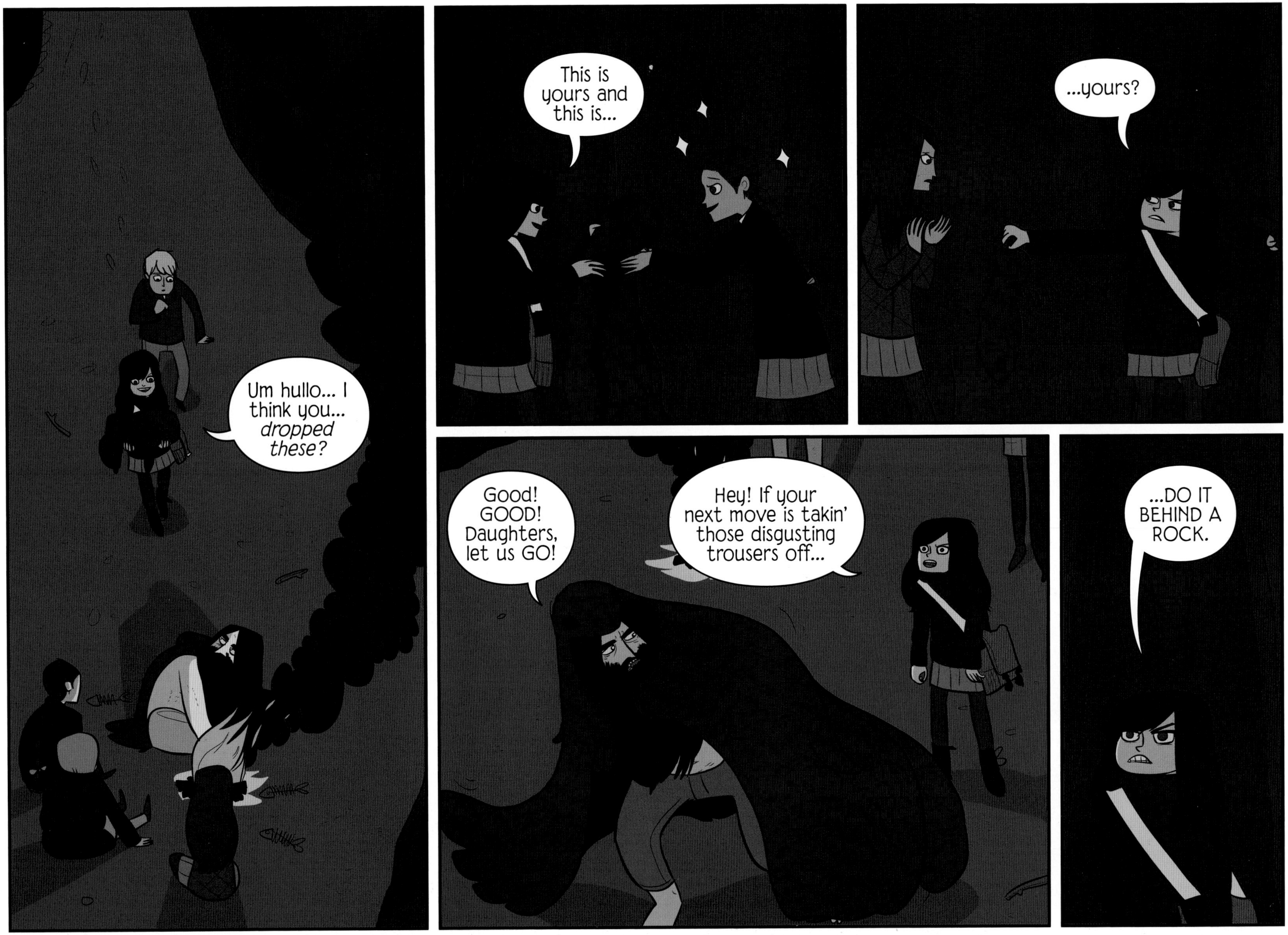
Um hullo... I think you... *dropped these?*
This is yours and this is...
...yours?
Good! GOOD! Daughters, let us GO!
Hey! If your next move is takin' those disgusting trousers off...
...DO IT BEHIND A ROCK.

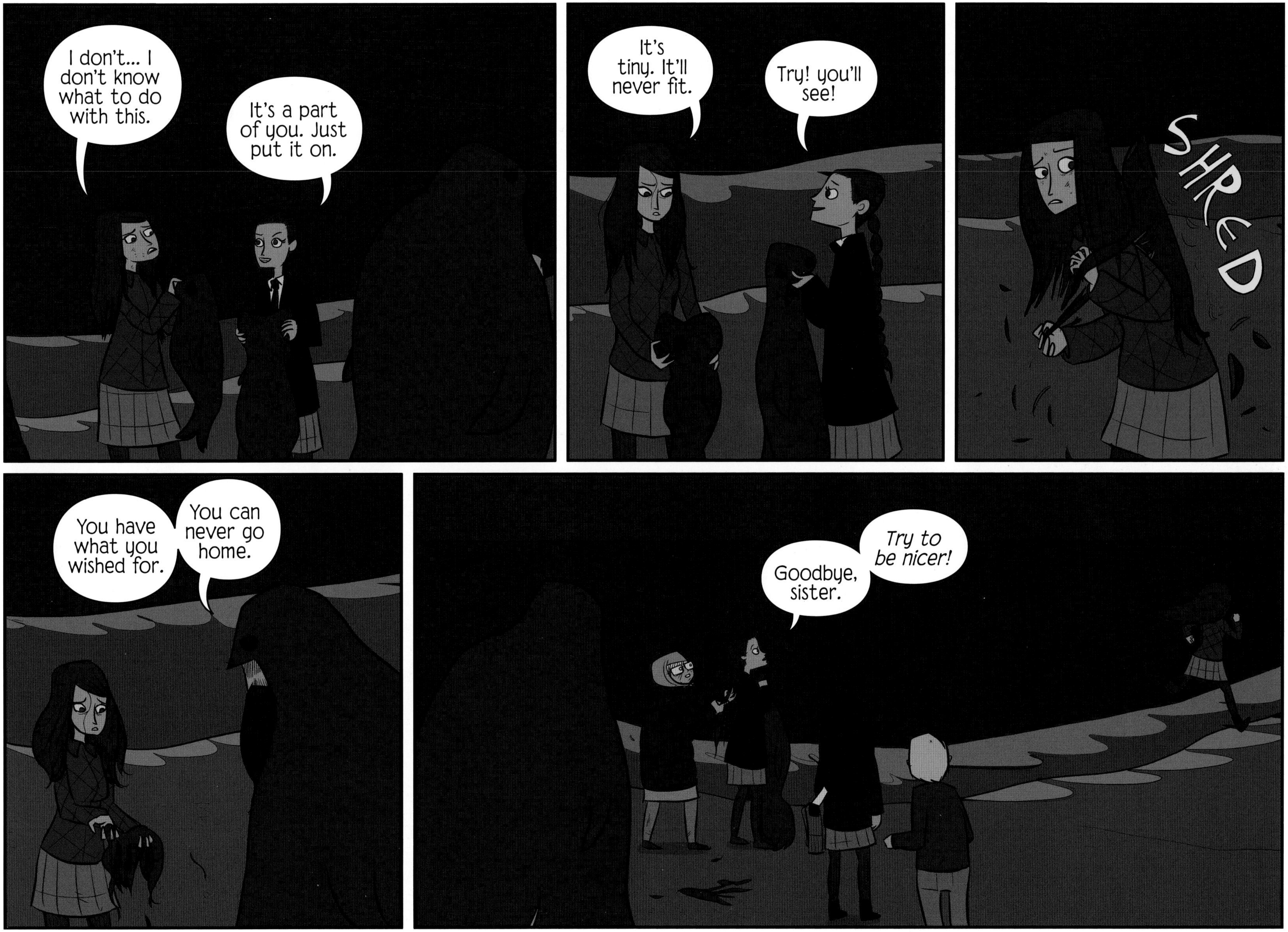
I don't... I don't know what to do with this.
It's a part of you. Just put it on.
It's tiny. It'll never fit.
Try! you'll see!
SHRED
You have what you wished for.
You can never go home.
Goodbye, sister.
Try to be nicer!

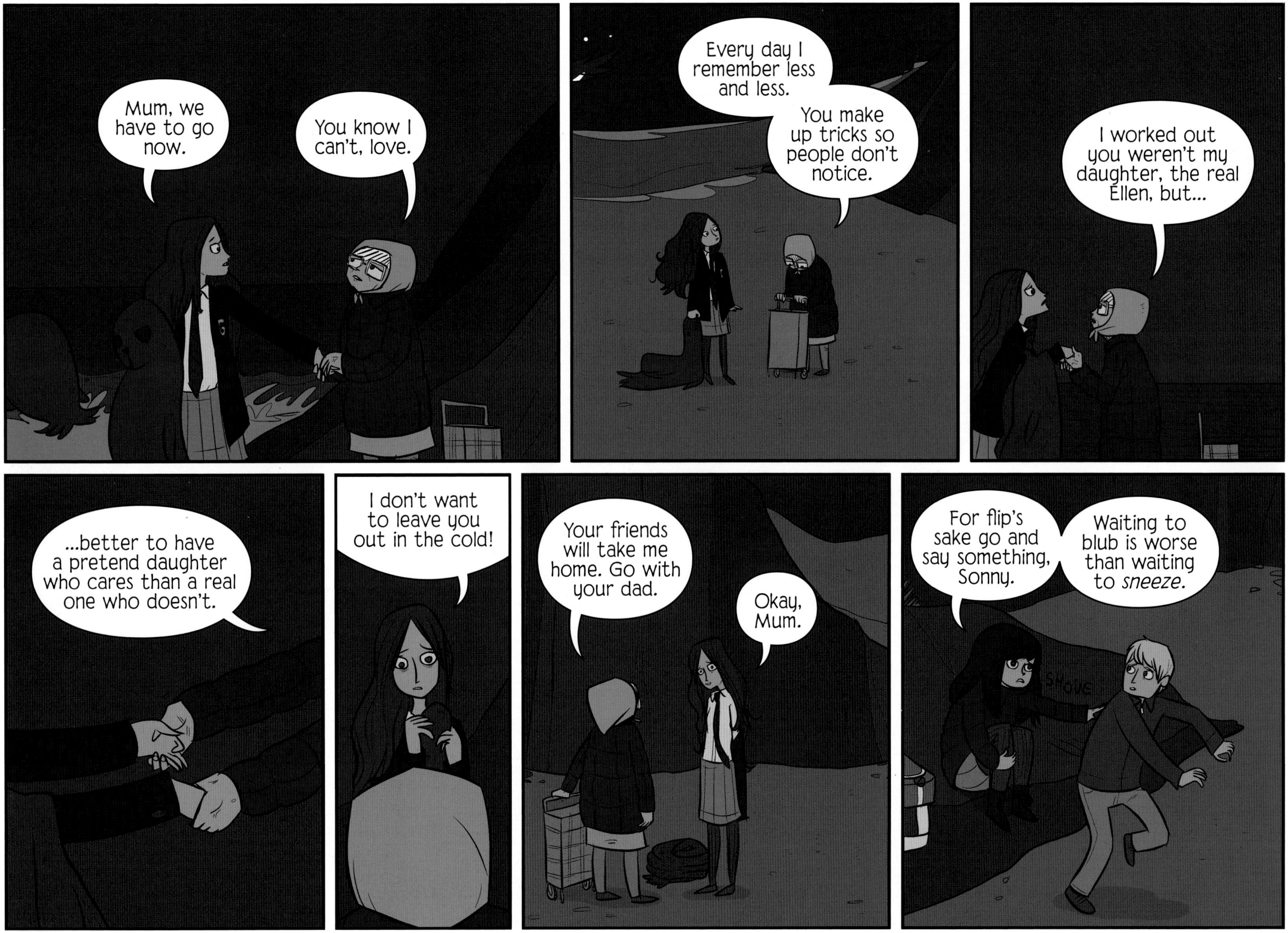
Mum, we have to go now.
You know I can't, love.
Every day I remember less and less.
You make up tricks so people don't notice.
I worked out you weren't my daughter, the real Ellen, but...
...better to have a pretend daughter who cares than a real one who doesn't.
I don't want to leave you out in the cold!
Your friends will take me home. Go with your dad.
Okay, Mum.
For flip's sake go and say something, Sonny.
Waiting to blub is worse than waiting to *sneeze.*
SHOVE

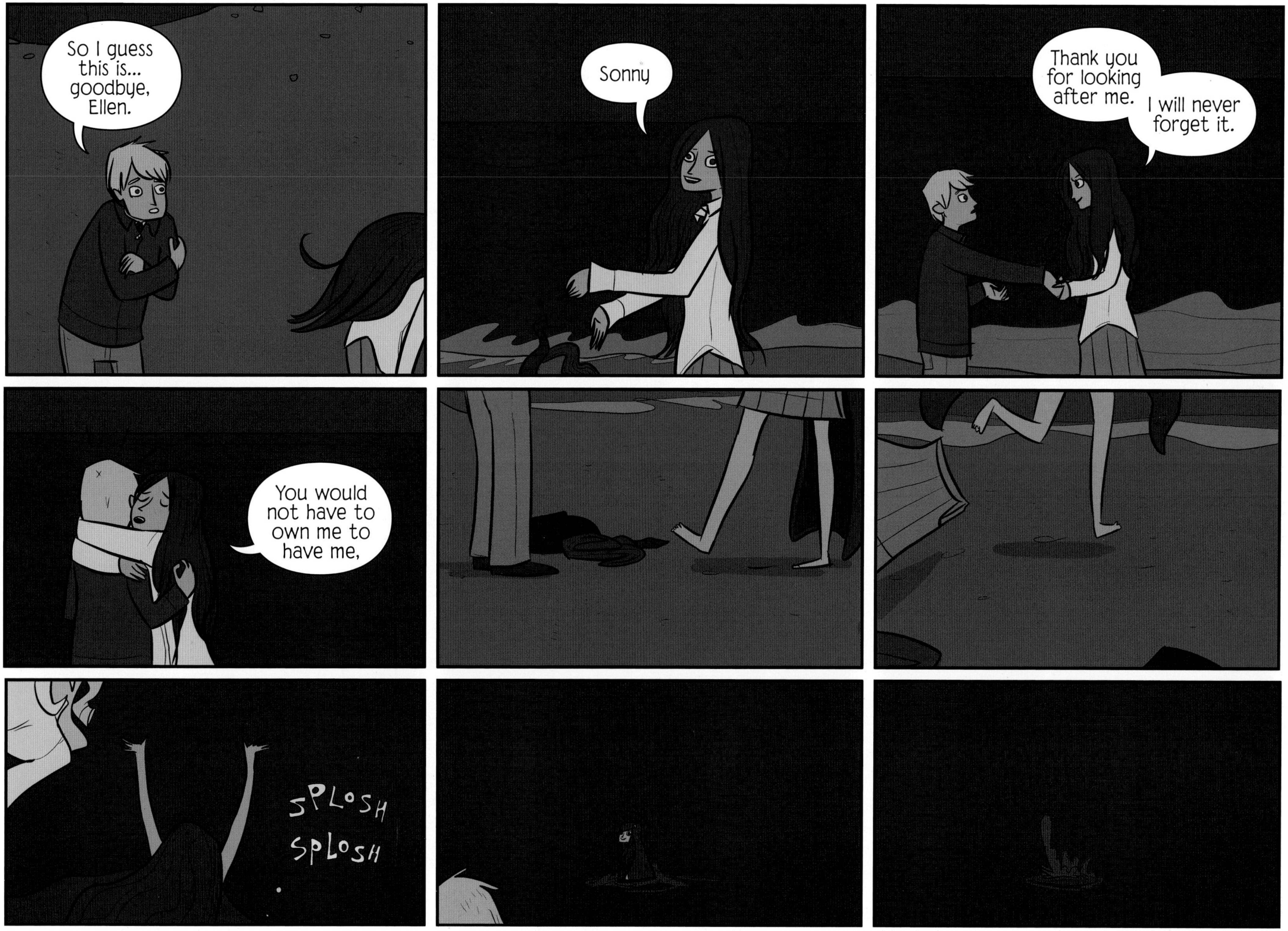
So I guess this is... goodbye, Ellen.
Sonny
Thank you for looking after me.
I will never forget it.
You would not have to own me to have me,
SPLOSH
SPLOSH

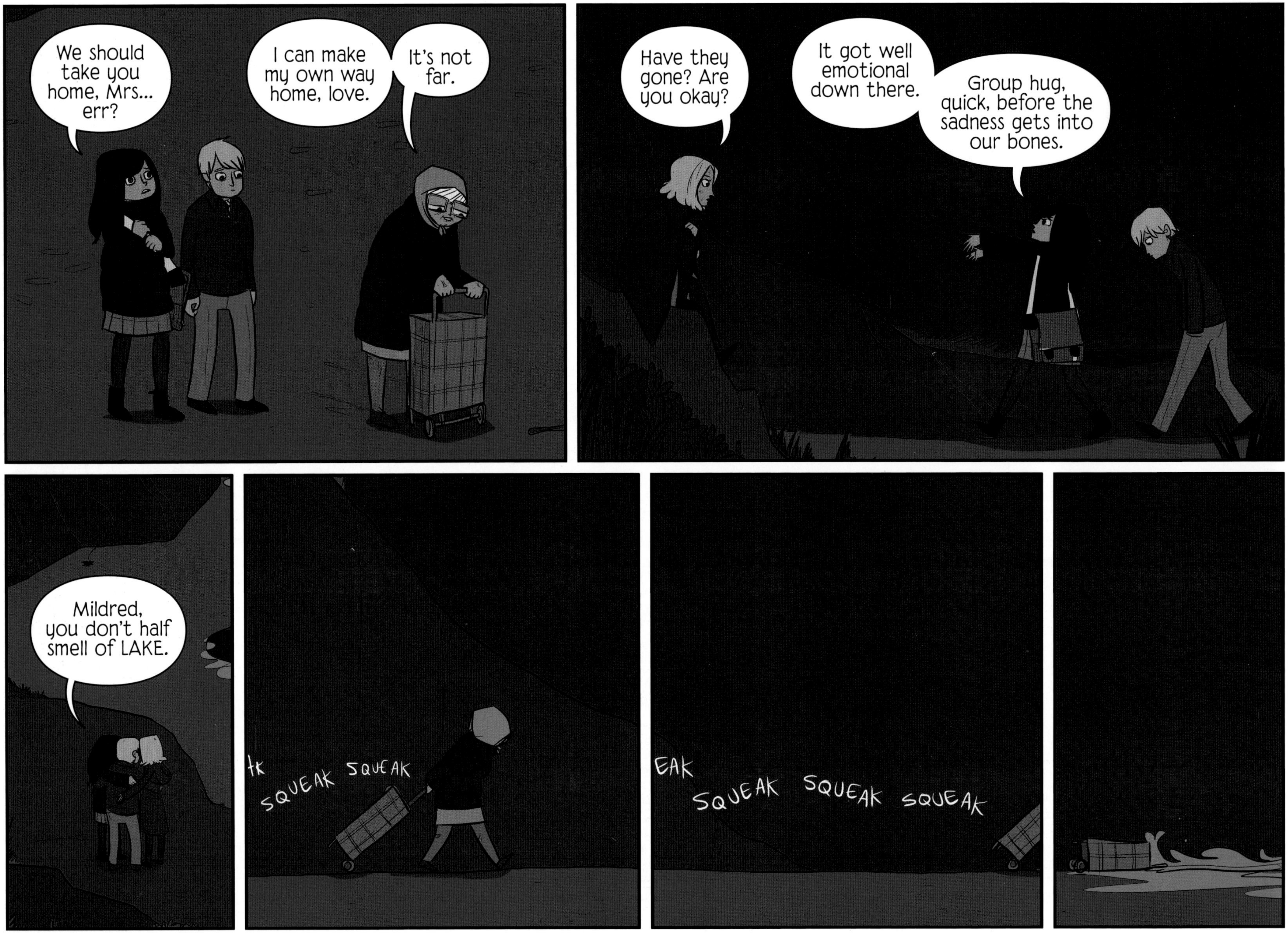
We should take you home, Mrs... err?
I can make my own way home, love.
It's not far.
Have they gone? Are you okay?
It got well emotional down there.
Group hug, quick, before the sadness gets into our bones.
Mildred, you don't half smell of LAKE.
tk
SQUEAK SQUEAK
EAK
SQUEAK SQUEAK SQUEAK

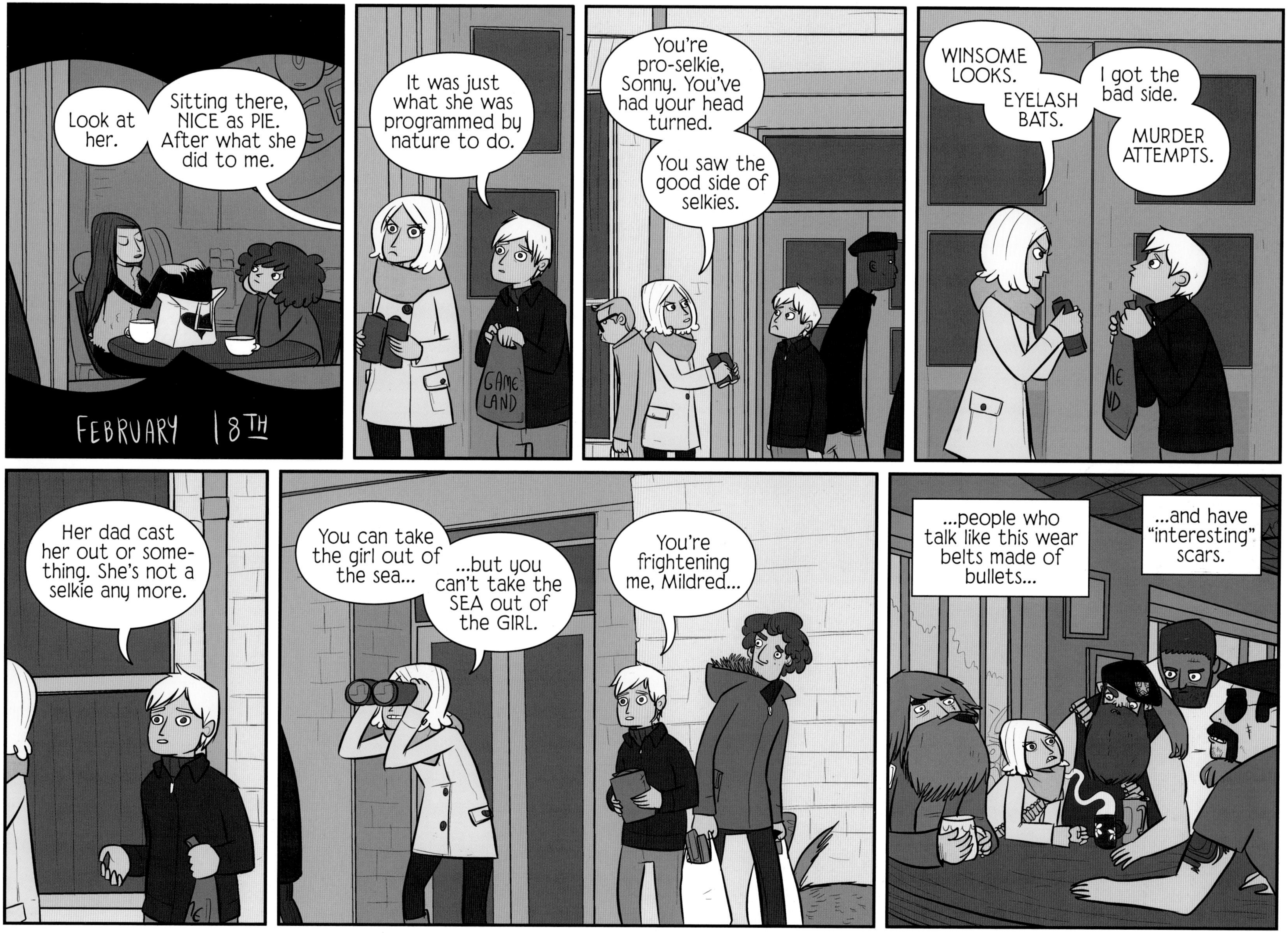
Look at her.
Sitting there, NICE as PIE. After what she did to me.
FEBRUARY 18TH
It was just what she was programmed by nature to do.
GAME LAND
You're pro-selkie, Sonny. You've had your head turned.
You saw the good side of selkies.
WINSOME LOOKS.
EYELASH BATS.
I got the bad side.
MURDER ATTEMPTS.
Her dad cast her out or some-thing. She's not a selkie any more.
You can take the girl out of the sea...
...but you can't take the SEA out of the GIRL.
You're frightening me, Mildred...
...people who talk like this wear belts made of bullets...
...and have "interesting" scars.

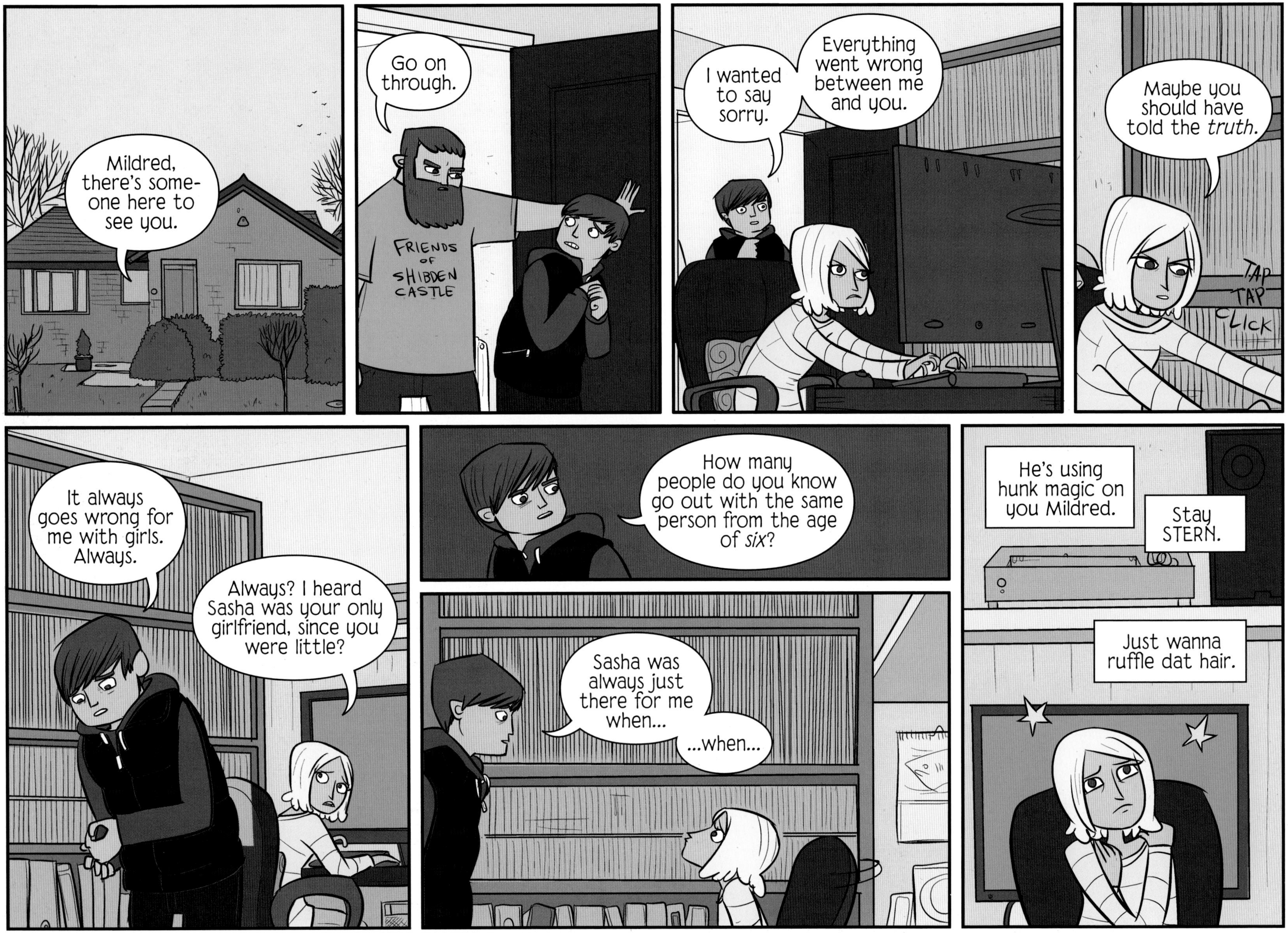
Mildred, there's some-one here to see you.
Go on through.
FRIENDS OF SHIBDEN CASTLE
I wanted to say sorry.
Everything went wrong between me and you.
Maybe you should have told the *truth*.
TAP TAP CLICK
It always goes wrong for me with girls. Always.
Always? I heard Sasha was your only girlfriend, since you were little?
How many people do you know go out with the same person from the age of *six*?
He's using hunk magic on you Mildred.
Stay STERN.
Just wanna ruffle dat hair.
Sasha was always just there for me when...
...when...

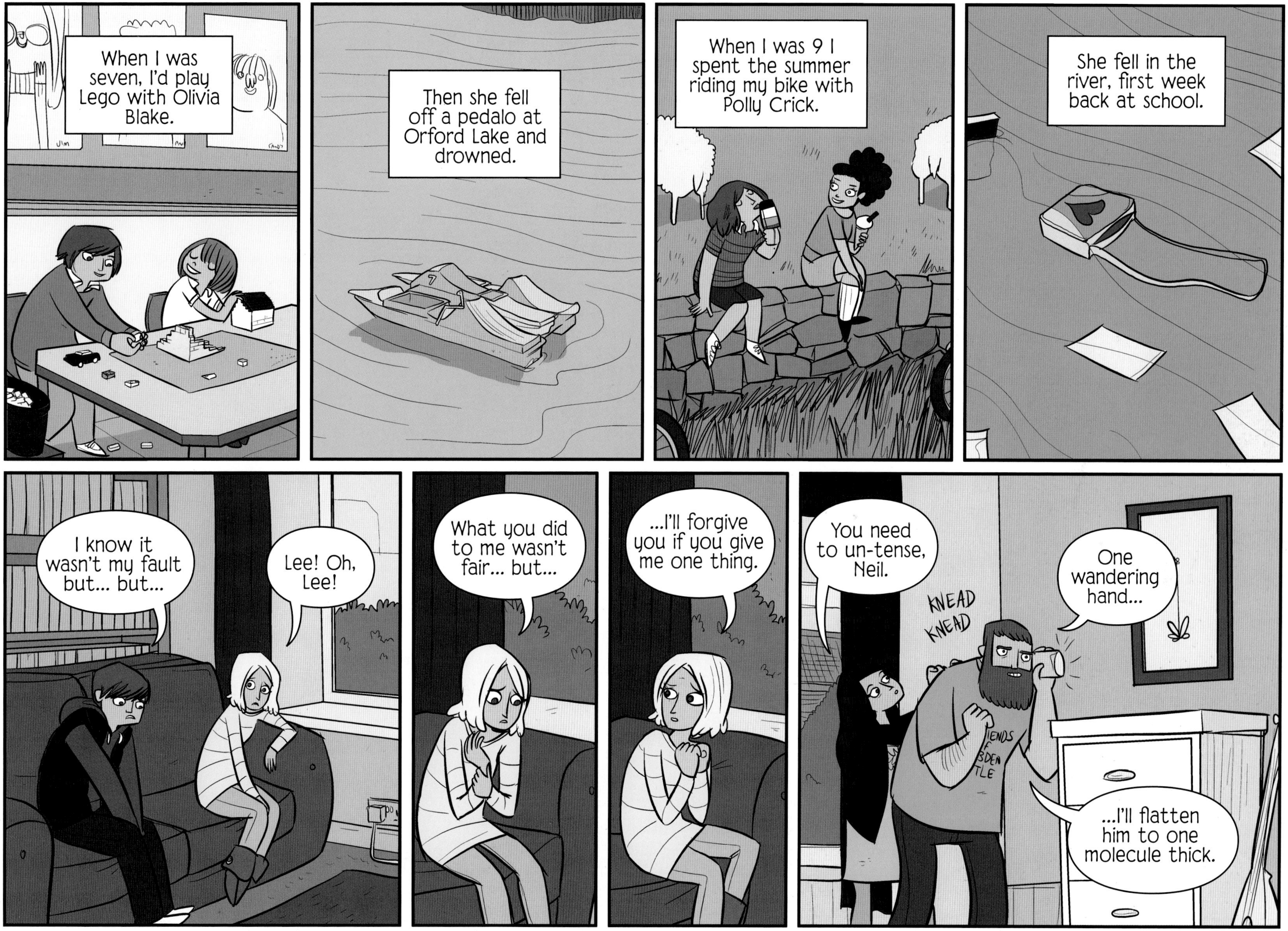
When I was seven, I'd play Lego with Olivia Blake.
Then she fell off a pedalo at Orford Lake and drowned.
When I was 9 I spent the summer riding my bike with Polly Crick.
She fell in the river, first week back at school.
I know it wasn't my fault but... but...
Lee! Oh, Lee!
What you did to me wasn't fair... but...
...I'll forgive you if you give me one thing.
You need to un-tense, Neil.
KNEAD
KNEAD
One wandering hand...
...I'll flatten him to one molecule thick.

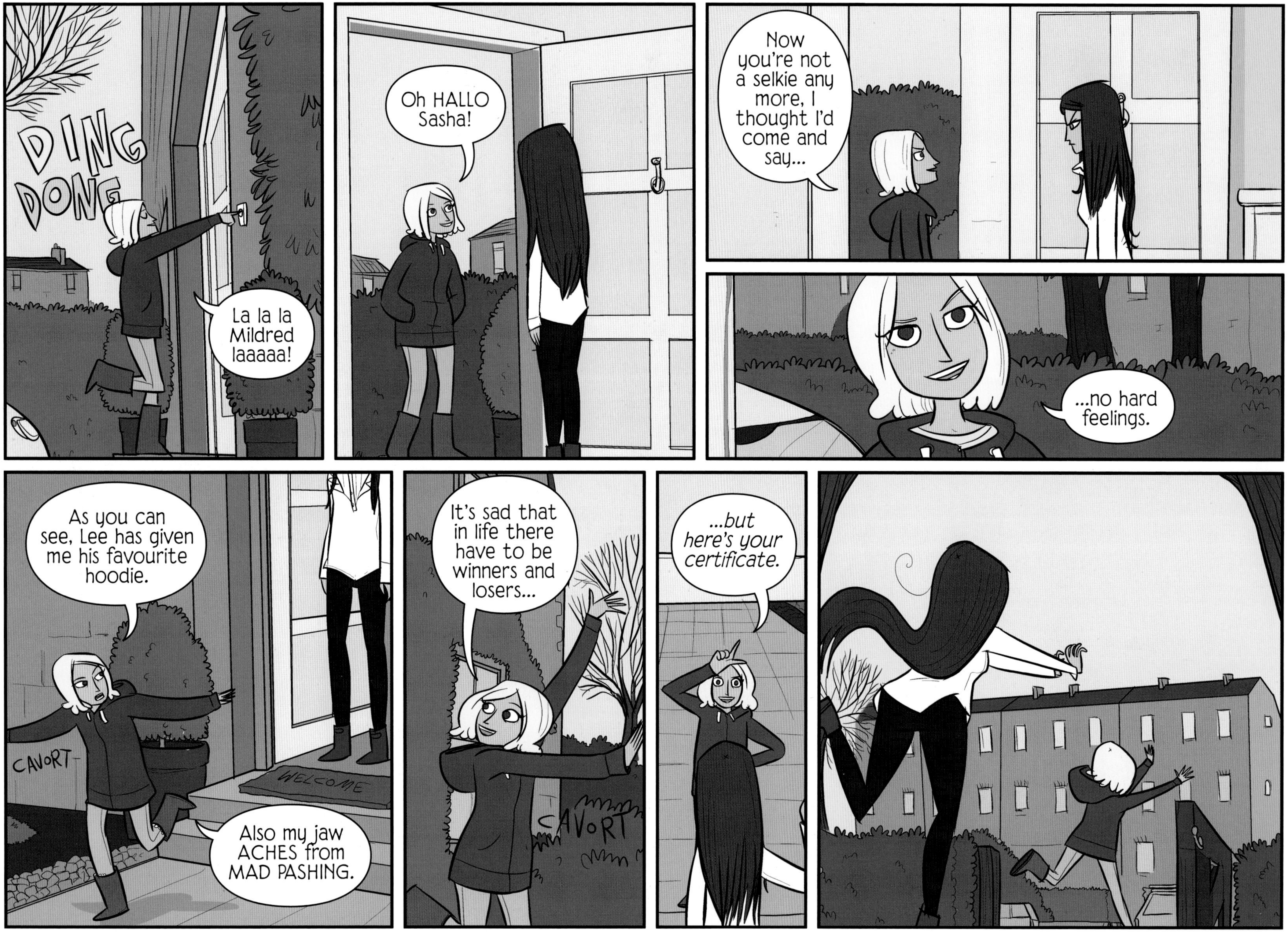
DING DONG
La la la Mildred laaaaa!
Oh HALLO Sasha!
Now you're not a selkie any more, I thought I'd come and say...
...no hard feelings.
As you can see, Lee has given me his favourite hoodie.
CAVORT
WELCOME
Also my jaw ACHES from MAD PASHING.
It's sad that in life there have to be winners and losers...
CAVORT
...but here's your certificate.

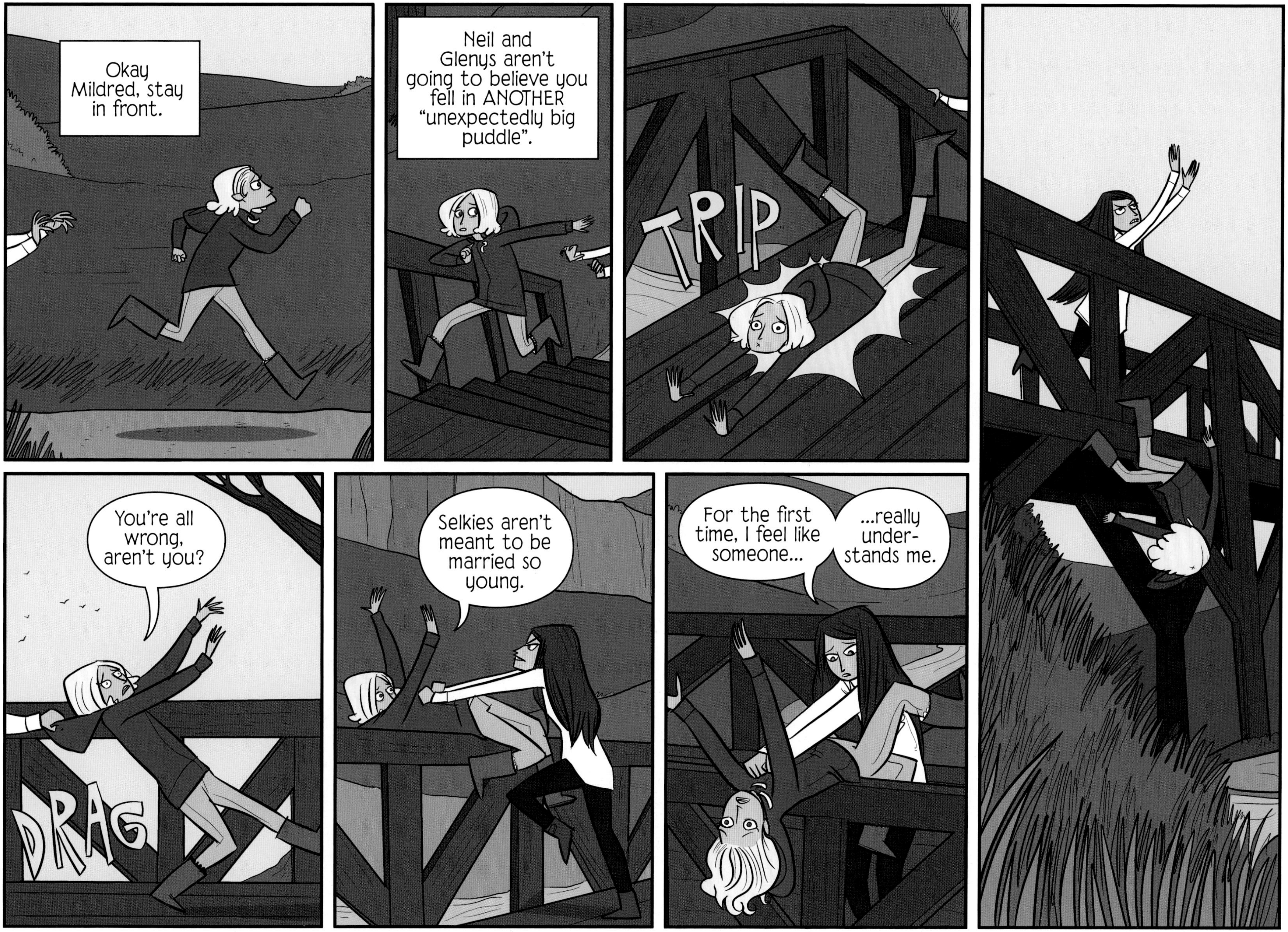
Okay Mildred, stay in front.
Neil and Glenys aren't going to believe you fell in ANOTHER "unexpectedly big puddle".
TRIP
You're all wrong, aren't you?
DRAG
Selkies aren't meant to be married so young.
For the first time, I feel like someone...
...really under-stands me.

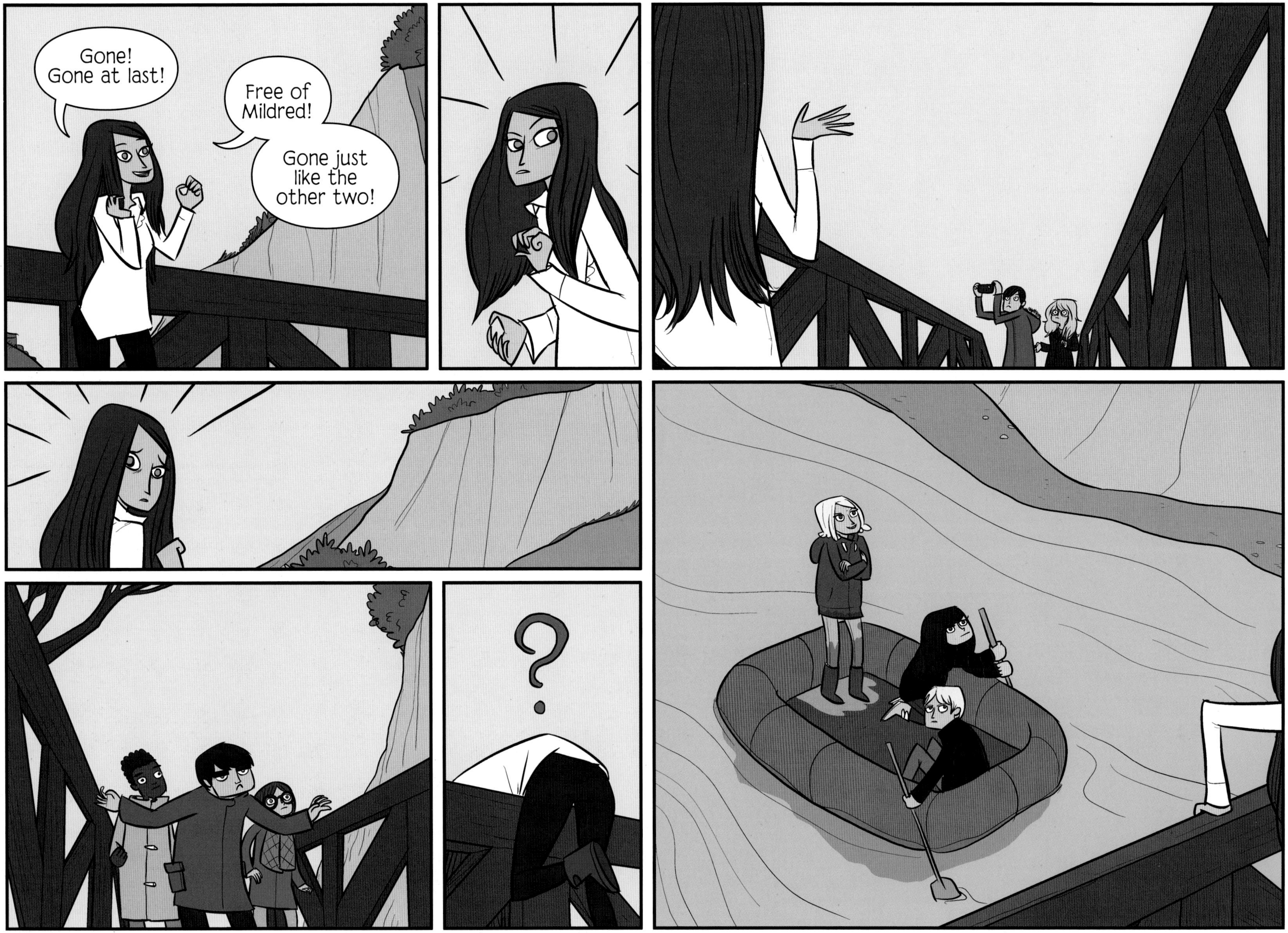
Gone! Gone at last!
Free of Mildred!
Gone just like the other two!
?

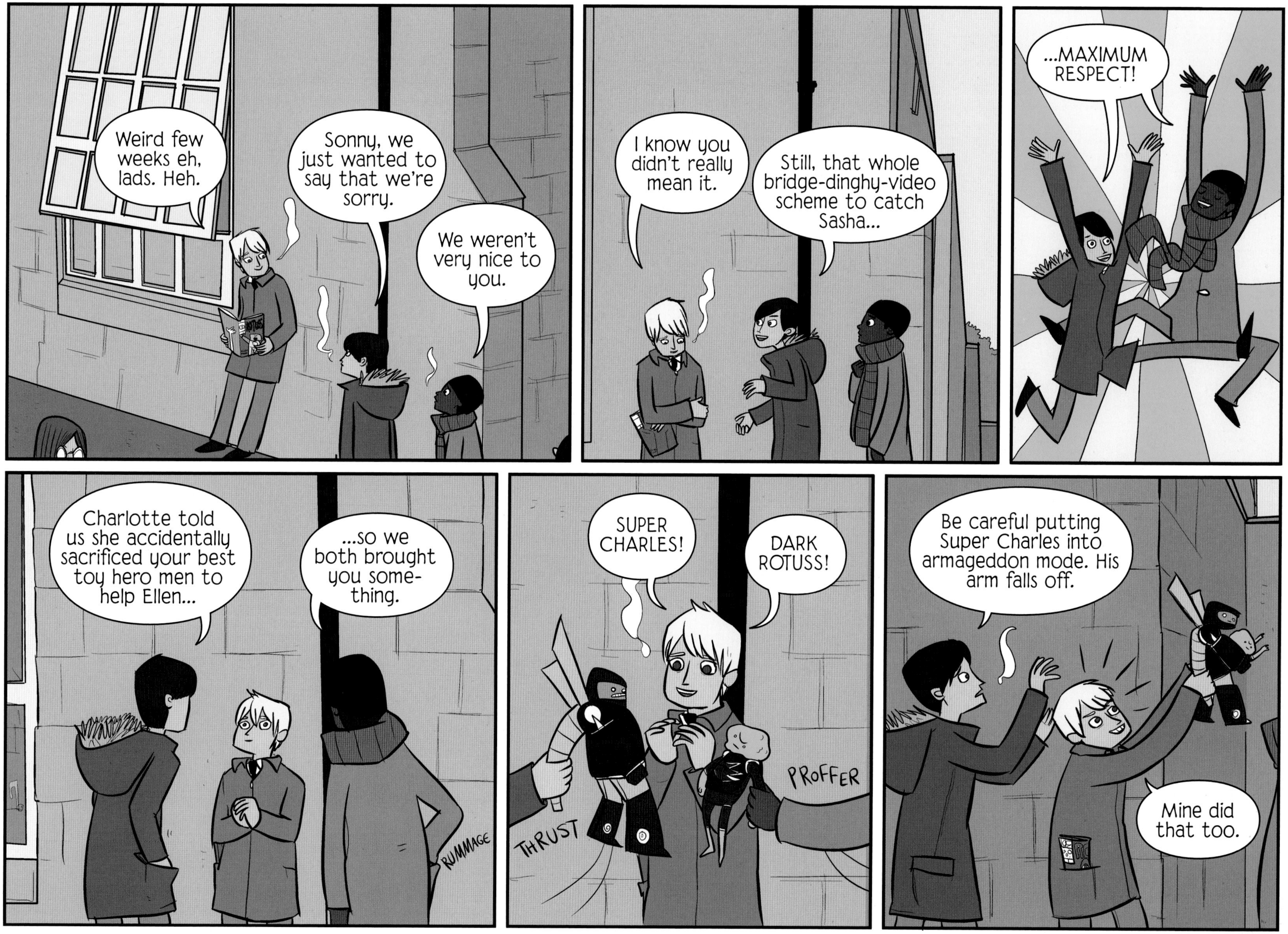
Weird few weeks eh, lads. Heh.
Sonny, we just wanted to say that we're sorry.
We weren't very nice to you.
I know you didn't really mean it.
Still, that whole bridge-dinghy-video scheme to catch Sasha...
...MAXIMUM RESPECT!
Charlotte told us she accidentally sacrificed your best toy hero men to help Ellen...
...so we both brought you some-thing.
RUMMAGE
SUPER CHARLES!
DARK ROTUSS!
THRUST
PROFFER
Be careful putting Super Charles into armageddon mode. His arm falls off.
Mine did that too.

Bad Machinery, Volume Five

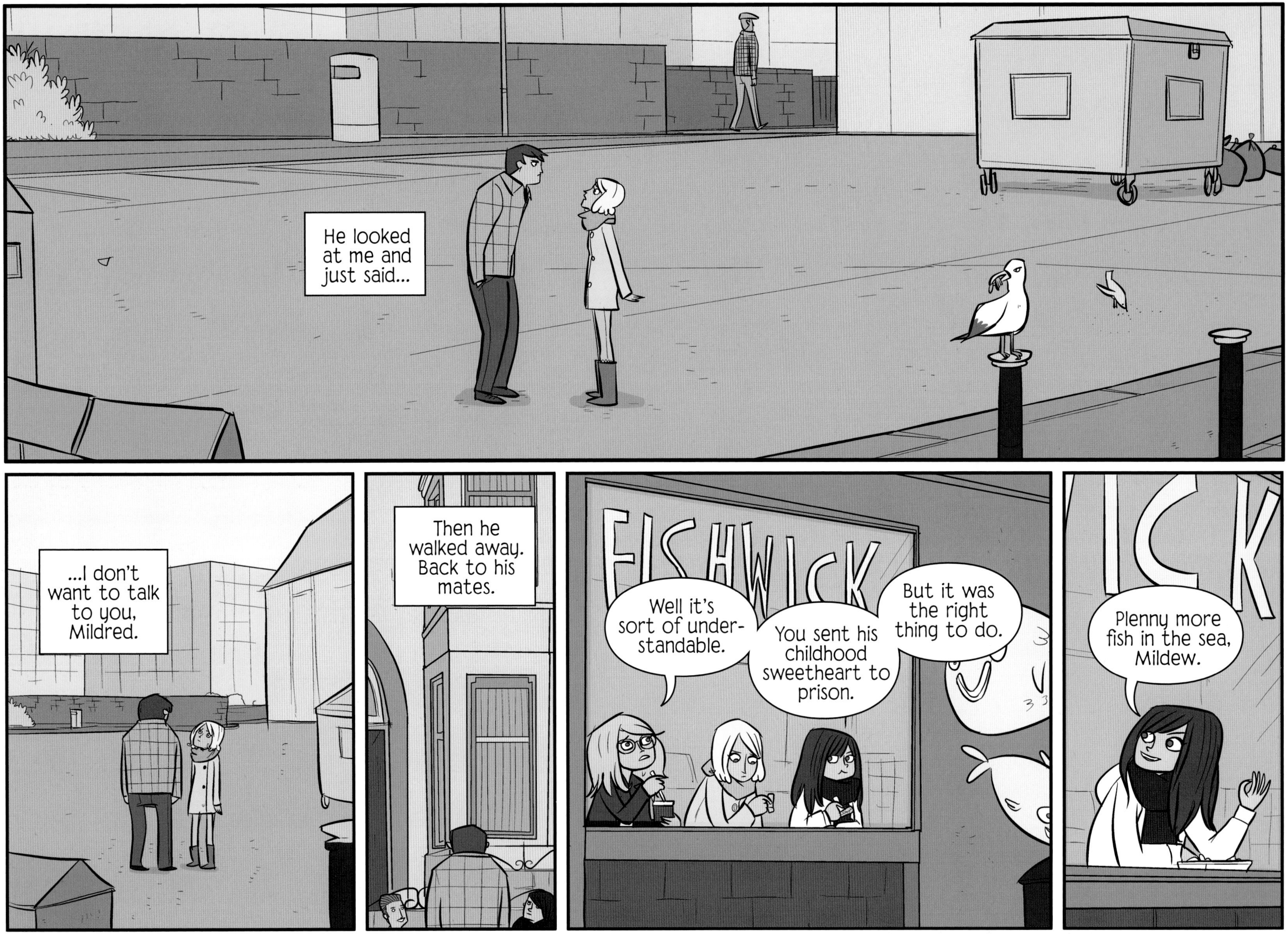
He looked at me and just said...
...I don't want to talk to you, Mildred.
Then he walked away. Back to his mates.
FISHWICK
Well it's sort of understandable.
You sent his childhood sweetheart to prison.
But it was the right thing to do.
Plenny more fish in the sea, Mildew.

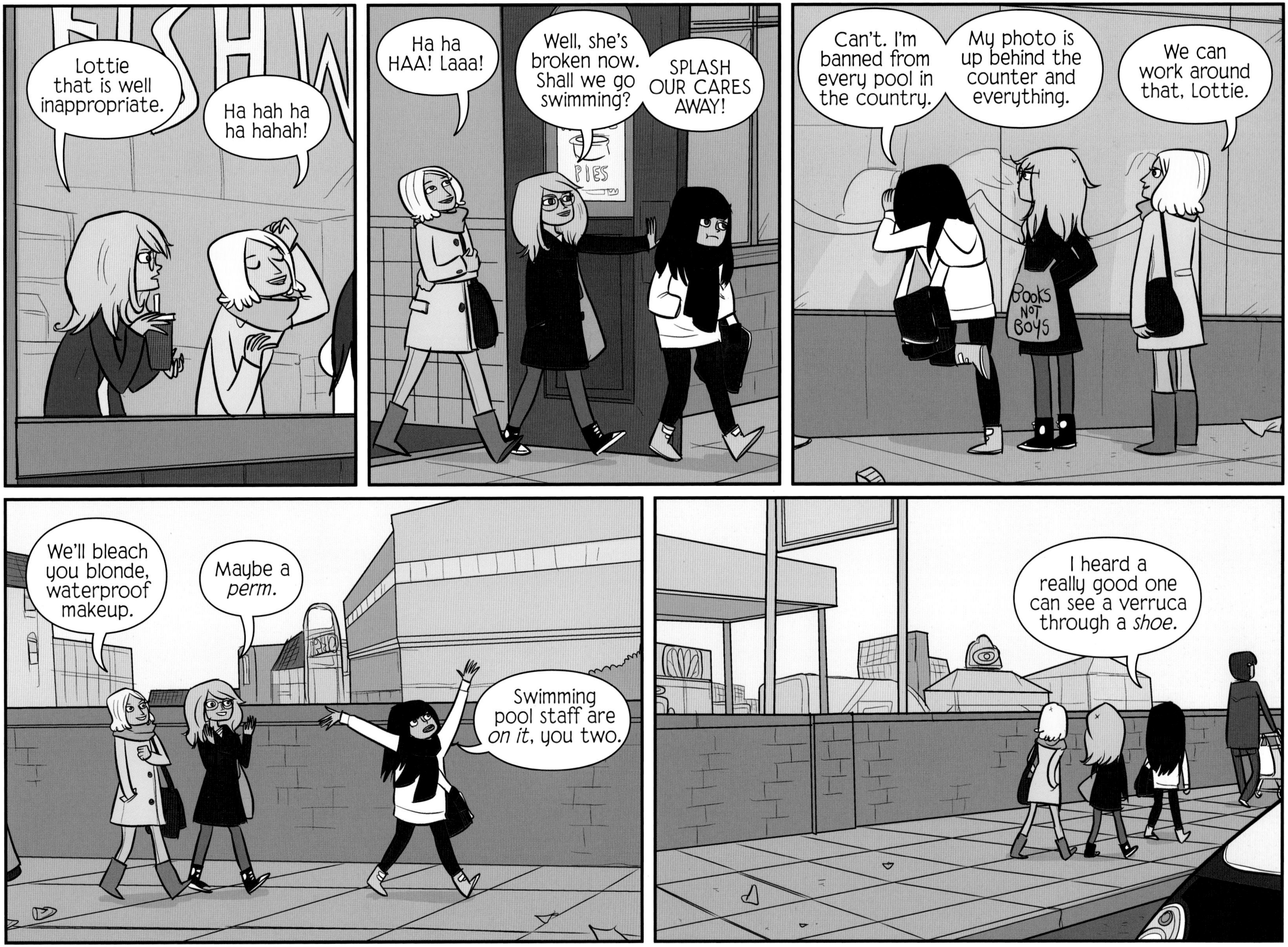
FISHW
Lottie that is well inappropriate.
Ha hah ha ha hahah!
Ha ha HAA! Laaa!
Well, she's broken now. Shall we go swimming?
SPLASH OUR CARES AWAY!
PIES
Can't. I'm banned from every pool in the country.
My photo is up behind the counter and everything.
We can work around that, Lottie.
BOOKS NOT BOYS
We'll bleach you blonde, waterproof makeup.
Maybe a *perm*.
Swimming pool staff are *on it*, you two.
I heard a really good one can see a verruca through a *shoe*.

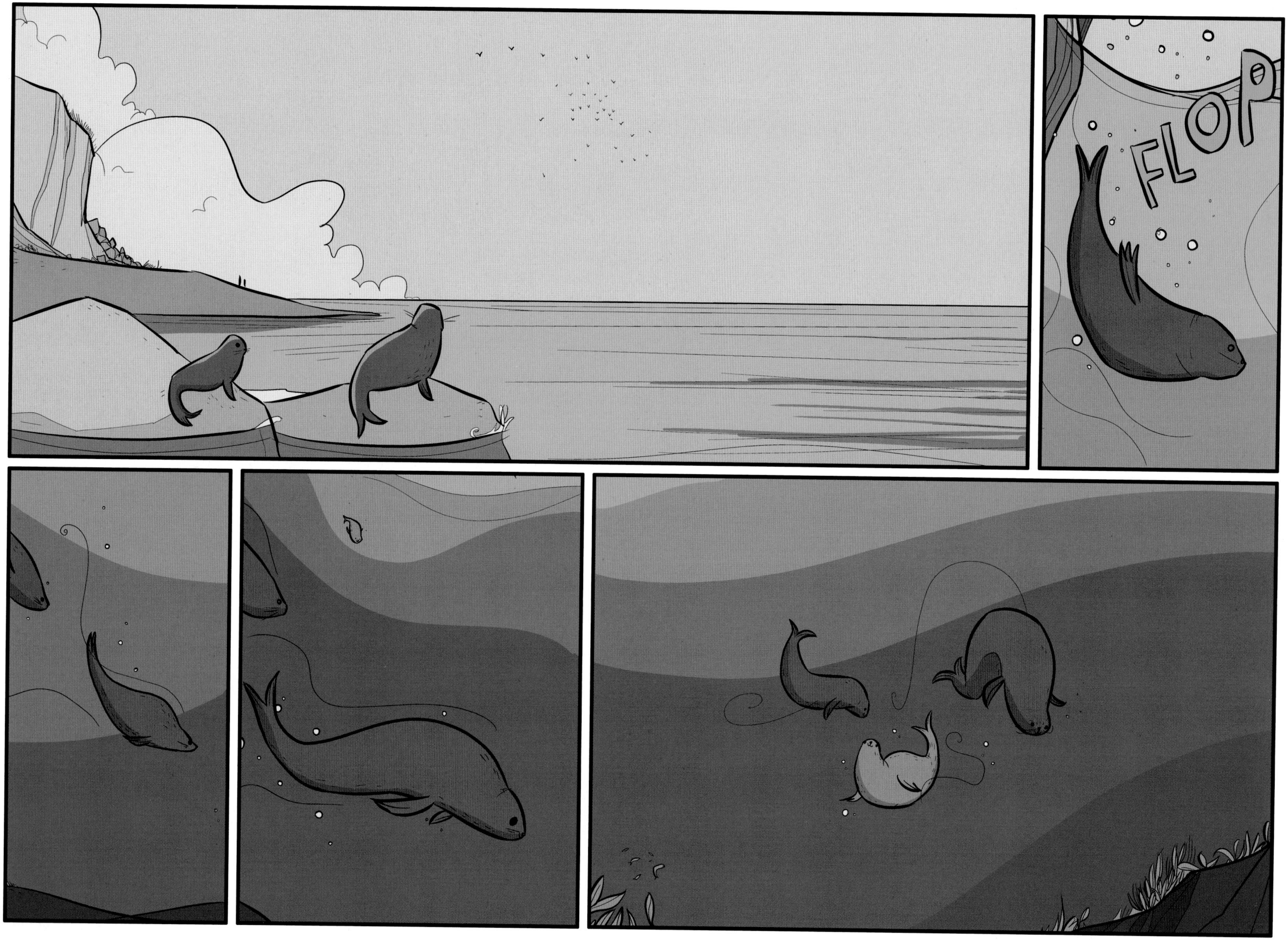
FLOP

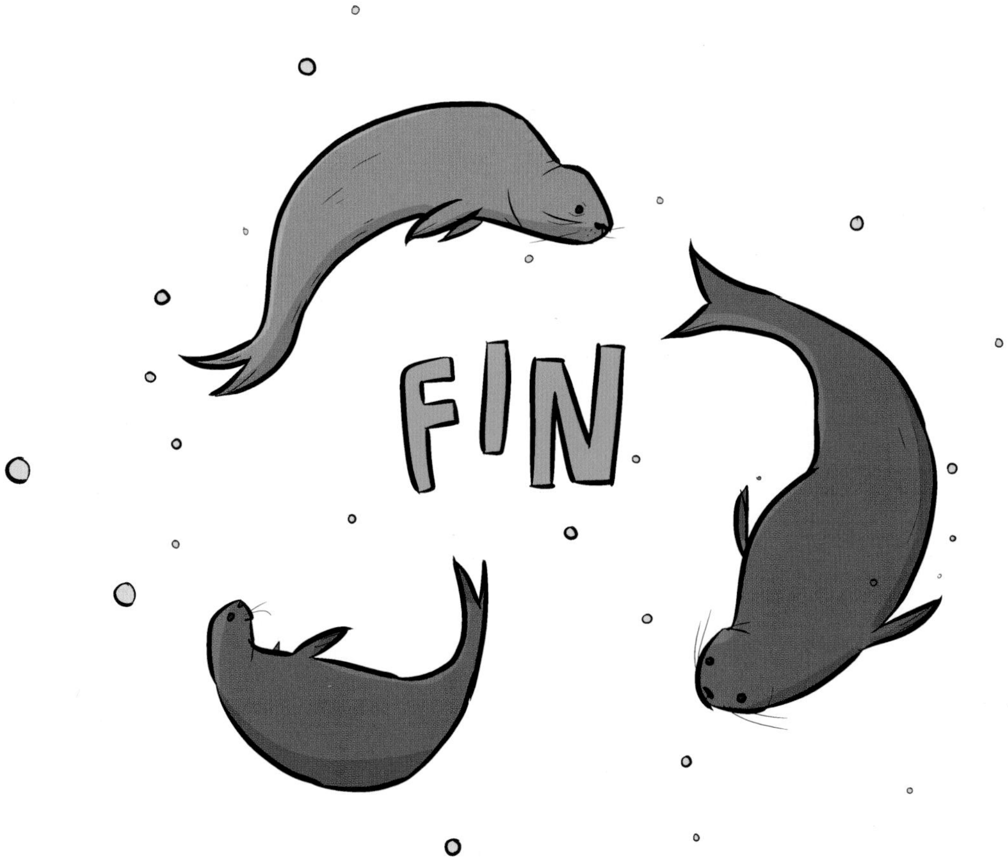
FIN

FIRE INSIDE SKETCHBOOK

ELLEN
(THE SELKIE)

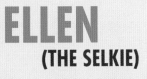

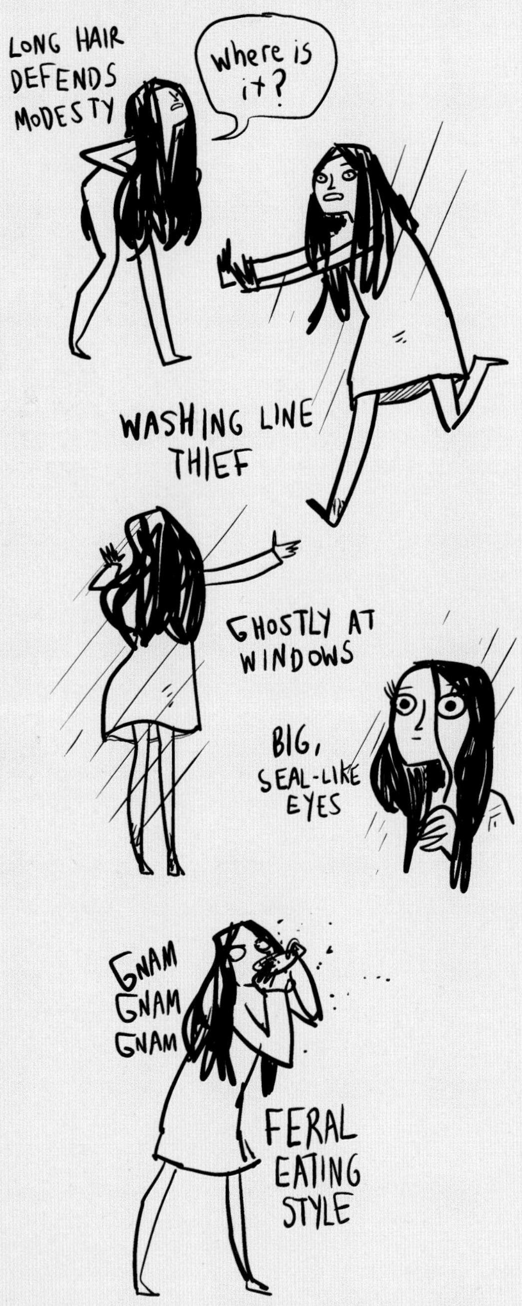
LONG HAIR DEFENDS MODESTY
Where is it?
WASHING LINE THIEF
GHOSTLY AT WINDOWS
BIG, SEAL-LIKE EYES
GNAM GNAM GNAM
FERAL EATING STYLE

Selkies are alluring mythological seal-people who emerge from the sea and make lovers of the men or women who find their sealskins. There are lots of variations on the myth, probably because at the time folklorists cooked up these tales, there was no Wikipedia to check your facts against. At best you had to get the Microsoft Encarta CD-ROM, and only rich kids had that.

Ellen the selkie is sweet-natured and kind, as you imagine a seal would be as you stare into its big liquid eyes. Sasha is more vindictive, as a seal probably actually is as it whacks you over the head with its big muscular tail after you looked sideways at half-eaten fish it was "saving for later". I don't claim to be an expert on seals any more than I am an expert on any other animal, but I do know that they are excellent players of the "arrayed honking horn", making them the only animal with musical talent apart from the praying mantis*.

**Note to self: check this on Wikipedia/Encarta '98.*

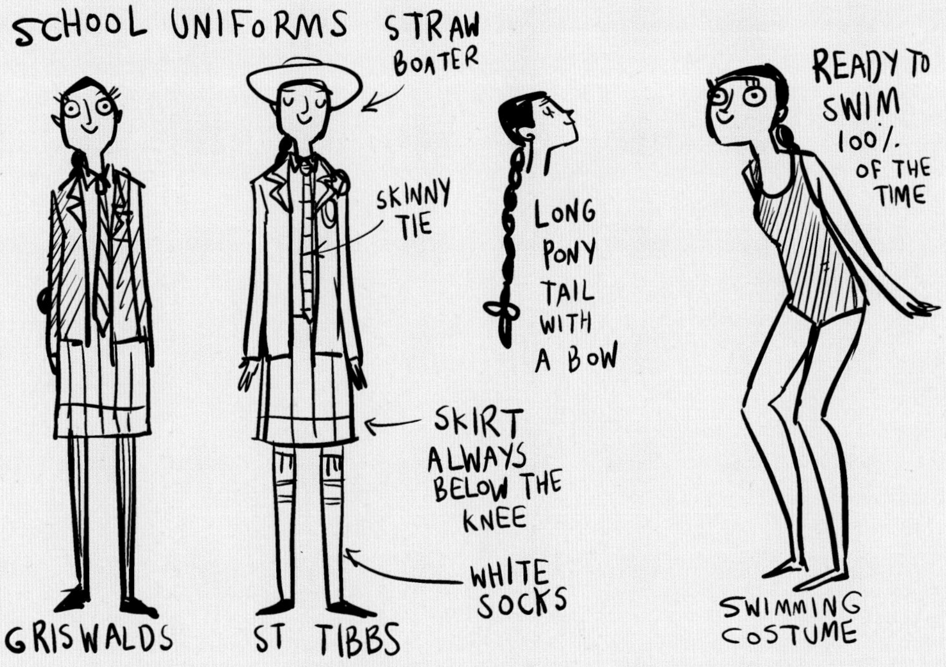
SCHOOL UNIFORMS
STRAW BOATER
SKINNY TIE
LONG PONY TAIL WITH A BOW
READY TO SWIM 100% OF THE TIME
SKIRT ALWAYS BELOW THE KNEE
WHITE SOCKS
GRISWALDS
ST TIBBS
SWIMMING COSTUME

SASHA
(ALSO THE SELKIE)

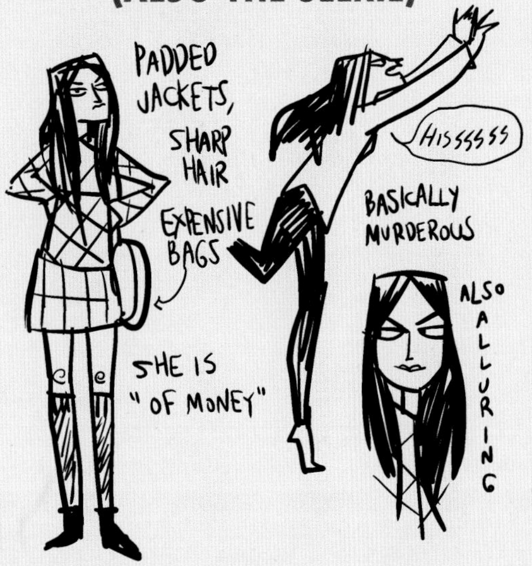
PADDED JACKETS,
SHARP HAIR
HISSSSSS
EXPENSIVE BAGS
BASICALLY MURDEROUS
SHE IS "OF MONEY"
ALSO ALLURING

One question this story never really answers about Sasha is, how did she manage to to find a family who buys her sweet padded jackets and nice bags and all that? My feeling was that she was adopted as a foundling by a rich family.

I don't think that family is to blame for the trail of drowned little girls Sasha has left in her wake, but at the same time, they should perhaps have noticed that the roll-call at their little angel's birthday parties was starting to look a bit sparse. Also, Lee must have spent a long time in denial. Either that, or he's not very bright. (He's not very bright.)

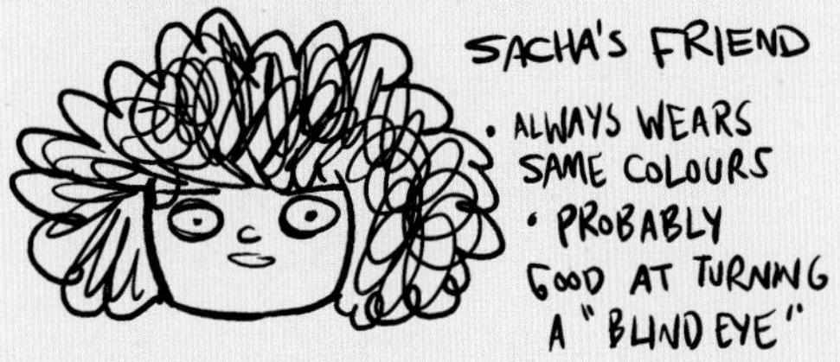
SACHA'S FRIEND
• ALWAYS WEARS SAME COLOURS
• PROBABLY GOOD AT TURNING A "BLIND EYE"

THE SELKIE-DADDY

FAMILY HAIRCUT

HE'S BIG

MUCH BLUBBER

GET HIM IN TROUSERS A.S.A.P

While Ellen and Sasha have no problem blending in on land (apart from the illiteracy and the drownings), their father resembles the kind of wild figure one would cross the road to avoid. While it is only fair to take each person on their personal merits, there is something about the combination of massive shirtless bulk, untamed beard and stinking, oily seal-cape that quickens the pulse in a primal way.

Your donation of seventy-five cents could buy this man a comb.

PROBABLY SHOULDN'T BE LIVING ON HER OWN ANY MORE

CLASSIC TARTAN SHOPPING TROLLEY

PADDED JACKET AT 45° TO THE YOUNGSTERS

A LOST FIGURE

THICK GLASSES, SELF-CUT HAIR

REVITALISED BY LOOKING AFTER "ELLEN"

THANK YOU, MUM!

A MUTUALLY BENEFICIAL ARRANGEMENT

MARCHES WITH PURPOSE

SOLID!

GOES INTO THE SEA

ENERGY CROW

I've written you a book, Barry! With COMPLIMENTS!

Energy Crow

by C. Grote

Between *The Case Of The Lonely One* and this book, I wrote a short story called "Murder She Writes", where Lottie is taken on a writers' retreat by the author Shelley Winters, and has to solve a murder. Having successfully foiled the killers, she pens her own book designed to expand young minds. That book is called *Energy Crow*.

Under no circumstances should any young minds be allowed to read the full manuscript of *Energy Crow*, which may be a the most degenerate publication ever aimed at under-5s.

I well reckon this book is "educational" heh heh

Energy Crow

ELLEN'S "MUM"

"Mum" is a sad figure. I felt very protective of her when I was writing this story. Her life isn't great until Ellen arrives, but somehow two people in quite dire circumstances make the best of things. When the story originally ran on the web, people asked me after Mum walked into the sea, "did she end her own life?" I made things a little bit ambiguous, which was mean, because a lot of people liked her and felt protective of her the way I did.

My feeling was that she was a selkie too, whose land-born husband had died, but stayed around for her children long after they had needed her, slowly becoming vague and disconnected. Ellen wakes something up in her, and she leaves with her own seal-skin in her tartan shopping trolley and returns to the sea.

So this version of *The Case Of The Fire Inside* has a happier ending than it did when I first made the pages. It's the same ending I always saw in my head, but I feel better for having finally put it on the page. That's assuming that the grey seal is Mum. It might not be. But I like to think that it is.

LEE

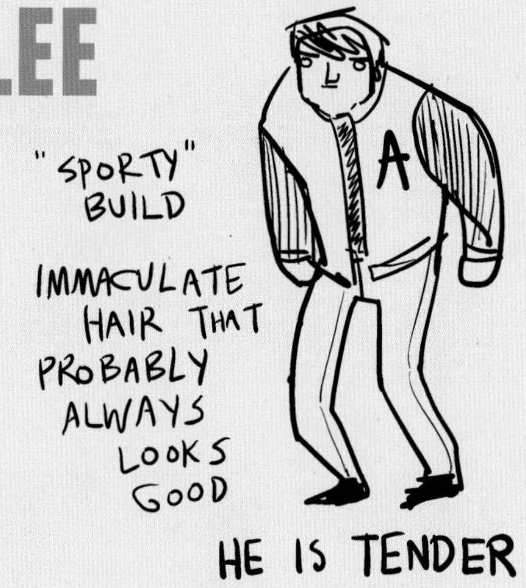
"SPORTY" BUILD
IMMACULATE HAIR THAT PROBABLY ALWAYS LOOKS GOOD
HE IS TENDER

Lee was first seen in *The Case Of The Lonely One* as one of the "bad kids" Mildred joins in detention. "Bad" is probably the wrong word, but one imagines that he is the sort of boy who would begin throwing a tennis ball around in class the second the teacher leaves the classroom to do a bit of photocopying. This isn't his fault, it's a medical condition suffered by many youths who were exposed at a young age to sporting goods stores.

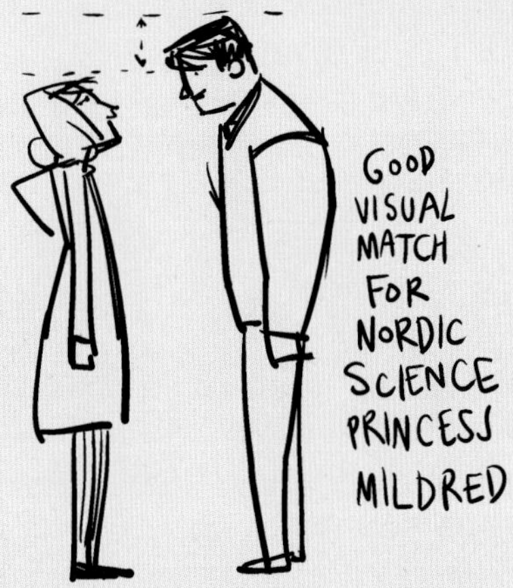
GOOD VISUAL MATCH FOR NORDIC SCIENCE PRINCESS MILDRED

CECILE

Cecile Craven isn't quite four in this story, but already she is beginning to develop a powerful agency. With just three summers under her belt, she's able to intimidate her mild-mannered brother Sonny. There's little telling what kind of person Cecile will grow up into, but I've long felt that she represents a "clear and present danger" to good order in Tackleford.

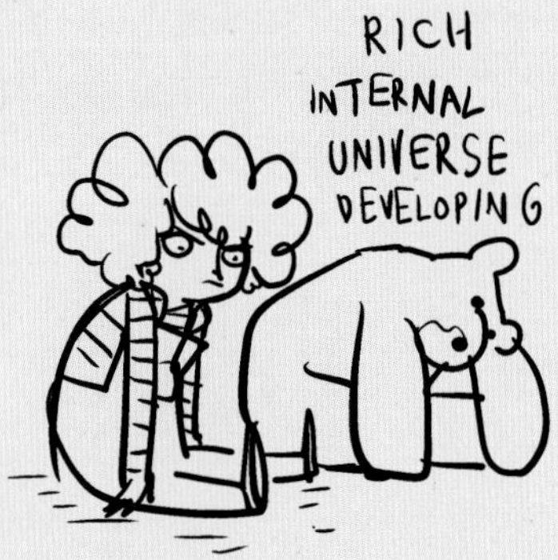
RICH INTERNAL UNIVERSE DEVELOPING

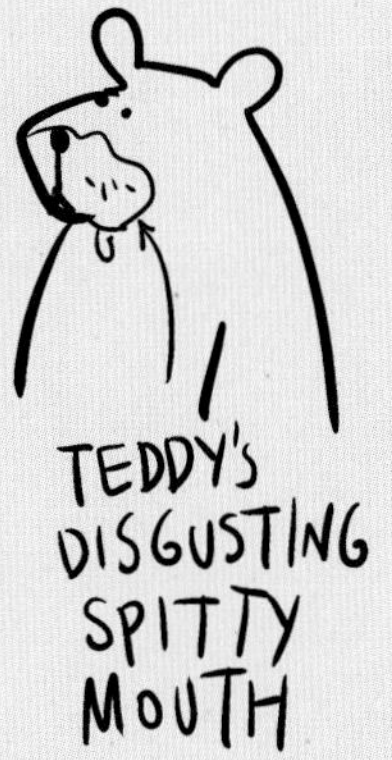
TEDDY'S DISGUSTING SPITTY MOUTH

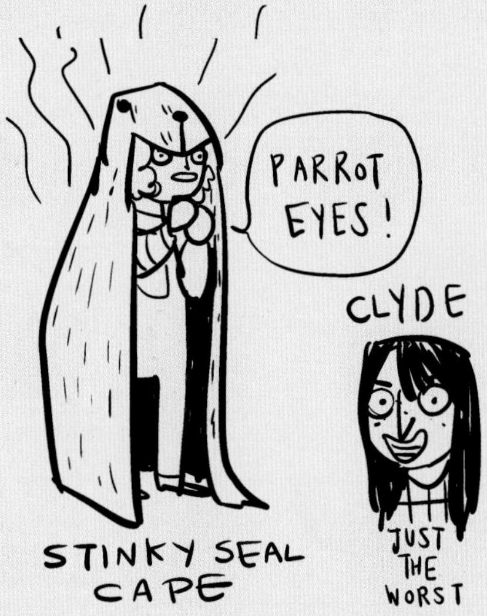
PARROT EYES!
STINKY SEAL CAPE
CLYDE
JUST THE WORST

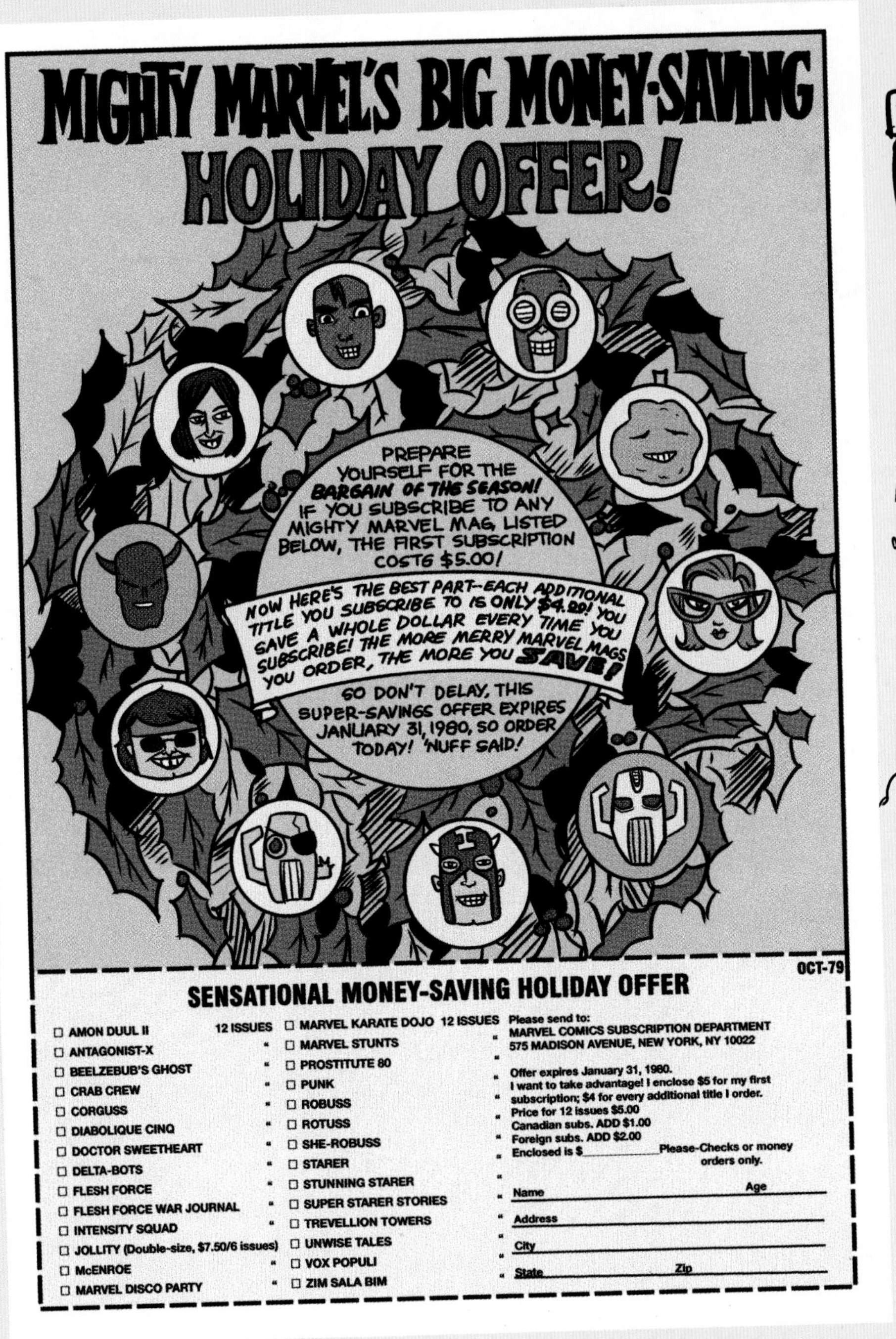
MIGHTY MARVEL'S BIG MONEY-SAVING HOLIDAY OFFER!
PREPARE YOURSELF FOR THE BARGAIN OF THE SEASON! IF YOU SUBSCRIBE TO ANY MIGHTY MARVEL MAG LISTED BELOW, THE FIRST SUBSCRIPTION COSTS $5.00!
NOW HERE'S THE BEST PART—EACH ADDITIONAL TITLE YOU SUBSCRIBE TO IS ONLY $4.00! YOU SAVE A WHOLE DOLLAR EVERY TIME YOU SUBSCRIBE! THE MORE MERRY MARVEL MAGS YOU ORDER, THE MORE YOU SAVE!
SO DON'T DELAY, THIS SUPER-SAVINGS OFFER EXPIRES JANUARY 31, 1980, SO ORDER TODAY! 'NUFF SAID!
OCT-79
SENSATIONAL MONEY-SAVING HOLIDAY OFFER
☐ AMON DUUL II 12 ISSUES
☐ ANTAGONIST-X "
☐ BEELZEBUB'S GHOST "
☐ CRAB CREW "
☐ CORGUSS "
☐ DIABOLIQUE CINQ "
☐ DOCTOR SWEETHEART "
☐ DELTA-BOTS "
☐ FLESH FORCE "
☐ FLESH FORCE WAR JOURNAL "
☐ INTENSITY SQUAD "
☐ JOLLITY (Double-size, $7.50/6 issues)
☐ McENROE "
☐ MARVEL DISCO PARTY "
☐ MARVEL KARATE DOJO 12 ISSUES
☐ MARVEL STUNTS "
☐ PROSTITUTE 80 "
☐ PUNK "
☐ ROBUSS "
☐ ROTUSS "
☐ SHE-ROBUSS "
☐ STARER "
☐ STUNNING STARER "
☐ SUPER STARER STORIES "
☐ TREVELLION TOWERS "
☐ UNWISE TALES "
☐ VOX POPULI "
☐ ZIM SALA BIM "
Please send to: MARVEL COMICS SUBSCRIPTION DEPARTMENT 575 MADISON AVENUE, NEW YORK, NY 10022
Offer expires January 31, 1980.
I want to take advantage! I enclose $5 for my first subscription; $4 for every additional title I order.
Price for 12 issues $5.00
Canadian subs. ADD $1.00
Foreign subs. ADD $2.00
Enclosed is $______ Please-Checks or money orders only.
Name Age
Address
City
State Zip

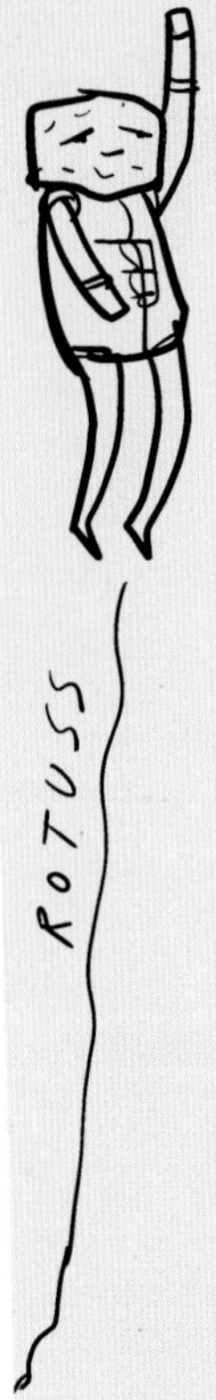
ROTUSS

SONNY'S TOYS

I have an irresponsible attitude to character creation, as the fake subscription ad above confirms. Stop me before I do it again.

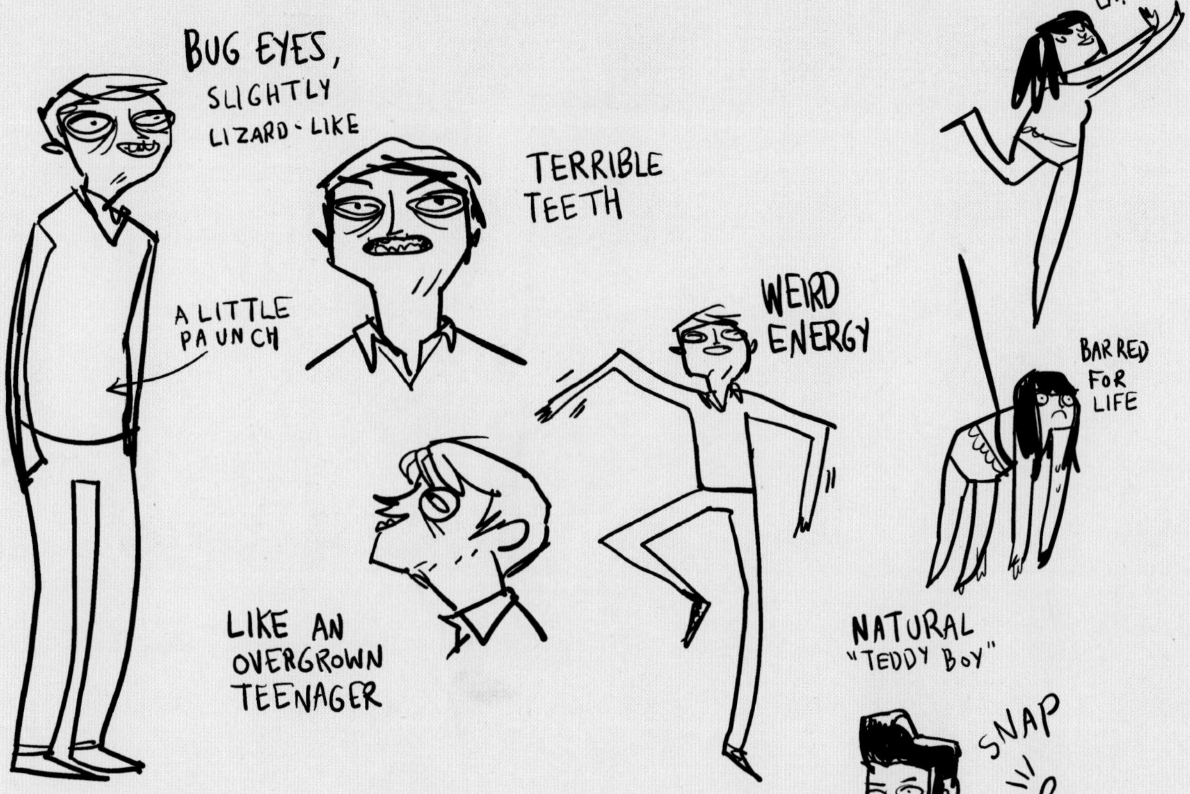
BUG EYES,
SLIGHTLY
LIZARD-LIKE
TERRIBLE
TEETH
A LITTLE
PAUNCH
WEIRD
ENERGY
LA!
BARRED
FOR
LIFE
LIKE AN
OVERGROWN
TEENAGER

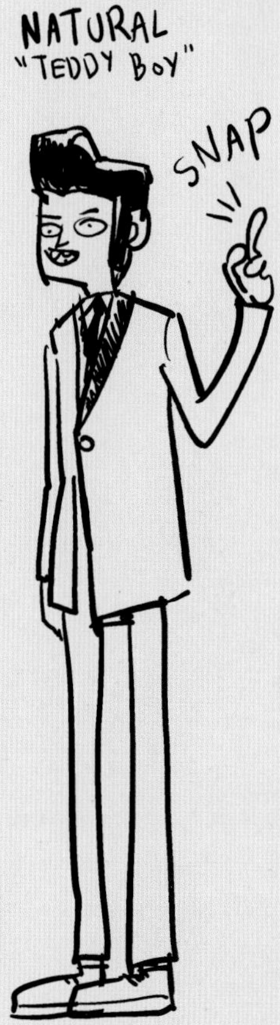
NATURAL
"TEDDY BOY"
SNAP

GRANPA JOE

Granpa (short for "Grandpa", which is short for "Grandfather", which is itself short for "Lord Prince Grandfather, Patriarch and Duke") Joe is a scallywag. His marriage to Grandma Josephine probably didn't last very long. It's likely that he never really connected with such concepts as "responsibility" or "being around". I imagine that the last straw was when he stripped down a motorcycle engine on the dinner table, while the best tablecloth was on it, and his mother-in-law was visiting. But the things that made Joe a terrible husband and a dangerous father make him a great grandparent. Freed of the need to do anything so quotidien as provide for his brood, he can concentrate on the important things—inappropriate anecdotes, forbidden treats, trips to not entirely on-the-level tradesmen with his descendents in tow. Not in toe, though. That mortoned monster needs to be kept firmly under wraps.

THE RULES OF THE POOL

The "Rules Of The Pool" poster is a British design classic, which is to say that the government didn't bother to update it for thirty years, and when they finally did, the person who did the new one did a terrible job of it. Generations of British teenagers were introduced to the word "petting" this way, long after it passed out of common use.

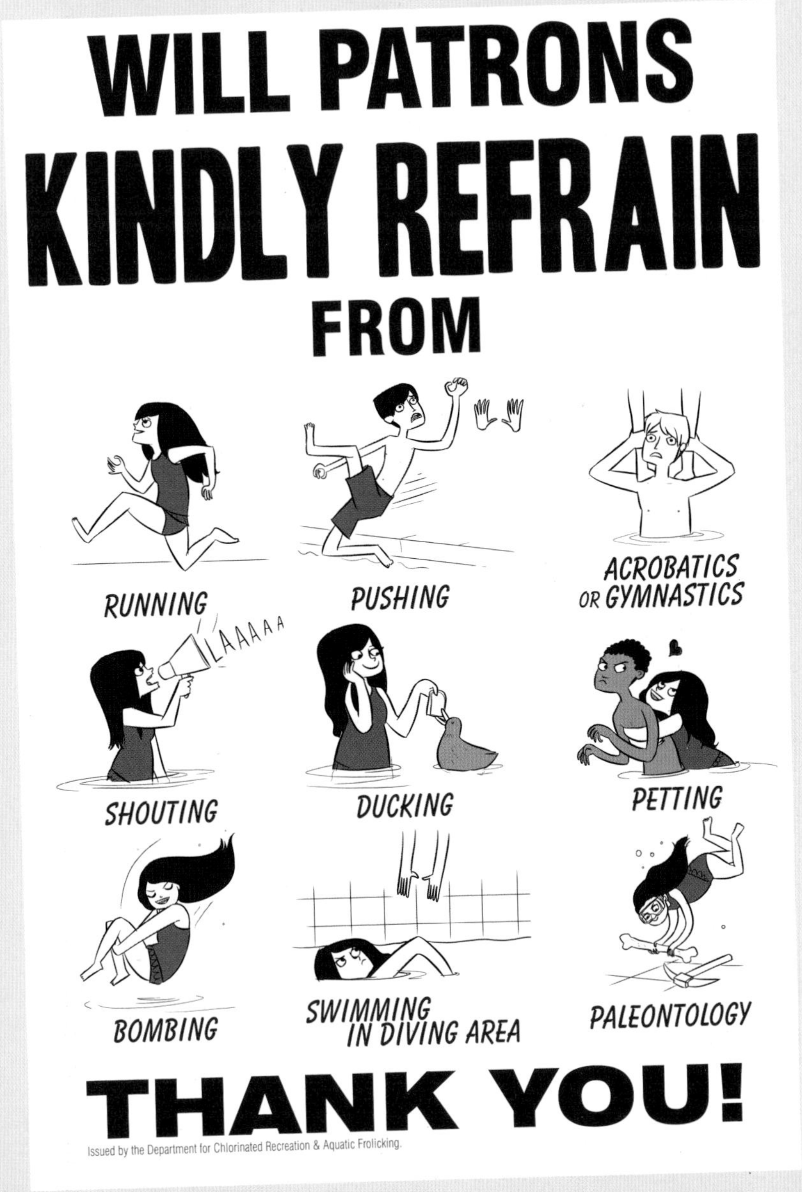
WILL PATRONS
KINDLY REFRAIN
FROM
RUNNING
PUSHING
ACROBATICS
OR GYMNASTICS
LAAAAA
SHOUTING
DUCKING
PETTING
BOMBING
SWIMMING
IN DIVING AREA
PALEONTOLOGY
THANK YOU!
Issued by the Department for Chlorinated Recreation & Aquatic Frolicking.

ALSO FROM JOHN ALLISON & ONI PRESS

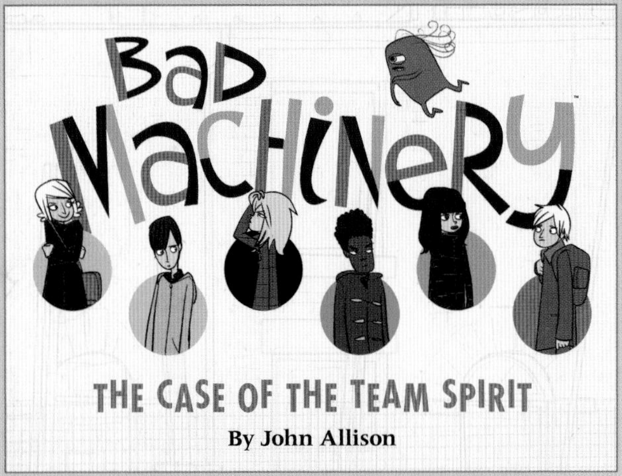

Bad Machinery
THE CASE OF THE TEAM SPIRIT
By John Allison

BAD MACHINERY, VOLUME 1:
THE CASE OF THE TEAM SPIRIT
By John Allison
136 pages, softcover, full color
ISBN 978-1-62010-084-4

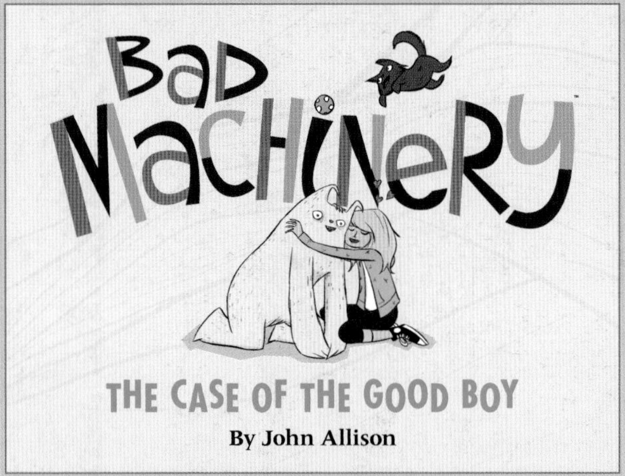

Bad Machinery
THE CASE OF THE GOOD BOY
By John Allison

BAD MACHINERY, VOLUME 2:
THE CASE OF THE GOOD BOY
By John Allison
144 pages, softcover, full color
ISBN 978-1-62010-114-8

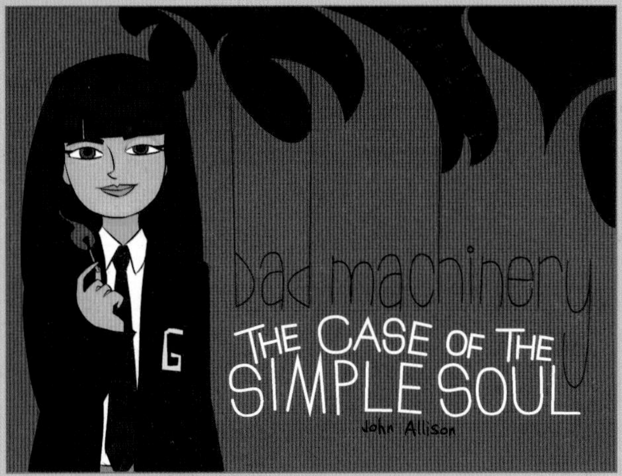

bad machinery
THE CASE OF THE SIMPLE SOUL
John Allison

BAD MACHINERY, VOLUME 3:
THE CASE OF THE SIMPLE SOUL
By John Allison
136 pages, softcover, full color
ISBN 978-1-62010-193-3

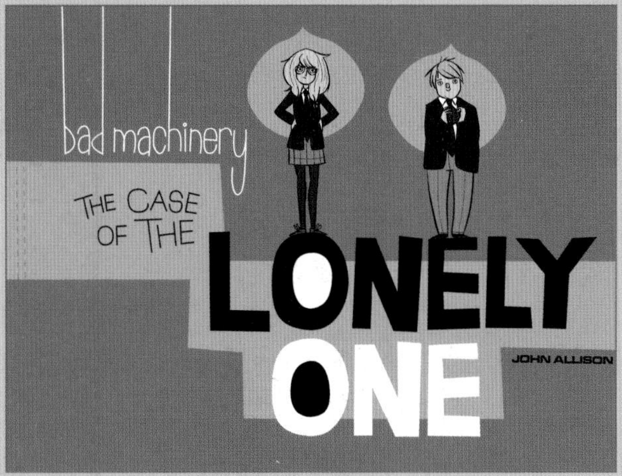

bad machinery
THE CASE OF THE
LONELY ONE
JOHN ALLISON

BAD MACHINERY, VOLUME 4:
THE CASE OF THE LONELY ONE
By John Allison
136 pages, softcover, full color
ISBN 978-1-62010-212-1

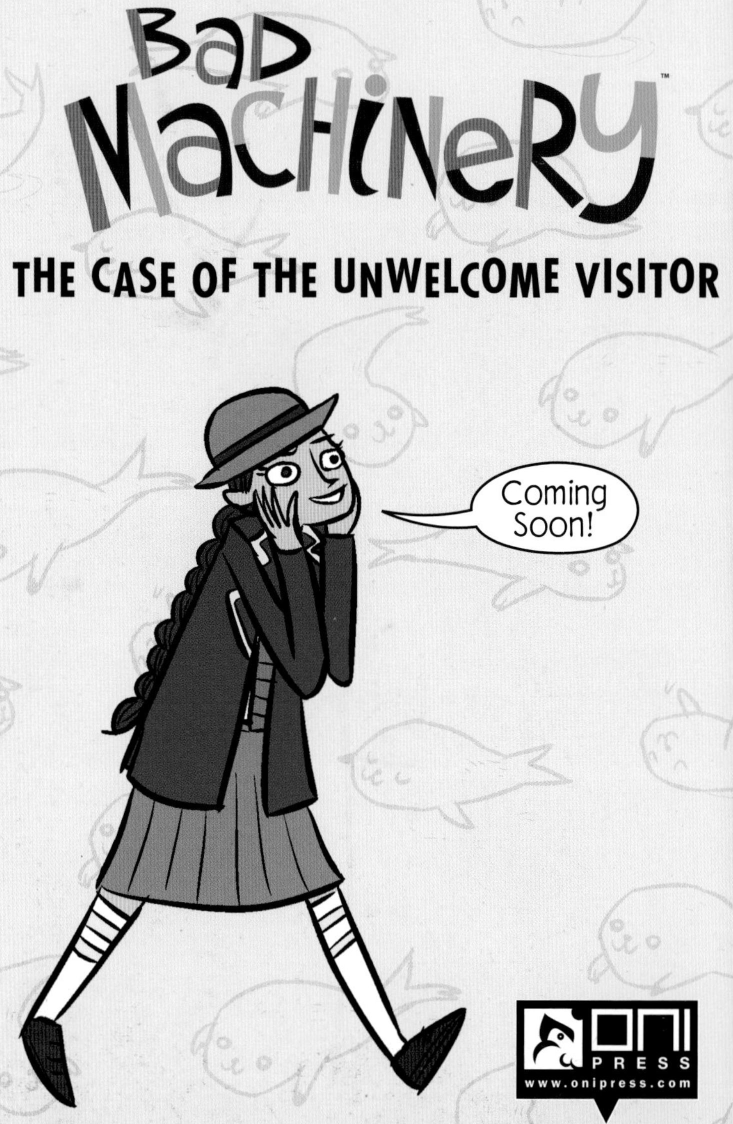

Bad Machinery
THE CASE OF THE UNWELCOME VISITOR
Coming Soon!

ONI PRESS
www.onipress.com